DIRECTING THE NARRATIVE
and
SHOT DESIGN

The Art and Craft of Directing

by

Lubomir Kocka

Series in Cinema and Culture

VERNON PRESS

www.vernonpress.com

In the Americas:
Vernon Press
1000 N West Street,
Suite 1200, Wilmington,
Delaware 19801
United States

In the rest of the world:
Vernon Press
C/Sancti Espiritu 17,
Malaga, 29006
Spain

Series in Cinema and Culture

Library of Congress Control Number: 2018933406

ISBN: 978-1-62273-399-6

CONTENTS

To my beloved father, thank you for your love, care, and confidence in me, and thank you for always supporting me and believing in me. I miss you so much. To my dear sons, Mišino and Ľubino. I am sorry, I didn't know, how to do it. I wish I could do it over, just one more take. And to my Donna, the center of my universe, my life would simply not be the same without you.

PREFACE

"I constantly see people rise in life who are not the smartest, sometimes not even the most diligent, but they are learning machines. They go to bed every night a little wiser than they were when they got up, and boy does that help, particularly when you have a long run ahead of you."

Charles T. Munger, American investor, businessman, and philanthropist.

ACKNOWLEDGEMENT

If you're willing to fight for something, to take a stand, to risk getting hurt, if you truly believe in something, if you love enough, it gives you power. You will feel justly entitled to do whatever you will be called for because you will do it heartily.

A man is defined by what he does. Film directing is more than simply a part of my life; it is an indivisible part of my being. I began a career as a child actor at age fourteen. I was able to apply this experience, along with my painting and photography experience, and film graduate education, toward the professional pursuit of my passion for film and television directing. As soon as my professional career took off, I got an offer from my alma mater to return as a film educator, which I gladly accepted. That was the moment when I discovered my passion for teaching. I tremendously enjoy teaching, mentoring, and inspiring a young generation of filmmakers. I owe much of that passion to my parents, who were educators as well and had great experiences.

Nothing is more rewarding for me than instilling a passion for the art of film into my students and seeing the results of their appreciation of cinema in their successful film and television productions. For me, it is like an extension of my own life. Students recognize that in today's workplace, they need to show that they are citizens of the world and that they have cross-cultural competencies that will help them to have more options down the line. Since I have specific overseas experience, I can introduce them to these competencies. I was and am aware of the role and responsibilities as a film educator. A few times in my career I felt that the burden is too heavy for me, that I can't carry this load anymore. When I was about to give up on teaching, my former student, Kevin Phillips *(Super Dark*

Times) sent me an e-mail: *"The weight we carry is as heavy as our passion for life - but don't sweat it. Just be true blue you and all will follow suit. I'd say go to class as you did all these past years, particularly when you had us as students - and know that if you can impact just one student, it's absolutely worth it!"*

Before you begin to read this book, I have to warn you – your life as a film or television director won't be paved with rose petals and sunlight all the time. Be prepared for your film not to be well received by audiences even though you put all your love, passion, talent, diligence, and a lot of money into it. Film critics will enjoy tearing you apart. You will feel like a bucking bull lying down in the arena with multiple hooks embedded in your shoulder, waiting for the final sword thrust, or "estocada," to kill you. At that point, you may try to comprehend the wisdom of the old adage that there is a certain freedom in having nothing left to lose. But then you will stand up, shake yourself off, and start working on another film. Someone once said, *"Obstacles and suffering are inevitable – change is the law of life. We all have inconveniences of one kind or another. How you deal with them ultimately determines how successful you are."*

You will constantly be challenged in your life, but there is a light at the end of every tunnel. If you are aware of your vital power, you will open your eyes and see yourself emerging from troubles with an enhanced awareness of your capabilities. You will again feel that if you want to, you can move mountains. That is when you will know you are ready to stand up from the ashes and direct a new film again. As a director, you will never know if the film you are currently working on is your last film or if you will ever get another chance to direct a film. Because of that uncertainty, you have to work on each film like it is your last chance to direct. So, if you are still interested in this book, I will be more than happy to share my professional experience with you.

Writing a book presents numerous challenges. I never thought that I would have enough courage to do it. I am grateful to a lot of people for helping me with this book. First and foremost, I must thank my SCAD students in the USA and my VŠMU students in Slovakia. Not all the college students who are quoted in this book are mentioned by name, and I would like to apologize in advance for this. These students gave me a chance to think about my own directing style and about the theoretical aspects of filmmaking. I think that one of the most enjoyable things for me in interacting with students is how much I learn about myself. I gratefully kept in mind those valuable pieces of wisdom in the process of writing this book, and now I'm able to share it with you all.

I want to honor the work of all my students, those named and those unnamed in this book. I wish to thank each and every one. This book reflects your work, and your talent is imprinted in the book. I would like to offer my heartfelt thanks to my former graduate student Jane Barr, who willingly offered her editing services. She just could not stand so many sloppy mistakes, errors, typos, omissions, and inaccuracies in my first draft of the manuscript. Later on, she took the position of line producer in organizing filming in the USA for the visuals for this book. Also, I would like to extend my sincerest thanks and appreciation to my graduate student, Joanna Brooks, a hardworking assistant director, executive assistant, and casting director for filming visuals in the USA. She is a living sample that success comes from hard work and dedication.

I would like to thank the film crew, who worked with me on visuals, the photographers: Lubo Kocka, Venkat Dilip Chunduru, Ernesto V. Fuentes, Sean Grimaldi, David Allen Jones, and Balša Gobović. I would also like to thank the gifted actresses and actors: Táňa Pauhofová, Róbert Roth, Branislav Bystriansky, Alexander Barta, Torsten Hillhouse, Corine Milian, Vitali Pushkar, Angelina Stanley, Geoffrey Wilson, Michael Foley, Misty Insel, Virginia Patterson, Remy Godwin, Ian Trottier, Liam Ireson, Tiara Maldonis, Geoffrey Insel, Drew Funk, Jarod Valvo, Rachel Valvo, Tiara Maldonis, Sara Wallace, Nick Bow, Cory Carpenter, Emily Huff, Donna Wright, Michal Kocka, Alexandra Hažíková, Marek Geišberg, Eva Sakálová, Hailey Vest, Madison Bildahl, Claire Price, Francesca Crichton, Milena Goncalez, Malikah Cobb, Quinn Lowsky, Claire Price, Dylan Ruggiero, Fairuz Ferrer Elwazir, Luis Felipe Mameri, Norbert Bodo, Andrea Papp, Martin Blažek, Western park Boskovice ensemble cast, Dakotah Terrace, and Colton Terrace. And thanks also to graphic designer Paul Rodecker. Thank you all so much for your incredible talent and work.

Book Cover credits: Cover designer - Vernon Press, Storyboard Artists - Ru Xu, Liss Villella, Costume Designer - Eva Farkašová, Photo - Lubo Kocka.

Photo Album credits: Alan Hyža, Ria Vaňová, Jozef Koršala and the author's archive.

I would like to thank and express my gratitude to the whole team of people from Vernon Press Publisher for taking a risk on this book that is just a hair outside the realm of their past projects.

The book extensively utilizes visuals and presents a deep probe into the core of the directing dilemma: shot design. Here, the shot design is introduced as a powerful, expressive tool and not just as a toolbox for mastering the mechanics of shooting. Over 200 different scenes with real actors in real locations were photographed for the book. Professional actors, actor-models, commercial talents, and non-professional actors were cast to embody scripted characters. A variety of different shooting locations in the USA, Europe, and Africa were used to mimic different periods and genres. Each scene demonstrates a particular situation described in the book and is portrayed through still pictures and floor plans with choreographed action for the actors and camera set-ups. Each scene was shot with a Canon 5D Mark II or Mark III or a Canon 7D. All photographs illustrate the outputs from those camera set-ups. Floor Plans/Overhead Diagrams and Schematics show the performers' blocking and their movement along with the camera set-ups and camera movement. Floor Plans/Overhead Diagrams and Schematics were created with Celtx pre-production software (www.celtx.com). All scenes were uniquely shot for the purposes of this book; plenty of them replicate the scenes from well-known and popular feature films. Even though I do not refer to existing movies explicitly, you might recognize some of them, like *Blue* (Dir. Krysztof Kieslowski), *Citizen Kane* (Dir. Orson Welles), *Amadeus* (Milos Forman), *Contempt* (Dir. Jean-Luc Godard), *The Graduate* (Dir. Mike Nichols), *In The Mood for Love* (Dir. Wong Kar Wai), *Manhattan* (Dir. Woody Allen), *Maria's Lovers* (Dir. Andrey Konchalovski), *Paris, Texas* (Dir. Wim Wenders), *Talk to Her* (Dir. Pedro Almodovar), *Once Upon a Time in the West* (Dir. Sergio Leone), *Dolores Claiborne* (Dr. Taylor Hackford), *Babel* (Dir. Alejandro González Iñárritu), and many more.

The book was funded in part through a Savannah College of Art and Design, Inc. Presidential Fellowship for Faculty Development.

Excerpt from the article *How Language Shapes Thoughts,* written by Lera Boroditsky, *Scientific American* (February, 2011). Reproduced with permission. Copyright © 2011 Scientific American, a division of Nature America, Inc. All rights reserved.

All killer no filler. An interview with Richard Raskin, Editor of Short Film Studies. Reprinted by permission of the author Mr. Richard Raskin.

AESTHETICS OF THE SHOT by Stephen Prince. Reprinted by permission of the author Mr. Stephen Prince.

SO YOU WANNA WORK IN MOVIES? Reprinted by permission of the author Mr. Oliver Stapleton.

PREVISUALIZATION: the film BEFORE "The Film." Author Chris Olsen. Reprinted by permission of MicroFilmmaker Magazine (www.microfilmmaker.com).

PROLOGUE

The film is about experience, story, and emotion. It can infuriate us, sadden us, bore us, or it can bring joy, laughter, and happiness. Being a filmmaker is both a privilege and a burden. We see life in a unique way but are expected to communicate that vision to the entire world. The attempted resolution of this problem can inspire a creative act whose closest emotional equivalent is motherhood. As in life, all films demonstrate the dark lows and staggering triumphs contained within every frame. The filmmaking is the noble art of creativity. For those who like scientific definitions, creativity is an exasperatingly slippery concept. Neurologist Arnold Scheibel from UCLA explains the process as *"the putting together of familiar information in an unusual way."*

Regarding creativity, I am frequently thinking about another statement. Fyodor Mikhailovich Dostoevsky *(Crime and Punishment),* the most important and influential Russian writer who ever lived and who has often been quoted, once said, *"Creativity isn't anything else but 2% of talent and 98% of sweat."* Also, I recall a statement credited to Sigmund Freud, an Austrian neurologist and the founder of psychoanalysis, which might seem like it has nothing to do with creativity, but for me, it does: *"Each energy is just transformation of sexual energy."* If you think that I am about to advise you to master your libido and sparingly harness this energy in order to transform it into spiritual energy, you are mistaken. But the opposite may be true. In this instance, maybe no advice would be better. Sex is the essence of creation, from the birth of the life to the birth of artistic expression. To this day, thousands of years after the arrival of Adam and Eve, man has tried to channel this energy into more fulfilling areas which could bring him greatest passion and the blissful joy and pleasure, and mental and intellectual gratification. The filmmaking is one of those areas.

I read an article in the *Scientific American* entitled *Inner Sparks* which was an interview conducted by journalist Alicia Anstead with the ear, nose, and throat specialist Charles J. Limb, who also happens to be a sax player. His research investigates what goes on in the brain when musicians improvise. It's worth reading the whole article, but here are a few things that stuck out to me:

Why should scientists study creativity?

While I think creativity is amazing, I don't put it on a pedestal. I view at it as a very normal biological process that some people are able to take to extremely profound levels,... (...) From a scientific perspective: if it's a biological behavior, if humans are creative beings, we really ought to study it like you study any other complex biological behavior.

What happens neurologically to the brain during creativity?

(...) When you're doing something that's creative, you're engaging all aspects of your brain. During improvisation, the prefrontal cortex of the brain undergoes an interesting shift in activity, in which a broad area called the lateral prefrontal region shuts down, essentially so you have a significant inhibition of your prefrontal cortex. (...) In the meantime, we saw another area of the prefrontal cortex—the medial prefrontal cortex—turn on.

What's next in your creativity research?

(...) The next real direction I'm headed into has to do with trying to clarify our study of reward mechanisms in the brain and their relation to creativity. Why is it that we like to be creative? Why is it that we like to perceive creativity? And what happens when somebody is improvising in terms of pleasure or reward centers? Where is the gratification neurologically, and how does that change according to the emotional content of the music? I've always wondered: Why do we love sad music? Why does it make us feel better and not worse? It's a funny inversion that takes place in the brain. Whereas we try to avoid sadness in life, in art, and especially in music, we almost gravitate toward it. By and large, the effect is very positive. Improvisation causes a similar response: When you're spontaneously creating music that is sad, what are you getting? Are you getting joy? Pleasure? What's the basis of the reward? That's one of the directions I'm heading.

This leads me to the point where I have to explain why I put in this book such a huge emphasis on directing with conceptual approaches and methodological practices while still maintaining an open door for instincts, intuitions, improvisation, and subconscious decision making. Dr. Li Zhaoping of University College London said, *"You'd expect people to make better decisions when given time to look properly, but this was not so."* He explained, *"The conscious or top-level function of the brain, when active, vetoes our initial subconscious decision – even when it is correct – leaving us unaware or distrustful of our instincts."* So, thinking too much about a decision can leave us worse off. This is what happens with the obsessive compulsive disorder: the subconscious knows very well that you have turned the gas off, but the conscious brain gets too involved and throws the whole thing into doubt, forcing you to second-guess yourself.

In a turmoil of producing the film, you will lead a lot to intuition. The rapid processing of facts is inevitable when you will be forced to make split-second judgments and split-second decisions.

A tremendous responsibility for the result is a huge burden, but trust your gut, you will be surprised by your capacity to make the right call just based on instinct alone. Research published in *Current Biology* shows that in some instances, snap decisions are better than endless pedantic pondering and logical weighing up. Test subjects were asked to pick the odd one out on a screen covered with more than 650 identical symbols, including one rotated version of the same symbol. They performed better when they were given no time to linger and were forced to rely on their subconscious to select the correct answer.

So now Milton Erickson's famous intuition to *"trust your unconscious"* is backed up by research. The booming science of decision-making has shown that more information can lead to objectively poorer choices, and to choices that people come to regret. Your conscious logical brain doesn't always make the best decisions. Sharon Begley wrote in her article published in *Newsweek*, March 7, 2011:

> *(...) an unconscious system guides many of our decisions, and that it can be sidelined by too much information. And it has shown that decisions requiring creativity benefit from letting the problem incubate below the level of awareness - something that becomes ever-more difficult when information never stops arriving.*

But I am in no way trying to convince you to stop reading this book just solely to rely on your gut instincts. No doubt, instincts can open many closed doors for you, but the best possible decisions come from weighing your instincts against your rational thinking. So my advice here would be the following: trust *your instincts* but *rely* on rational thought. Many great discoveries have been made by chance. Louis Pasteur, a French biologist, microbiologist, and chemist, renowned for his discoveries of the principles of vaccination, microbial fermentation, and pasteurization, said, *"Chance favors the prepared mind,"* when he discovered the vaccine for chicken cholera while accidentally using an old and forgotten bacterial culture for inoculating fowl only to find that the fowl became ill but did not die. This statement has stayed with me for a long time. I had the privilege of portraying one of Louis Pasteur's students in the 1977 TV film *Louis Pasteur* directed by Igor Ciel, my film professor.

You will try to figure out your own way around filmmaking without realizing that some of your "discoveries" have already been discovered. You can go back and look at the history of cinema or at the work of others and see how our predecessors intuitively solved their problems. Just look at years of intuitive filmmaking and realize that there are some very simple principles. You can attempt filmmaking intuitively by wandering around and seeing where you get to, but with the "maps" I will teach you, you can plan a route that you know in advance will make some sort of sense. But I have to warn you, they might make an O.K. director good, but they won't make a good director great. I have borrowed that idea from the composer and music theorist Dmitri Tymoczko and largely adapted it to film. *"I don't want to sell maps as the royal road to composition,"* he advises. *"They don't substitute for the hard work of learning how to move notes around. But they can help show when a new idea is promising and when it will probably lead to a dead end."*

I am not the first director in the world, and I certainly will not be the last one who came to the realization – after having had a long and substantial career as a director of produced fictional feature films inside the studio system and in independent films – that it wasn't until I started teaching that I truly began to understand my own directing process. Also, I found that along with my love and aptitude for teaching others, teaching deepened my directing. I found passion in sharing the knowledge and insights gained from my personal journey. Harvard's first tenured black law professor, Derrick Bell, once said about his major effort in teaching *"(...) they (students) should be ready and able to take risks and make sacrifices for the things they believe in, and their real success in life will come from making those sacrifices and taking those risks, regardless of outcome."*

With this quote, I am not opposing my previous declaration regarding learning; I just want to introduce the concept of learning through practice and explore the concept of effective practice in developing new directing skills. In this book, you will find a lot of practical exercises that are aimed at helping you to master some important directorial concepts. These concepts will not just provide you with a toolbox; you will also learn how to use individual tools from that toolbox. I am going to teach you how to use them in just a moment. Thereafter, I want you to respond to them either by adopting them or very consciously rejecting them for some reason.

ABOUT THIS BOOK

The landscape of film is rapidly changing – this book can be a "directing-altering book," since it provides high-quality learning resources that encourage and challenge film enthusiasts, aspiring directors, film students, and professionals to break through to new levels of excellence and impact in their film directing, television directing, and new media directing.

The directorial concepts introduced and presented in this book, along with the practical exercises, provide a foundation of theoretical and practical knowledge that any person can learn and apply. The goal of this book is to teach specific directorial skills through specific directorial concepts and specific directing exercises, and to teach, develop, and evolve film enthusiasts', film students', and cineastes' narrative filmmaking skills and visual storytelling abilities, to educate and train them to make professional films of a high artistic level and to develop their artistic talents and film craft skills related to directing. After studying all directorial concepts covered in this book, readers will be able to execute their vision with clarity and decisiveness.

The forms and methods of teaching the art and craft of directing are still changing, but not the basic principle. The method of teaching is based on the knowledge that the best way to learn how to make a film, TV show, or new media product is to go through the entire creative process of writing, shooting, and editing your own project. This principle is applied to the structure of the book with an emphasis on blending the theoretical and the practical aspects of filmmaking. A huge emphasis is put on directing with conceptual approaches and methodological practices, while still maintaining an open door for instincts, intuitions, improvisation, and subconscious decision making.

What makes this book stand out is that it covers a set of clearly defined directorial concepts universal to all filmmakers. Methodology and visual strategy for rendering a scene based on a character's perspective is one outstanding feature of this book. When a director conceptualizes a scene, he has to give it precision and clarity. Critical director's choices discussed in the book make this book stand out. This book also offers other unique features that have not yet been covered in a single published book on directing, which makes this book stand out from existing texts:

- Psycho-physiological regularities in left-right/right-left orientation transferred to a shot design. How directors can manipulate the viewer's perception of a character and of the journey they are on using screen direction.

- Methodology and visual strategy for rendering a scene based on character perspective.

- Directorial concept of emotional manipulation.

- Demystifying the 180-degree rule.

The Target Readers

This book is designed for everyone from beginners to graduate-level film students. It shows readers how to unlock the full potential of their creativity using shot design, as well as the psychological effects of shot design. Film educators can use this book as a primary source in directing classes, a resource I've often wished I had throughout my years as a film and television professor.

- **Novices and Film Enthusiasts** without any formal film training, who want to make films and videos accessible to the public via the Internet on diverse video-sharing film platforms, virtual galleries and digital archives, and private websites.

  - This book assumes the reader has no knowledge of the field; therefore, basic concepts and terminology are introduced.

  - Novices will learn how to skillfully and creatively use the expressive tools and means of the film medium as well as how to design shots in a way that effectively develops and carries out their vision.

- **Aspiring Directors and Young filmmakers** who want to make professional shorts and then showcase them on mobile devices for film industry representatives who are looking for new talents.

  - This book encourages learning by doing.

  - Aspiring directors are faced with tackling how to develop the vision for a film and how to carry out that vision.

- **Undergraduate Students** who want to learn how to make films and afterward are looking for a chance to break into the industry.

  - Since the core of the book presents the methodology for translating a vision to the screen, it teaches students from the very beginning of their careers to be precise and well organized in their creative process.

  - Students develop narrative filmmaking skills and visual storytelling abilities.

- Students integrate theoretical and practical knowledge with hands-on experience.

- Students learn basic blocking, staging methods and principles, staging style, and staging pattern.

- Students learn how to design a film scene by integrating and implementing the newly acquired theoretical knowledge and directing skills related to the aesthetics of the shot.

- Students learn to make critical choices, which include the mood and tone of the scene, character perspective, and the director's choices in designing a shot.

- Students learn how to creatively master the relation of the shot to the emotional meaning of the situation.

- Students learn how to translate the inner feelings, motivations, and insights of their characters into filmable situations.

● **Graduate Students**

- The book presents a focused approach to film directing and therefore is an invaluable contribution to their theoretical and practical growth.

- Students continue in examining all aspects of director's art and craft through theory and hands-on work.

- Students evolve their ability to interpret a script, choose every element within the frame, shape the actor's performance within a shot, and develop overall visual storytelling skills.

- Students evolve their ability to visualize the inner state of mind of a character.

- Students learn how to control the design of the shot and how to fashion each visual element to create a strong emotional and psychological connection with the viewer.

- Students learn how to efficiently use their deep knowledge of modeling character perspective for the sake of engaging the audience with the events and emotions in a scene.

- Students are encouraged to discover their own view of the world around them and then taught how to interpret it. On this basis, each student can find his/her own special, solitary and inimitable artistic expression from which they can create their own unique directing style.

- Students will discover that breaking the rules can be a very creative way to achieve excellent results.

- Students learn how their own temperament, emotionality, and mannerisms can impact the vision, abstraction, and interpretation of their films.

- **Professional Filmmakers and Cineastes** associated professionally with filmmaking.

  - No matter how skilled a director may be, no matter if he/she has been directing for many years or just for the first time, he/she will always face the same problem: how to conceive a vision, develop that vision, and execute it. This book will help them to rationalize this largely intuitive process, expand their creative capacity, and speed up the process of making critical directorial decisions.

    The book presents a focused approach to film directing and therefore is a vital contribution to a filmmaker's consistent theoretical and practical growth.

- **Film Educators**

  - The way the material is organized, the book can be used as an invaluable source for teaching directing classes based on the quarterly system, semester system, or one-year system.

  - Since the book contains many handouts for practical exercises, film educators can use them in classes and adapt them to their own teaching methods.

  - Practical guidance in the planning, execution, and implementation of the theory-based directorial concepts makes this book very hands on.

  - Other pedagogical features in the book include: floor plans, tests, quiz, a scene from a screenplay, examples of written homework of students on the given topics, the assessment assignment, and students' self-assessment, which is a written analysis on what students have learned or discovered from all the practical exercises and assignments that they found valuable and can apply to their future work.

Exploring original and unique ways of the art of storytelling, as well as examining my own experience verifying and evaluating alternative methods for solving dilemmas creatively within the films I have directed, is the very essence of this book. Bias is an inclination to present and hold a partial perspective. Because I wanted to postulate more generalized directing concepts related to film and television directing, which are not just derived from my directing experience, and therefore they can generally be applied all over the board, I have chosen not to include too many examples from films I directed. Referring to my own films would make me feel self-centred, even self-obsessed, it would make me feel that I am bragging about myself, and don't credit others around. Later in the book, I have a quote from the Polish film director Andrzej Wajda *(Man of Iron)*, which comprises my whole philosophy implemented in the book: *"There should be less lecturing by directors on how they made their own films and more practical hands-on experience offered to students. How I made my films is unimportant to young film-makers."* I am using quotes from great filmmakers or from film theorists and film historians after postulating specific directorial concepts, in order to add credibility, sort of "universal" gravity to those directorial concepts postulated by myself. Something like reassuring the readers that those concepts are not composed from a limited and contingent perspective, and they haven't been invented by me and that they have no just limited application to my films, and they have been here for a pretty long time, but nobody put them in concise statements/definitions.

PART I: DIRECTORIAL CONCEPTS

CHAPTER 1:
DIRECTOR

Talent and Practice

Before going any further, I feel obliged to explain why the combination of crafts-manship and artistry together make the profession of a director, and why there is a need to go far beyond a familiarity with the expressive tools of the medium.

"So what makes one director better than another? Being a director can absolutely be done with no experience and no training, but like anything else, the more knowledge and practice you have, the better you'll be at it." That's what Bethany Rooney and Mary Lou Belli claim in their book: *Directors Tell the Story* (Rooney, B. and Belli, M. *Directors Tell the Story: Master the Craft of Television and Film Directing*, 2nd Edition. Focal Press, 2016, ISBN-10: 1138948470). But this is something that Malcolm Gladwell, an English-born Canadian journalist, author, and speaker, might disagree with because he claims:

> *The idea that excellence at performing a complex task requires a critical minimum level of practice surfaces again and again in studies of expertise. In fact, researchers have settled on what they believe is the magic number for true expertise: ten thousand hours. The emerging picture from such studies is that ten thousand hours of practice is required to achieve the level of mastery associated with being a world-class expert in anything.*
> (From *Outliers: The Story of Success* by Malcolm Gladwell. Copyright © 2006 by Malcolm Gladwell. Reprinted by permission of Little, Brown and Company. All rights reserved.)

Gladwell, citing the neurologist Daniel Levitin, also writes:

> *In study after study, of composers, basketball players, fiction writers, ice skaters, concert pianists, chess players, master criminals, and what have you, this number comes up again and again. Of course, this doesn't address why some people get more out of their practice sessions than others do. But no one has yet found a case in which true world-class expertise was accomplished in less time. It seems that it takes the brain this long to assimilate all that it needs to know to achieve true mastery.*

Later in the book, he states the following:

For almost a generation, psychologists around the world have been engaged in a spirited debate over a question that most of us would consider to have been settled years ago. The question is this: is there such a thing as innate talent? The obvious answer is yes. Not every hockey player born in January ends up playing at the professional level. Only some do – the innately talented ones. Achievement is talent plus preparation. The problem with this view is that the closer psychologists look at the careers of the gifted, the smaller the role innate talent seems to play, and the bigger role preparation seems to play.

The success roadmap can be built either on the strength of your natural talent, or on the circumstances of your birth, or both, but not without experience, hard work and practice. When I am talking about practicing your craft, I just want to point out something interesting. The old wisdom says that we learn more from failure than from success. Unfortunately, you may be surprised to learn that this is not necessarily true but just a common myth. Researchers at the Massachusetts Institute of Technology showed monkeys a series of pictures and trained them to turn their heads left or right depending on which image was presented. When the monkeys chose correctly, they received a reward. The scientists found that when the monkeys made the right choices, the neurons involved in learning and discrimination were very active. The neurons *"learn better when the animal had a recent success,"* MIT researcher Earl Miller tells. *"Success breeds success because the rewards it produces raises attention levels. When monkeys made mistakes and got nothing, their ability to respond correctly didn't improve. Success breeds motivation, failure breeds frustration and lack of motivation."* We may have more to learn from our successes than from our failures.

Conventional wisdom says if you want to play at Carnegie Hall, Madison Square Garden, even your local talent show, it's going to take a lot of practice. But too much faith may be put in the saying "practice makes perfect." Researchers from McGill University recently published a study in the journal *Cerebral Cortex* that shows that while certain parts of your brain get molded by experience, others are based on talent ("Learning A Skill? Raw Talent Might Trump Hard Work." http://www.newsy.com/videos/learning-a-skill-raw-talent-might-trump-hard-work/ Accessed December 19, 2016).

The Role of a Director

Most likely, you are familiar with the following definition of a director, because it is the definition used the most, and because of that, I do not even know whom should be given credit for it: *"The director breaks down the screenplay, visualizes how the film should be shot and works with cast and crew to carry out his vision. The director is a movie's main creative source."*

Although we generally assume that the term "director" refers to the person's role in directing (steering) the work of production personnel, the term actually has a more important meaning: one who directs the attention of viewers. ("A Director Directs Attention." http://www.cybercollege.com. Accessed December 19, 2016)

(...) the most important part of your job is to understand the script - what the story is about, the themes, the story points, the characters. A director is a storyteller, and to be a good storyteller, you need to understand every detail about the story you are telling. ("Director as Story-teller." http://actioncut print.com. Accessed December 19, 2016)

Director – Visionary

Wherever you look, you will hear that a film director has to have a vision and know how to carry out the vision.

What first separates the good director from the great director is the creative vision, because, without that, you're just a technician. (...) We have to figure out what each scene really means, how each scene contributes to telling the whole story, and then design how to communicate that visually. (Rooney, B. and Belli, M. *Directors Tell the Story: Master the Craft of Television and Film Directing*, 2nd Edition, Focal Press; 2016, ISBN-10: 1138948470)

Bethany Rooney and Mary Lou Belli list in their book the four necessities a great director must be able to fulfill in order to achieve their creative vision:

1.   *Interpret the script*
2.   *Choose every element within the frame*
3.   *Shape the actors' performances*
4.   *Tell the story with the camera*

Once you have a vision, you want to tell people about it. There are a couple of steps in developing and communicating your vision, but the whole process begins with you clarifying your vision. Try to formulate a *Vision Statement*, which is a general statement that expresses your most important ideas, and then you can move on to looking for different ways of communicating your vision. "*If a director has no concept (vision, interpretation) the simplicity is nothing! Directors must have something to say on their own.*" (http://direct.vtheatre.net. Accessed December 19, 2016)

Visions give birth to images. You have to see things in order to show them, you have to notice them in order to learn how to reconstruct them, you have

to dream in order to lead your audience through a couple hours of day-dreaming. ("FILM DIRECTING: the BASICS."
http://afronord.tripod.com/direct.html. Accessed December 19, 2016)

The director is the visionary who takes the cast and crew on their creative journey toward the completion of a film. Directors tell their stories with images, and it is their intention to manipulate the emotions of the audience. (Frost, J. *Cinematography for Directors: A Guide for Creative Collaboration.* Michael Wiese Productions, 2009, ISBN-10: 1932907556)

Cennino d'Andrea Cennini (1370–1440), an Italian painter influenced by Giotto (an Italian painter and architect from Florence, generally considered the first in a line of great artists who contributed to the Renaissance), provides a practical handbook (*Il Libro dell'Arteon*) on the basic techniques for the apprentice painter. He declares in his book – and I just changed the word "painting" for "directing" – that "*This is an occupation known as 'directing,' which calls for imagination, and skill of hand, in order to discover things not seen, hiding themselves under the shadow of natural objects, and to fix them with the hand, presenting to plain sight what does not actually exist*" (Boorstin, D.J. *The Creators: A History of Heroes of the Imagination,* reprint edition. Vintage, 1993, ISBN-10: 0679743758). From my perspective, it is the best definition of film directing.

Director – Manipulator

The whole process of film directing is about manipulating, from conception to completion. It is an undeniable fact that a film director manipulates, controls, and regulates the audience's perception by using all the means that are at his/her disposal. He/she does it for the sake of satisfying the dramatic and emotional needs of the stories. Unquestionably, the director must manipulate the actors as well, because their performance is the best way to manipulate audience perception and evoke emotional responses. So many times, in order to get the real and raw emotion at the moment, rather than getting actors to "act," a director creates conditions in order to get actors to react the way he/she wants them to react – manipulating them to react in a specific way.

Actors are the human material of the film, so directors manipulate actors by different means to get the desired result, many times by *"angering or exciting or causing them anxiety by artificial means."* The following anecdote, about director Elia Kazan *(A Streetcar Named Desire)*, a Greek-American director, producer, writer and actor, can serve as a good example. During the filming of *Viva Zapata*, he apparently told Anthony Quinn that Marlon Brando was saying things about him behind his back to sharpen the conflict between their two characters on screen. Brando approvingly called the director an *"arch-manipulator of actors' feelings."*

Let's assume that you have a God-given talent, and some experience. What else do you need? Directing skills! Gain requisite skills! Directing is a learned skill. In order to do directing masterfully, you have to secure requisite skills. Of course, directing is not something you can learn overnight, but it is something that comes naturally as you grow professionally and personally. Even though there is no universal course of training to become a film and television director, we know that any academic and real-world experience that contributes to creativity, communication, leadership, management, and technical skills will help any filmmaker tremendously. But in order to achieve the greatness and mastery, you have to study stories, formulas, and the masters, and you must practice telling your own stories – a lot of practice. Directing is the most coveted and most challenging of any filmmaking position.

I am citing here the article written by Oliver Stapleton (*The Cider House Rules*), B.S.C (Director of Photography), who photographed a broad spectrum of critically hailed, influential films. He has worked with a wide array of critically acclaimed filmmakers to make some of Hollywood's best stories. Stapleton's collaborations with directors like Lasse Hallström (*Chocolat*) and Stephen Frears (*Philomena*) prove him a cinematic force to be reckoned with. I see this article as the best bridge to transfer you to the first real comprehensive chapter of this book, CHAPTER 2: VISUAL CONCEPT.

I want to Direct. Doesn't everybody. It's the control thing, and the power. All those people doing what you tell them. Or maybe YOU'VE GOT SOMETHING TO SAY. Or maybe not. You want a career, power, and glory. The big question is: DO YOU SEE PICTURES IN YOUR HEAD? If not, forget about being a Film Director, or a Cinematographer. Directors and Cinematographers can string pictures together in their head like a Composer can "hear" music and then write it down. Now some musicians (like me) tinkle about on an instrument until they work out a tune: this is not being a real musician. Real Musicians hear music in their heads, then write it down, or play it. The rest of us are just larking about, and a lot of fun it is too.

Some people say Directing is a vocation, like being a Priest or a Doctor. It's not remotely like being a Priest or a Doctor, but it may be a vocation because no-one in their right mind would voluntarily go through the kind of hell that a Film Director has to go through.

Film Directors not only have to be able to visualize in their heads, but they also have to be able to deal with a lot of very demanding and very different types of people. Occasionally someone like Kurosawa or Hitchcock appear. People like them are so brilliant that they clearly don't live in the same world as us mere mortals. And it is up to us to Protect and Preserve People like Them - the Brilliant Ones. In the Good Old Days (a phrase banned from my vocabulary, but I'm allowed to write it), the Brilliant Ones were revered by society: Philosophers, Writers, Composers, and Artists. Nowadays Film Directors of all kinds get the treatment, but most of them are not The Brilliant Ones but are just Ordinary Mortals trying to get in the limelight and make a decent movie. Good luck to them.

I don't like working with Directors who don't have anything to say, and are horrid to everybody because they perceive themselves as being important. They don't like working with me much either (fortunately). Some Directors are really nice people but not very good Directors, and some of them are really Brilliant but not very nice. Occasionally you will find one who is really Brilliant and Really Nice. Try and work with these!

The thing to remember if you aim to become a film director is that it is not necessary to behave badly (unless you're a Genius, in which case you can't help it.) And also that the one person on the film set who doesn't have to know anything technically is the Director. He or She can have their heads completely immersed in the Script and the Actors, and that's all right by me. Because that's what we do - the Crew: we supply the technical expertise.

Actually, when I wear a free T-shirt that says CREW on a film, I can't work out whether the DP (Director of Photography) is really Crew or Management. Anyhow, the DP, Operator (maybe the same person) and the Script Supervisor can work out how to shoot the film with the Director. Directors who dictate everything are really boring to work with - especially when they are nasty. If they are a Brilliant One people, forgive them, but if they are just dull, then they don't. ("SO YOU WANNA WORK IN MOVIES?" http://www.cineman.co.uk/. Accessed December 6, 2017. Reprinted by permission of the author Mr. Oliver Stapleton.)

Directing – Calling

When someone asks me about my profession, my knees start to shake with fear – will my answer be satisfying enough? This fear, which I still can't get rid of, took over when my grandma asked me after my high school graduation, *"My sweetie, what are you going to study?"* When I saw that my answer, *"Film and television directing,"* didn't satisfy her – well, how could it when she was born in the nineteenth century (just one year after the Lumière Brothers publicly exhibited *L'Arrivée d'un train en la Gare de la Ciotat* for the first time), without any affection for movies –I started adding onto my answer. The more she looked like she had no clue what I was talking about, the more I kept adding to my explanation. And all of a sudden, she said, *"My sweetie, why did you choose such an unrespectable, disreputable, and irresponsible profession?"* And since then, I have tried to persuade my grandmother that this profession is decent and highly respectable.

I remember the very first lecture of my film professor, film and television director Igor Ciel (*Inferno, Vivat Beňovský*) in Czechoslovakia at the College of Muse and Dramatic Arts, Department of Film and Television. He told us:

> *If you decide to be a director, you will never again live a normal life. When you look at a tree, you will see it differently than a "normal" man. Every book you will read, you will read it through director's eyes. An everyday situation you will assess as a possible situation for your film. The decision to be a director is a decision for a profession, which takes 24 hours every day of the year. You will never have a break, you will fall asleep with your profession, and you will wake up with your profession. Are you sure, you want to live this kind of life?*

And then he added, *"Now is your last chance to stand up and leave this room. All of you have five minutes to make up your mind."* I remember those five silent minutes. No one made even the slightest sound. I'm sure that everybody in the class realized at that point what decision they were going to make. After those five minutes, the professor turned back and evaluated all of us with a long sigh and said, *"Ok. Now we can continue."* I never wondered what direction my life would've taken if I'd walked out of the room. Of course, I had a lot of doubts, wondering if I am good at what I am doing - but I never regretted the decision to become a film director. I feel I was doing in my life what felt right to my heart.

Directing is not just about crossing the finish line. Just doing it will bring you joy and lot of endorphin. Enjoy the process! Of course, that the finished film, which has been a goal driving you, makes you feel accomplishment, but also it will make you feel empty. Directing is a career of pain and suffering, but it's the most exciting thing in the world. It's the way of life. Directing is not just the thesis, *"I don't have to do what I don't want to do,"* but it is about the fact that what you are doing is making you fulfilled. Needless to say, that work is most fulfilling when it's a calling.

CHAPTER 2:
VISUAL CONCEPT

Conceptualization – Visual Concept
(Visual Look, Visual Design, Visual Style, Visual Treatment, Visualization, Visual Stylistic Pattern, Visual Unity of Film, Codes of Visual Conventions)

Intro

Conceptualization refers to the planning and designing process (creative) that goes into every film. During the conceptualization process, a script is translated into the director's artistic vision, and the film begins to take shape.

Directing is defined in this book as a unique act of creation where talent, imagination, sensitivity, and workmanship play a vital role. At the same time, film and television directing is introduced as a painstaking process of translating the director's vision into images. Taking directing to a new level in terms of study, student-directors learn that it is not only craft and technicalities that can have an impact on the vision, abstraction, and interpretation of the film, but that their own temperament, emotionality, and mannerisms can affect the entire process of directing as well. When you want to set yourself apart from others, let your inner voice be heard. Be unique! If you direct a film that you did not write, make sure to be personal, emotional, and impose yourself on the story. Even an impersonal story can become a personal one through your personal approach to it.

Emir Kusturica *(Underground)*, the Serbian film director, said:

> *The worst mistake a young filmmaker can make is to believe that the cinema is an objective art. The only true way of being a filmmaker is not only to have a personal point of view but also to impose it on the film, at every level.* (Tirard, L. *Moviemakers' Master Class: Private Lessons from the World's Foremost Directors*, 1st edition. Farrar, Straus and Giroux, 2002, ISBN: 978-057121102)

Visual Concept

It doesn't matter if filmmaking for you is an art form or commerce, it doesn't matter if you want to create spectacle or entertainment, or you want to make films for the central audience, or art house film moviegoers; or you prioritize blockbuster mentality over non-formulaic productions; you must learn which filmmaking techniques are best used for communicating the meaning, ideas, and emotions of your film to the audience. In this chapter, I want to draw your attention to the importance of the *Visual Look* of your film and to the *Genre* you will set the interpretation of your story in. For me, the visual look is like a vehicle for a story – without a vehicle, the story won't be delivered to the audience. And the genre, as a class or category of artistic composition characterized by a particular style, form, content, and technique, directly influences the visual look of the film. Actually, the *Genre* dictates a *Visual Treatment*.

A *Visual Concept* is necessary for the strength and continuity of every film. It is one of those things that if done right, no one will notice. However, if it's done wrong, everyone will notice, even if they can't identify specifically what the problem is. It is important to discuss and set the rules that will govern your visual concept before you begin shooting, as it can easily break down once you enter principal photography, the phase of film production in which the movie is filmed. It has to be a core element of your conceptualization process, and the result will be evident in the quality of your work.

Film Genre

When a director gets an offer to direct a film, the first thing he/she is thinking about is the genre the story is written in and which genre he/she will employ for interpreting the story. Usually, the interpretation of the story will be set in the same genre the story is written in, but not always! It is director's responsibility to choose the genre that will serve the story in the best possible way. You are permitted an artistic license in order to overcome the limitations of a written genre or heighten the impact of the story by modifying the original genre, or setting the interpretation of the story at the crossroads between genres, or combining visual and narrative conventions of a few genres. The freedom to create artwork entitles you to make adjustments. In 2008, when I got the offer to direct the theatrical feature film *Oblivious*, which was written as an action/thriller where a simple plan to scam a celebrity turns out to be the cover for weapons smuggling operations, I have decided to interpret it as an action-adventure genre, combined with elements of a love story genre.

Film genre can be defined, or, if you will, identified, as a category (group, classification, type) of films of common (recurrent) features (subject, theme, setting, events, values, film techniques, patterns, conventions, tradition, standards). *Genre Conventions* can be defined as a group of similar thematic, stylistic, and structural elements as well as a group of similar cinematic approaches used by filmmakers. Genre itself is a sort of collective understanding of conventions and boundaries. Filmmakers create their films within the restrictions of the genre that audiences have come to expect.

While scholars dispute definitions and systems, the audience is already a genre expert. It enters each film armed with a complex set of anticipations learned through a lifetime of moviegoing. (Robert McKee, *Substance, Structure, Style and the Principles of Screenwriting,* ReganBooks; 1st edition, 1997, ISBN-10: 0060391685)

You can either fulfill audience's anticipation or risk their confusion and disappointment, as Robert McKee says. But boundaries of specific genres are constantly changing as individual films challenge conventions. There are many films where the interpretation of the story intersects the crossroads of two or more genres or is based on a derivation, deviation, and deflection of a particular genre. Rejections of standard conventions can put you on the radar if you want to stand up. Freshness and new voices are expected and welcome.

Hong Kong film director Wong Kar Wai *(2046),* internationally renowned as an auteur for his visually unique, highly stylized films, states:

The only thing that I try to make very clear when I start a film is the genre that I want to place it in. (Tirard, L. *Moviemakers' Master Class: Private Lessons from the World's Foremost Directors,* 1st edition. Farrar, Straus and Giroux, 2002, ISBN: 978-057121102)

Genre and Suspension of Disbelief

There is still another reason for you to clearly determine the genre you will be using for your film, and it is the *Suspension of Disbelief,* the phenomenon, which was defined as *"a willingness to suspend one's critical faculties and believe the unbelievable; something surreal; sacrifice of realism and logic for the sake of enjoyment."* It will help you make your film work. The audience will accept implausibility in the story when they know that they are watching sci-fi, horror, or a fairytale.

If you successfully set the interpretation of the story, for instance in the science fiction genre, utilizing stylistic elements and narrative conventions, let's say of supernatural sci-fi comedy, and you do it for the sake of narration (for the sake of narrative and dramatic purposes), then you will convince the audience to accept the main twist in the story as a real, and you will convince the audience to believe that they are watching a real drama. And from there, you can depart in your own way and create a "make-us-believe story."

Let me summarize: The genre will guide you to the extent/level to which you can depart from reality and still convince the audience that they are watching a real drama, or at least make them willing to suspend disbelief. To suspend their disbelief, you have to make things believable, and the genre is here to help you with this. Think about the norms and limitations of the genre, how these limitations work for you, and how you can obey or stretch them for the sake of engaging the audience.

Visual Style – Codes of Visual Conventions

(Sets of visual conventions, genre visual style, stylistic patterns, and stylistic organization of film)

My former student, Kevin Phillips, while he was still my student, shot me an e-mail, apologizing for being late for class in the morning, awoke in a cold, sweat, presumably from an awful nightmare.

> *There is no reason to limit oneself in style if the story being told is aesthetically in harmony with the visual devices in use. Once again...I've broken it down to a restrictive formula...whereas we have interpreted the ideologies of a SYMPHONY and are adapting them to the screen in order to create a VESSEL for our VISUAL LANGUAGE. This is in order to keep a strict congruity within the film, and hinder ourselves from indulgence.*

Kevin Phillips' feature debut (2017) - *Super Dark Times* – "a sensitive coming-of-age story astutely captures the moment when a teen's carefree perspective turns into a traumatic loss of innocence" – is now receiving numerous accolades and worldwide recognition.

> *Film style matters because what people call content comes to us in and through the patterned use of the medium's techniques. Without performance and framing, lens length and lighting, composition and cutting, dialogue and music, we could not grasp the world of the story. Style is the tangible texture of the film, the perceptual surface we encounter as we watch and listen, and that surface is our point of departure in moving to plot, theme, feeling – everything else that matter to us. And since filmmakers devote painstaking care to fine points of style, we must dig into details. (…) Yet most film scholars don't analyze style, particularly visual style. Ironically, as films have become more available for close analysis than ever, interest in stylistics has waned. Why? Partly because film studies has for some time attracted scholars of a literary turn of mind, more comfortable with hermeneutics than stylistics – which remains a minor discipline in literary studies. In addition, even scholars have difficulty attending to the minutiae of technique. As we watch a film, we absorb its images but seldom notice how they're lit or composed. So critics and scholars find it more natural to talk about characters' psychological development, about how the plot resolves its conflicts and problems, or about the film's psychological or cultural or polit-*

ical significance. (Bordwell, David. *Figures Traced in Light: On Cinematic Staging.* © 2005 by the Regents of the University of California. Reprinted by permission by the University of California Press.)

David Bordwell, in another book *Narration in the Fiction Film*, states: *"In order for style to come forward across the whole film, it must possess internal coherence. This coherence depends on establishing a distinctive, often unique, intrinsic stylistic norm."* (Bordwell, D. *Narration in the Fiction Film.* University of Wisconsin Press, 1985, ISBN-10: 0299101746)

Geoff Andrew, in his book *The Director's Vision*, states: *"Film style is how you exploit the cinematic arts – composition, color, camera angle and movement, lighting, sound, sets, action and performance – to convey your thematic obsessions and artistic visions."* (Andrew, G. *The Director's Vision: A Concise Guide to the Art of 250 Great Filmmakers*, 1st edition. Chicago Review Press, 1999, ISBN-10: 1556523661)

Style is defined by *Film Terms Glossary* as a recognizable group of conventions used by filmmakers to add visual appeal, meaning, or depth to their work that can be applied to any genre.

- Classical style
- Art cinema style
    - Avant-garde cinema
    - French impressionist cinema
    - Surrealist cinema style
    - Italian neorealism
- "Cinéma vérité" style
- European "artistic" filmmaking style
- New Hollywood
- MTV style
- Cop-show style/NYPD Blue style (fabricated style)
- DOGMA 95 style
- Soap opera – sitcom style
- Reality show style / docu-soap style (implied stance of "reality effect"/faked "observational stance")

Michael Rabiger, in *Directing: Techniques and Aesthetics*, states:

The style of a film is really the visible influence of its maker's identity. (...) Partly this is content, partly it's the kind of tale and the characteristic forms each chooses, and partly it's because the films have the mark of individual personalities and tastes written all over them. (Rabiger, M. *Directing: Film*

Techniques and Aesthetics, 4th edition. Focal Press, 2008, ISBN: 978-0-240-80882-6)

Directing Style

The second thing I want to discuss in this chapter that is directly linked to a *Visual Style* is *Directing Style,* as well as *Directing Style Conventions.* Directing style is a characteristic, identifiable, visual, formal, and personal imprint (mark, signature, stamp, POV, personal touch of the director) that reflects a director's identity and is immediately recognized. Directing style conventions are all elements of visual style, form style, theme selection, and personal identity that help to define a specific directing style.

Cennino d'Andrea Cennini, in his book *Il Libro dell'Arteon,* wrote almost six hundred years ago: *"If nature has granted you any imagination at all, that you will eventually acquire a style individual to yourself, and it cannot help being good; because your hand and your mind, being always accustomed to gather flowers, would ill know how to pluck thorns."*

I encourage you to discover your own way of perceiving and interpreting the world. With this foundation, you can develop your own special, solitary, and inimitable artistic expression, which will help you create your own unique directing style. Think about your unique perception of the world and your interpretation of your perception.

Michael Rabiger, in his book, *Directing: Techniques and Aesthetics,* states:

> *This search for your own path, for the truths underlying your formation and patterns, starts feeding itself once you make a commitment to expressing something about it. This willingness to begin the journey sustains the artistic process (...)* (Rabiger, M. *Directing: Film Techniques and Aesthetics,* 4th edition. Focal Press, 2008, ISBN: 978-0-240-80882-6)

Arthur Schopenhauer, a German philosopher, best known for his work *The World as Will and Representation* said: *"Talent hits a target no one else can hit. Genius hits a target no one else can see."* Robert Bresson *(Balthazar),* an acclaimed French film director, said: *"Make visible what, without you, might perhaps never have been seen."* Marcel Proust, the French novelist, said: *"The real voyage of discovery consists not in seeing new lands but in seeing with new eyes."* And one more time Cennini's advice: *"(...) discover things not seen, hiding themselves under the shadow of natural objects, and fix them with the hand, presenting to plain sight what does not actually exist."* Think about the following in searching for your own directing style:

- Unique theme or topic (something unique, never seen before, or seen before but with a personal imprint imposed on it).
- New and unseen subjects.
- Turning generic themes into unique content.
- Meaningful, life-enriching stories.
- Dealing with universal human subjects.
- A genuine commitment to the basic moral and ethical problems.
- Passing your sense of wonder and positivity onto others.
- Manifestations of humanity.
- Radical approaches.
- Something that reflects your identity, professionalism, artistry, and industry.
- Innovations – the invention of a new language true to the nature of the film.
- Art-house approach.
- Art-cinema narration (breaking the conventional narration, chance events, fortuitous discoveries, subconscious, dreams, emotions).
- Crossover of genre visual style.
- Genre deviations.
- Stylistic replications.
- Rejections of standard conventions (new system of conventions, disorder as a rule).
- Breaking all the rules of conventional cinematographic practice set by traditional Hollywood filmmaking.
- Fully embracing new technologies.
- Artistic risks.
- A need to stand out from the crowd.
- A "wow" factor.

Visual Look

Orson Welles *(Touch of Evil)*, American director, actor, writer, and producer, said: *"Create your own visual style... let it be unique for yourself and yet identifiable for others."*

The visual look of a film is determined first and foremost by the nature of directorial vision, and then by modes of lighting/light design, camera treatment, shot design, location, production design, costume design, set design/set dressing, makeup, cast, special effects, editing, color palette, color grading, and color correction.

While seeking how to express the look and feel of your film during the conceptualization process, you have to figure out and then determine how to:

- Set the tone for the entire film through a visual look.
- Establish a visual look of the film.
- Enhance the expressive potential of the film through a visual look.
- Comment on the narrative through a visual look.
- Maintain that visual look all the way through the film.

When designing and shaping the vision of the mental picture of your film, work
out all components below. It will help you in articulating your vision.

- VISUAL STYLE OF FILM
    - Elements that relate to a visual look of a location
      (photographic opportunities, visual possibilities,
      visual potential; atmosphere and mood of the
      place; contribution to the mood and emotional
      tone: INT. vs. EXT., DAY vs. NIGHT, color, texture,
      design; lighting; set dressing, design, adjustments,
      layout, modification)
    - Genre visual codes and conventions
    - Settings (location or studio, realistic or stylized,
      historical or contemporary)

- MODES OF LIGHTING
    - Realistic/naturalistic
    - Expressionist/stylized
    - Motivated
    - Low key
    - High key
    - Chiaroscuro
    - Frontal, side, or back
    - Hard or Soft
    - Emotional
    - Special

- PICTURE COMPOSITION
    - Fragmented or continuous
    - Camera angle
    - Shot sizes
    - Shot design

- Composition of shot
- Framing
- Open/closed frame composition
- Picture plane

- LENSES

  - Wide
  - Long
  - Standard/normal
  - Zoom
  - Selective focus
  - Depth of field (shallow focus, deep focus, rack focus, pull focus, zoom in/out)
  - Filters

- COLOR

  - Warm tone
  - Bluish tone
  - Omitting colors
  - Mixing colors
  - Tonal balance

- FILM STOCK

  - Fast film
  - Black and white or color
  - Over/underexposed

- CAMERA MOVEMENT

  - Moving shot, static shot, handheld, crane shot, "shaky" camera style/"snapshot" documentary style, spectacular shots/abnormal perspective

- STAGING AND BLOCKING

  - Stationary, on movement
  - In-depth or online
  - Open-frame composition
  - Closed-frame composition (frame is carefully composed – self-contained)
  - Frame makes an indirect comment on a character's inner state of mind

- Movement of characters (from left to right, from right to left, toward and away from the camera)
- Group shots, single shot, isolated character, obscured character
- Short take
- Shot based on inner montage
- Pace and rhythm (traditional/nontraditional narrative pace)

Visual Structure

The director manipulates, controls, and regulates the audience's perception of events within the film, and that is an undeniable fact. Since film is a visual medium, visual communication is the primary system for communicating information. A director uses visual control as a narrative tool or device.

I do believe in two rules in film. The rule of *Continual Progression* and the *Rule of Unity*. In order to keep the story development continuous, a film must be structured the way that one event leads to the next event and so on, creating the chain of events linked or related to one another; ensuring the progression of the story to its completion in a continual manner. The unity and wholeness is the essential quality of a good film, and every director has this on his/her mind when he/she designs the film. From a practical point of view, a director strives to create a film that represents a blending of high-quality film elements, including art direction and all its components, like production design and costume design. Shot design and the physical appearance of the actors help the director create a special look for the film that suits the story in the best possible way. You will learn later in this book how to use specific directorial tools for creating a style-consistency film; tools for accomplishing the outer and inner cohesion of the film, which will support the unity of the film, and heighten the emotional impact on the audience. All directorial components - directing actors, cinematography, shot design, art direction with all its aspects - all have to come together in a unified and seamless way.

You are a director, and you are using your visual literacy, a well-developed graphic sense, and an understanding of 3D design concepts for visual storytelling. You are using the camera for a comprehensive visual interpretation of the story that works in harmony with the plot. You try to be in full control of the subject matter and attempt to exhibit a creative strategy in accomplishing your vision. One of the most effective tools at your disposal while working on a *Visual Concept* is creating a *Visual Structure* of your film. An inspirational source book is Bruce Block's book *The Visual Story: Creating the Visual Structure of Film, TV and Digital Media*.

The structure you've picked for space, line, shape, tone, color, movement, and rhythm will help you find the correct lenses, camera angles, locations, wardrobe, and architectural elements for your production. The visual rules will give your production visual unity, style, and (...) visual structure. (Block, B. *The Visual Story: Creating the Visual Structure of Film, TV and Digital Media*, 2nd edition. Focal Press, 2008, ISBN: 978-0-240-80779-9)

When I accidentally bumped into Bruce Block's book, I said to myself, "This will not work; the art of filmmaking cannot be bound by rules, graphs, and charts." Just out of curiosity, I checked out the feature film *Fallacies of our Traditional Moral*, I wrote and directed in 1989, the story about the unwanted pregnancy of 14-year-old girl, and to my surprise, I have to confess that Bruce Block is right. *"When the story structure gains intensity, the visual structure must do the same."* I've wished I had this source of information years ago. My films would definitely look and work better. Now I instruct my film students to construct a visual structure for every film they work on before they start shooting.

Bruce Block says:

Draw the graph for story structure (story intensity) and then the graph for visual structure (visual intensity). Create a visual structure that parallels the story structure. At the climax of the story you will have maximum contrast, and in the story's resolution, the visual contrast will change to affinity. (Block, B. *The Visual Story: Creating the Visual Structure of Film, TV and Digital Media*, 2nd edition. Focal Press, 2008, ISBN: 978-0-240-80779-9)

Here, I have decided to provide you with a couple of statements from guru directors, all of which are related to the topic I have discussed in this chapter. Consider it a "director's master class."

To me, style is just the outside of content, and content the inside of style, like the outside and inside of human body. Both go together, they can't be separated. – Jean-Luc Godard, French-Swiss film director, screenwriter *(Breathless)*

There is no point in having sharp images when you've fuzzy ideas. – Jean-Luc Godard,

I keep persuading younger colleagues to whom I teach scriptwriting and directing, to examine their own lives. The years in which you don't work on yourself like this, are in fact wasted. – Krysztof Kieslowski, Polish art-house film director and screenwriter *(Three Colors trilogy)*

You don't make a movie, the movie makes you. – Jean-Luc Godard

My movie is born first in my head, dies on paper; is resuscitated by the living persons and real objects I use, which are killed on film but, placed in a certain order and projected on to a screen, come to life again like flowers in water. – Robert Bresson

I always direct the same film. I can't distinguish one from another. – Federico Fellini, Italian film director and screenwriter (*8½*)

I've realized that basically, I don't give a shit for society, which in the case of Poland, is forty million people. But what I really care about is the individual human being. - Krzysztof Kieslowski

To shoot a film is to organize a complete universe. – Ingmar Bergman, Swedish film director and screenwriter (*Persona*)

Film can do amazing things with abstraction, but it rarely gets a chance. People are treated like idiots, and people are not idiots. We're hip to the human condition, the human experience, and we love mysteries. – David Lynch, American film director and screenwriter (*Blue Velvet*)

I never made a film which fully satisfied me. – Roman Polanski, French-Polish film director (*Rosemary's Baby*)

A film has to be like a stone in the shoe. – Lars Von Trier, Danish film director and screenwriter (*Dancer in the Dark*)

Realism is a bad word. In a sense, everything is realistic. I see no line between the imaginary and the real. – Federico Fellini

Film is not the art of scholars, but of illiterates. – Werner Herzog, German film director and screenwriter (*Fitzcarraldo*)

Only cinema narrows its concern down to its content that is to its story. It should, instead, concern itself with its form, its structure. – Peter Greenaway, British film director and screenwriter (*The Cook, the Thief, His Wife & Her Lover*)

Making films has got to be one of the hardest endeavors known to humankind. Straight up and down, film work is hard shit. – Spike Lee, American film director (*She's Gotta Have It*)

The theater is like a faithful wife. The film is a great adventure - the costly, exacting mistress. – Ingmar Bergman

The directing of a picture involves coming out of your individual loneliness and taking a controlling part in putting together a small world. A picture is made. You put a frame around it and move on. And one day you die. That is all there is to it. – John Huston, American film director *(The African Queen)*

Cinema is interior movement. – Robert Bresson

I have formulated my own directing style in my head, proceeding without any unnecessary imitation of others. – Yasujiro Ozu, Japanese film director and screenwriter *(An Autumn Afternoon)*

It's not where you lift it from, it's where you lift it to. – Jim Jarmush, American film director *(Coffee and Cigarettes)*

I'm tempted to divide the history of humanity not into before Christ and after Christ but before Lumière and after Lumière. Milos Forman, American film director *(One Flew Over the Cuckoo's Nest)*

In the lecture, Andrey Tarkovsky *(Nostalghia)*, Soviet director held at a special event called *Thieves of Cinema* on September 9, 1982, in Rome, he said: *There are two basic categories of film directors. One consists of those who seek to imitate the world in which they live, the other of those who seek to create their own world. The second category contains the poets of cinema, Bresson, Dovzenko, Mizoguchi, Bergman, Bunuel and Kurosawa, the cinema's most important names. The work of these filmmakers is difficult to distribute: it reflects their inner aspirations, and this always runs counter to public taste. This does not mean that the filmmakers don't want to be understood by their audience. But rather they themselves try to pick up on and understand the inner feelings of the audience.*

When you have finished surveying this chapter, return to the beginning and read in more detail. Then you can proceed to the next step – practicing this directorial concept in: I. STUDIO – APPLICATION OF GENRE CONVENTIONS. Information related to this studio can be found in Part II: STUDIOS – DIRECTING EXERCISES.

CHAPTER 3:
CONCEPT OF VISUAL UNITS

Applying the Concept of Visual Units for Rendering a Scene

Intro

Nicholas T. Proferes, in his book *Film Directing Fundamentals*, states:

> *For nearly a century the concept of a beat has been used in acting as a unit of action or nuance from the perspective of a character. However, it is also possible to think of beats from a director's perspective as units that progress the narrative.* (Proferes, N. *Film Directing Fundamentals: See Your Film Before Shooting*, 2nd edition. Focal Press, 2005, ISBN:0240805623)

The *Concept of Visual Units* is the methodology for translating a script to the screen. You will learn in this chapter how to break down a scene into directorial units, how to translate directorial units into visual units, and how to break down visual units into individual shots. This chapter also compares two different styles of filming: the standard formula/pattern for shooting a scene using the "classical" approach of "coverage" and the non-standard formula/pattern for shooting a scene using a shot-by-shot style based on the concept of visual units.

A scene (a unit of the story that takes place in a specific location and time) can be shot in an infinite variety of ways, but there is only one way to do it that will best serve the story and emotional needs of your film, and reflect your individual style and personal identity. It's up to you to find the "face" of the scene. If you have a feeling about how the scene should be portrayed, or you "see" the scene in your head, prepare shots in advance and stick to your vision. If you do not see the scene in your head but want to assure the consistency of a scene – which will contribute to the unity of the film and its wholeness – then analyze the scene beforehand by breaking it down into individual units.

The concept I will explain here will help you to translate dramatic scenes to the screen. The concept of visual units is loosely based on the *Concept of Dramatic Units*, where dramatic units are defined as fundamental building blocks of drama, based on the unity of time, the unity of place, and concentration on the development of a single plot, that means the unity of action. The three unities of time, place, and action observed in classical drama and specified by an ancient Greek philosopher Aristoteles in his Poetics, are three dramatic principles of a scene.

The process described below is applied to each previsualization process. For each scene you work with, follow the procedure step by step. Although you might have an intuitive sense for visualizing a scene (overall, this process is largely intuitive), examine your intuition. Maybe it contains something else you have overlooked. Don't settle for less when more is available to you.

Visual Units

You must understand the structure of the scene and its progressive elements. Since each unit must fit into the whole of the scene, units make up the scene and create a unified whole. For visual-storytelling purposes, you have to delineate units because they can help you to define the shots. The term *Visual Units* refers to fundamental building blocks that help a director communicate the idea and meaning of the scene, as well as achieve his/her unique artistic interpretation. You'll likely see other terms like: sub-events, fragments, segments, bits, sections, dramatic blocks, dramatic action, narrative beats, action units, units of action, sections of actions, lines, subunits, rhythmic beats, acting beats, director's beats, directing elements, textual elements, emotional events, and moments. All these terms have different origins, but they can be used interchangeably and mean essentially the same thing – the smallest structuring components.

You need to identify units for the sake of visual narration. Why? Because these units might imply the shots – and they do. The procedure you should follow in identifying visual units is very simple. The simplest and most effective way to identify units is by changes in the scene. All changes you see in the scene have a mutual denominator, and that mutual denominator is called a *Principal Key* - a fundamental instrument of traceability in mappings distinctions in a dramatic scene. So, when you sense or when you can rationally recognize that the changes in a physical action are the most frequent changes in a scene, the principal key is focused on "changes in physical action." Now, when you know what the principal key is for a particular scene, try to apply this key throughout the entire scene, since you might have overlooked some distinctions. By applying the principal key, you will figure out all visual units within that specific scene.

Guidelines for Breaking a Scene to Visual Units in three easy Steps

1.   Break the scene into units – apply an intuitive approach:
     Look at the scene intuitively, allow the intuition and subjectivity to guide you, and every time you feel a shift in the action, or a change in something within the scene, draw the horizontal line separating the division. Keep doing this throughout the scene and do not intellectualize. Identify and designate (frame) the units by drawing lines separating one division from another.

2. Break the scene into units – apply an analytical approach:
    For an analytical approach, set up a principal key for defining the units
    and use it for the purposes of clarifying these distinctions within the
    scene.

    Principal Key:

    a. Changes in subject (new subject of interest, a character changes
        the subject)
    b. Changes in information (presentation of information relevant
        to the story, revealing information, withholding information)
    c. Changes in character perspective (shifts from one character to
        another, changes in subjectivity)
    d. Changes in character feelings, motivations, and insights
    e. Changes in action (shifts in action, rising action, falling action)
    f. Changes in objectives
    g. Changes in mood
    h. Changes in physical action
    i. Changes in story intensity
    j. Changes in emotional intensity (excitement, empathy, increase
        of tension, increase of curiosity)
    k. Changes in time (time interval)
    l. Changes in lines
    m. Changes in storyteller's perspective
    n. Changes in visual interest
    o. Shift in power balance
    p. Pauses

Now compare the results from both approaches, the first one – intuitive approach – and the second one – analytical approach, and decide which one:

- Better serves the story
- Helps the audience to understand the action and characters
- Better emphasizes dramatic and emotional intensity of a
  story
- Better articulates a point of interest for the audience (asso-
  ciative point)
- Better maps emotional and dramatic twists, turning points,
  fulcrum points, and pivotal moments
- Better communicates the idea and meaning of the scene
- Better communicates the essence of the scene
- More effectively visually narrates the story
- More intensively translates your (director's) intentions

3. Translate the units into shots – mentally:
    When the scene is broken down into the smallest units, move on to the
    next step, which is translating these units into shots. Does each unit im-
    ply an individual shot? Does each unit indicate just one individual shot
    or more shots? Do two or three or four units indicate a shot? Although
    the goal is to create a scene that will be perceived by the audience as an
    unbroken event (or should be perceived as an unbroken event), no
    doubt you will not always shoot the scene in one long, unbroken take.
    Therefore, when you want to create a flow of invisible shot changes (and
    you probably want to, since you don't want to expose the mechanism of
    filmmaking and by doing so divorce the audience from the action and
    shift the viewers' attention to the camera work), you have to break down
    the scene into individual shots, which are seamlessly tied together. Once
    the scene is already broken down into units that are seamlessly narra-
    tively tailored together, use them as a matrix for breaking down the sce-
    ne into individual shots. These units imply the shots because these units
    are actually fundamentals of shots.

I know there is doubt and skepticism and that some of you are condemning the
concept of visual units before it's even had a chance to show you that it might
work. As a director, you have an obligation and a supreme creative responsibility;
therefore, try and see if this concept is something that will work for you. Later on,
you might find this concept so obvious that you decide to adopt it for each film
you work on, but first, you need to try it. I've seen many student-directors adopt
this concept to the benefit of their films.

Verbal Storyboard

The undeniable benefit of working on the *Verbal Storyboard* (the written output
of the concept of visual units*)* is the fact that your work is nurtured by the driven
power of dramatic and emotional necessities of a scene. By working on a verbal
storyboard, you do not get bogged down in the minute visual details, which can
be elaborated on later; you are totally focused on the essence of the scene. So, the
biggest pay off of this process is that you will work out a "visual blueprint" of the
scene, which will guide you in visual storytelling and help you to design individual shots.

A verbal storyboard is a mental image of a scene, where each intended shot is
described by words.

Keep in mind that a verbal storyboard is the director's first stage in the previsualization process. It is the first time the script will be translated into images –
mental images. Since the basic concept for visualization comes from the dramatic

and emotional necessities of the story, you can start by analyzing the scene. Although you might have an intuitive sense for visualizing the scene (as I've mentioned before, this process is largely intuitive), start with breaking the scene into units. For visual-storytelling purposes, you have to define the units, because they can help you to define the shots. The undeniable benefit of working on a verbal storyboard is the fact that your work is nurtured and driven by the power of the dramatic necessities of the story and the emotional needs of each scene.

Working on a verbal storyboard allows you to focus on the essence of the scene. Verbal storyboards do not have to indicate the size of shot, composition, camera angle, or camera movement. You are distilling a scene, you are "boiling" it down to its dramatic and emotional essence, which is revealed in a "visual essence." Impurities in a scene are "vaporized", and its pure, high-emotional and dramatic condensation is collected in a verbal storyboard. Since you are translating the scene into its "visual essence", you can begin to work on a verbal storyboard without having your locations locked down, or even without having scouted them. As a matter of fact, the verbal storyboard can help you to outline locations that might work for your film. In 1997, I was scouting a location for the TV Series entitled *Mountain Rangers*. I insisted on visiting a scripted location, *The High Mountain Cabin*. At the time, I was convinced that I could not write a shooting script without visiting all the scripted locations ahead of shooting. *The High Mountain Cabin* is situated in the High Tatras mountains in Slovakia, and because of the altitude, and snow, it was only accessible by helicopter. And what God didn't want, the helicopter fell down. I was not supposed to survive the helicopter crash landing, but my time has not yet come. I knew there were valuable lessons to be learned from that accident, and the first one I learned was that I don't have to see the location before I start working on a shooting script. That accident taught me an important survival lesson, which was translated to the concept of a verbal storyboard, I am sharing now with all of you.

These photos taken on May 7, 1997, shows the site where the helicopter crashed.

Guidelines for Creating a Verbal Storyboard in Steps

1. Break a scene into units. Apply a naïve/intuitive approach and, afterward, an analytical approach, as discussed earlier. To use the analytical approach, set up a principal key for framing the units. Compare the results from both approaches and decide which one better communicates the idea and meaning of the scene and which one more intensively and more effectively translates your intent.
2. Identify and separate the units by drawing lines separating one unit from another one.
3. Express the essence of each unit in one sentence.
4. Break the sentence into phrases or words.
5. Indicate a visual image: Translate the sentences, phrases, words, meaning, emotion, essence, or whatever is important for you in a scene into visual images. Does each sentence indicate an individual visual image? Does each phrase or word indicate an individual visual image? Do two, three, or four words or phrases or sentences indicate a visual image? A visual image is actually a visual unit. Your visual unit does not have to inevitably indicate the size of shot, composition, camera angle or camera movement.
6. Verbally describe the visual image (visual unit) – verbal description of a visual image = the content of a visual unit.
7. Assign a shot to the verbal description of the visual image. Now take into consideration: size of shot, composition, camera angle, and camera movement. For the meantime, you can exclude from your consideration the following, unless the following are the part of your narrative devices: lens selection (prime or zoom lenses), framing (arranging and enclosing objects within shot frame), and screen time (time allotted to the shot.) You will elaborate on this later on when you have an actual location for your shoot.

Simple-minded Sample in Steps

Scene: John is standing close to the desk when he suddenly leans across the desk to reach for his keys. He grabs them and holds them against his chest like a treasure.

Steps 1–4:

Step 1: Principal key: changes in action.
Step 3: Sentence: John reaches for his keys, grabs them, and holds them against his chest.

Step 4: Phrases: John reaches for…his keys…grabs them…and holds them against his chest.

Step 4a: Words: John…reaches…for his keys…grabs them…and holds them…against his…chest.

Steps 5–6:

	WORD	INDICATED VISUAL IMAGE	VERBAL DESCRIPTION OF VISUAL IMAGE
A	John …	character	John standing close to the desk.
B	…reaches…	movement	John leans towards the desk.
C	…for his keys…	keys	Keys lying on the desk.
D	…grabs them….	a hand grabs the keys	Quick action – a hand grabs the keys.
E	…and holds them…	a hand holding the keys reaches the chest	Quick action – hand holding the keys reaches the chest.
F	…against his chest.	character holds his keys against his chest	John stands close to the desk and holds the keys.

Step 7:

	WORD	INDICATED VISUAL IMAGE	VERBAL DESCRIPTION OF VISUAL IMAGE	ASSIGNED SHOT
A	John…	character	John standing close to the desk.	MFS of John; direct front-face shot; eye level
B	…reaches…	movement	John leans towards the desk.	MS of John leaning to-wards the keys out of the shot; profile shot; low an-gle
C	…for his keys…	keys	Keys lying on the desk.	CU of keys; high angle

Ca				**CU** of John looking at the keys out of the shot; low angle
D	...grabs them...	a hand grabs the keys	Quick action – a hand grabs the keys.	**CU** of keys – a hand enters the shot and grabs the keys and leaves the shot; eye level; profile shot
E	...and holds them...	A hand holding the keys reaches the chest	Quick action – hand holding the keys reaches the chest.	**CU** of hand "moving through the space"; moving shot
F	...against his chest.	character holds his keys against his chest.	John stands close to the desk and holds the keys.	**MS** of John holding his keys; eye level

Coverage vs. Shot-by-Shot Style

A standard formula/pattern for shooting a scene using the "classical" approach of "coverage" requires *Lining a Script* (a technique to show visually what coverage will be shot for each scene) using straight vertical lines. Vertical lines indicate camera shots through the scene. Each line represents the anticipated camera set-up, with a desired type of shot. A non-standardized formula/pattern for shooting a scene using a shot-by-shot style requires using horizontal lines based on the concept of visual units explained above. Here, I compare and contrast both approaches. When you learn more about both concepts, you might discover possibilities of combining the *Vertical Pattern* with the *Horizontal Pattern*

	COVERAGE Standardized coverage of classic studio system, where a scene is shot from a variety of angles and distances, using different shot sizes.	**SHOT-BY-SHOT STYLE** Non-standardized style of shoot, where every shot is carefully planned out.
	Characteristics	**Characteristics**
The main characteristic	The classic studio feature film and the contemporary television drama depend almost exclusively on the use of coverage.	The contemporary feature films use the dynamic qualities of shot-by-shot blocking, staging, and shooting.
Conceptualization	Sometimes it lacks a comprehensive and detailed control of all aspects of shot design.	Every element of the shot is designed to serve the overall impact.
Pre-production	It can be properly planned in advance and some key elements identified, but a lot is left to chance.	Everything is planned out, and nothing is left to chance.
Blocking and Staging	"Shooting for the edit" – shooting each scene multiple times from various angles and distances to obtain proper coverage.	Each shot is individually staged and carefully planned out.
Framing	Retain an unobtrusive and functional style of framing and editing. The coherent representation of the action.	Some filmmakers reject invisible technique tradition, obtrusive cutting, and camera movement divorced from action.
Spatial Treatment	The director "records" the action from a set of basic camera positions, which usually stay on one side of the line as if it were being shot through a proscenium arch.	The director "interprets" the action from various camera set-ups and from both sides of line of action.

Editing	Editing is functional, motivated by the characters' interaction, and stays with the performers.	Editing is used expressively, and sometimes obtrusive cutting is used.
Cinematography	The classic narrative cinema technique, maintaining stylistic coherence, maintaining control at all times, and producing a narrative, which is easy to read. Less versatile photography.	Each shot is taken independently. More versatile photography.
Directing Style	Does not represent a substantial degree of directorial autonomy.	Recognizable individual style. Achieving a specific directorial style. Some filmmakers completely reject conventional visual codes and favor an indirect and oblique presentation.
Actors' Performance	The performance is carefully controlled to meet the demands of continuity editing using coverage as the primary blocking technique.	The visual image carries as much of the emotion of the scene as the performers.
Output (Footage)	Raw material.	Elaborated material.

	COVERAGE		SHOT-BY-SHOT STYLE	
	Advantage	Disadvantage	Advantage	Disadvantage
Editing	More footage for the film editor to work with.			Less footage for the film editor to work with
Economy		Wasting time, money, and energy.	Economy of the shoot.	

Cinematography		Losing discipline for excellence in cinematography.	Artistic freedom – room for creativity and experimentation	

Footage		Plethora of unusable shots		Lack of variety.
Solving potential problems	Producing different insight than was originally planned out, and ultimately better.			Cemented in original vision.

There is a skeptical attitude, even among my colleagues, when I do not allow my students to shoot the coverage and instead ask them to apply dynamic qualities of a shot-by-shot style while they work on in-studio directing exercises and on a final film. Even with my overwhelming support for the use of a shot-by-shot style in small video exercises, some student-directors, including some of my own colleagues, remain skeptical. But in the end, I think that the skeptical attitude is a good thing. There may not be one obvious "right" or "wrong" way of shooting. I do not anticipate that all student-directors will dutifully use a shot-by-shot style. But to refine and enrich your own style of shooting in order to be better equipped for a big film, I recommend you to adopt a shot-by-shot style even though you may think that the standardized style of shooting a film using "coverage" will work better for you. I am aware that my European formal film training, and years of directing films in Europe, and my prone to auteur film make me naturally incline toward a shot-by-shot style.

The following samples can be the answer to those, who still question the power of the shot-by-shot style, where every shot is carefully planned out.

Stanley Kubrick *(A Clockwork Orange)*, one of the world's most influential, and inspiring film director, known for the painstaking attention he paid to every detail of the film, and for exerting complete control over every aspect of his films, never used a storyboard (except the special effect shots in *Full Metal Jacket*) to visualize a shot in advance. But he specified a scene in great details in advanced, and composed shots on a film set, still giving every shot its precision. He was obsessed over every visual element in every frame.

Martin Scorsese *(Taxi Driver, Raging Bull)*, American director.

> *Scorsese's insistence on thinking everything through in advance makes a*
> *cinematographer's job easier, though nothing is ever set in stone. It can't be,*
> *because so much of filmmaking is problem-solving, particularly when va-*
> *garies of weather, or even just shifting light, enter the picture. (...) Prieto*
> *loves the day Scorsese finally sits down with him to explain the shot list.*
> *"That day for me is one of my favorite parts of production with Marty," he*
> *says, "because he'll explain his process of why he wants to do that medium*
> *shot, or why does the camera move? Or is it completely static? Are we tight or*
> *are we wide, and why? No shot is random." Those storyboards also give Prie-*
> *to a sense of the movie-to-be as an organic whole. "Marty thinks a lot also in*
> *terms of editing. It's not just covering a scene in the regular sense of wide*
> *shots and close-ups. He really does think about the end result, once it's all*
> *put together. Listening to that process helps me understand how he's pictur-*
> *ing it, and I can translate that into images. Not just shots, not just the fram-*
> *ing or the camera movements, but the emotion behind it." Knowing why*
> *Scorsese chose "a specific language for the camera," Prieto says, helps him to*
> *grasp the mood of a scene so he can figure out the appropriate lighting for it.*
> *(TIME, February 20, 2017, pg.42–43)*

The legendary cinematographer Gordon Willis *(The Godfather, Manhattan, An-*
nie Hall) also cautions against *"dump-truck directing"* – a term he coined to describe the bad habit of directors who aren't discerning when shooting. Willis's
sage advice comes in handy for the digital filmmaker, whose temptation to fix
everything in the post can overshadow the simplicity of doing it right the first
time. Here's the portion of the text of the Gordon Willis ASC interview for *Cinema-*
tographer Style, Volume 1:

> *What is shotgun moviemaking? It's like, "Let's spray the entire room. Let's get eve-*
> *ry single cut we can think of, including the doorknobs. Let's do everything. Let's*
> *take every shot. Let's take a long shot, a close-up, a medium close-up." There's no*
> *real structure in that thinking. And then it gets turned over to an editor, and the*
> *editor makes the movie. That's what I call "dump-truck directing," and I don't par-*
> *ticularly care for it. I've been fortunate enough to mostly work with people who will*
> *look at a scene and say, "What do we have to accomplish in the scene?" Whether we*
> *take one cut or four cuts, that's what we'll do. We'll lay it out and shoot those four.*
> *We'll lay it out and shoot 20 if that's what it takes, but it's never mindless machine-*
> *gun shooting.* (Jon Fauer, "Remembering Gordon Willis." ASC, http://www.
> fdtimes.com/2014/05/20/remembering-gordon-willis-asc/. Accessed March 11,
> 2017)

This book teaches the art and craft of directing in a specific way, one in which
academic freedom is maintained, and autonomy is nurtured. From my perspec-

tive, it is a precondition for distinguished contribution to the film education of all student-filmmakers. An abundance of creative and intellectual diversity, different professional experiences, different cultural experiences, different perspectives, different information, the different attitudinal point of views, and different opinions are things that can be brought into a film education by different directors through different assignments, different exercises, and different lectures. Having different directors with different backgrounds and cultures together in the same environment, and working for the same goals, is a prerequisite for diversity. Diversity and differences are necessary for promoting growth and learning among student-filmmakers around the world. The mantra is dissimilarity and not uniformity. Sameness is wrong! The efficiency justifies some consistency and uniformity in the educational process; we know that. This is a realistic perspective. But if we believe in diversity, uniformity is not the right road. Sameness is always easier to accommodate than difference. Let's push the envelope a little bit. I am not looking at this issue only from an academic perspective, but also from the perspective of the business-oriented film education. To develop directing skills among student-directors, different teaching approaches should be welcomed, along with different professional backgrounds and experiences, teaching perspectives and diversity of teaching styles, and a variety of teaching methods and approaches. The same applies to different directing styles and filming methods shared with student-directors.

When you have finished surveying this chapter, return to the beginning and read in more detail. Then you can proceed to the next step – practicing this directorial concept in I. STUDIO – APPLICATION OF GENRE CONVENTIONS. Information related to this studio can be found in PART II: STUDIOS – DIRECTING EXERCISES.

CHAPTER 4:
MANIPULATING FILM TIME

Techniques/Tools/Methods

The film is a time-based media. Anyone who has seen a film is aware that the time it takes to tell a story on the screen does not correlate to real time.

Time is everything. I think it was Polish film director Andrzej Wajda *(Ashes and Diamonds)*, recipient of an Honorary Oscar and a director I admire, who said that the film is only *"what"* and *"how long"* and nothing else. How simple! Certain things in the universe require deep evaluation, critical analysis and genius-level intelligence, but certainly not this one to figure out what he meant by that. As a film director, if you consider a subject, story, or script, you won't be far away from what he meant by the *"what."* Most likely, *"how long"* will appear to be a baffling concept, but only at first glance. When you look deeper into *"how long,"* you quickly realize that you have only three *"times"* in a film: *Dramatic Time* (time in the story), *Screening Time* (the length of a film/running time), and *Psychological Time* (viewer's perception of time.) Since screening time is more or less a given circumstance, you need to figure out how to compress a love story that spans over three years into a 90-minute or two-hour-long film that makes viewers feel like they have experienced it along with characters over a span of three years.

There are some proven scriptwriting methods that will help you to accomplish this goal. You have already learned them, or you will learn them very soon, but there are also a couple of "tricks" that are a part of the visual literacy of a director that you need to master as well.

Andrzej Wajda was never overly concerned with the reactions of critics when it came to his films. His real concern was the public, especially if he was not succeeding in communicating with the audience. Said Wajda: *"One could argue that a great many bad films are commercially successful. This is surely true, but it is also certain that there is no way films could ever serve any useful public purpose if the theaters were empty."* Why such a big diversion from the main topic? Wajda was an excellent director and master film educator. He also claimed that *"There should be less lecturing by directors on how they made their own films and more practical hands-on experience offered to students. How I made my films is unimportant to young film-makers."*

What you need to do with "time" is basically either compress it or expand it. In the vast majority of instances, you will need to compress time, but other instances will be about expanding time. The charts below describe different ways of achieving the time-expanding effect and time-compressing effect in film because different situations call for different strategies of time manipulation. As a storyteller, you have to master all the time-manipulation techniques; therefore, it is imperative and vitally important that you learn how to do so. Think about different ways to compress or expand time and practice the different methods indicated in the charts below.

EXPANDED TIME	
TECHNIQUES/TOOLS/METHODS	**GOAL/OBJECTIVE/PURPOSE/USAGE/ FUNCTION/ NOTABLE FILMS**
Slow-motion replay (An action sequence that took place in real time over a few seconds is slowed down and repeated until it takes half a minute or more.)	To make a fast action visible; to make a familiar action strange; to emphasize a dramatic moment. To add impact, additional information, or to help the viewer process information that would be too fast in real time. To focus audience attention on some detail. Films: *American History X; Kick-Ass; Fight Club; Cash Back; Inception; Faceoff; Zombieland; Girl, Interrupted; The Untouchables; X-Men: Days of Future Past; The Hurt Locker; Furious 7*
Time remapping (The speed can be varied smoothly over time. A scene can start off in real time and gradually or quickly increase in speed.)	To add intensity. To show how the character experiences the world around him or how the character sees the event. Films: *300; Blow; Snatch; The Matrix, Clockstoppers, Fight Club, Ip Man; Contact*
Freeze frame (To extend the length of a shot.)	To emphasize "now." Films: *Snatch; Kick-Ass; The Breakfast Club; Harry Potter and the Prisoner of Azkaban, Butch Cassidy and the Sundance Kid; Thank You for Smoking, The Dukes of Hazzard; Cash Back*
Repetition (The same action and shot can be repeated and shown from same camera position.)	To add more drama to the scene. Films: *Sin City; Fight Club; Groundhog Day; The Sandlot, Die Hard, Memento, Richie Rich; 28 Days Later*

Repetition and different angles (The same action can be shown and repeated from multiple angles, from different camera positions, or from different perspectives.)	To add more drama to the scene. Films: *The Fast and the Furious*; *Transformers*; *The Bourne Identity*; *Family Guy*, *Independence Day*, *Bonnie and Clyde*
Sequencing (Things that happen simultaneously in different locations can be shown in sequence; a number of scenes are shown one after the other that are supposed to have taken place at the same time.)	To exaggerate narration for dramatic effect. Films: *Pulp Fiction*; *Babel*; *Love Actually*; *Ocean's Eleven*; *Inception*; *Phone Booth*; *Run Lola Run*; *Atonement*
Cutaways (Adding cutaways and different angles can drag out an event that would be very quick in real time.)	To make the audience accept the wait and engage in the suspense. Films: *Live Free, Die Hard*; *Saving Private Ryan*; *Reservoir Dogs*; *Evil Dead*; *American Beauty*; *Red Cliff*; *Her*
Camera movement (The camera moves around or toward a stationary object.)	To reveal new information related to the character. To externalize a character's feelings, emotions, mental processes, inner states of mind. Films: *The Big Lebowski*; *The Matrix*. *Finding Neverland*; *Jurassic Park*; *Revolver*, *Death Proof*
Long take	To stretch time. To align the audience more closely with the character. To make the audience contemplate what the character is thinking about. Films: *2001: A Space Odyssey*; *In Bruges*; *Magnolia*; *Dear John*; *There Will Be Blood*; *Children of Men*; *Atonement*; *Russian Ark*; *Nine Lives*; *Death Proof*, *The Place Beyond the Pines*; *True Detective*; *Gladiator*
Frame composition, size of shot, depth of field	To align the audience more closely with the character. To emphasize the importance of the character. Films: *Rushmore*; *The Godfather*; *The Lord of the Rings*; *American Sniper*

Editing	To expend the time. To slow down the pacing and rhythm of the scene by applying the pattern of repetition. Films: *Requiem for a Dream; Charlie's Angels; The Kids Are All Right; Back to the Future; Memento; Malcolm X; Home Alone*
Flash-forwards (a scene that temporarily takes the narrative forward in time from the current point - spatial and temporal discontinuity)	To slow down the pacing and rhythm of the scene by indicating the character's imagination about the future. Films: *127 Hours; The Social Network; Push*
Flashbacks (a scene that takes the narrative back in time from the current point in the story - spatial and temporal discontinuity)	To slow down the pacing and rhythm of the scene by revealing something from the past. Films: *Casablanca; American History X; The Social Network; Now and Then; Inglourious Basterds; Oldboy*

COMPRESSED TIME	
TECHNIQUES/TOOLS/METHODS	**GOAL/OBJECTIVE/PURPOSE/USAGE/ FUNCTION/ NOTABLE FILMS**
Editing (The basic tool of time compression is the cut.)	To build up and structure a scene that is longer in real time. To portray the passage of time and time lapse. To speed up the pacing and rhythm of the scene by applying a pattern of alternation. Films: *Domino; A Clockwork Orange; Catch Me If You Can; Gone in Sixty Seconds*
Fast Motion (The simplest way to compress time is simply to speed up the motion.)	To accelerate the event. Films: *Requiem for a Dream; Crank; Garden State; A Clockwork Orange; Cash Back*
Time Remapping (The speed is sped up at various rates.)	To accelerate the event. Films: *Donnie Darko; The Transporter; Party Monster; Vanilla Sky*

Transitions (Dissolves, fade-ins/fade-outs)	To indicate the passage of a relatively long period of time. To suggest that more time has passed. Films: *Paris, Texas; The Notebook; Star Wars; Lucky Number Slevin*
Different time lapse techniques (Montage sequence; night turns to day; darkness turns to light; time-lapse of clouds; use of recurring patterns; contrasting screen direction; cutting to a CU of the subject in one space and then to a wider shot with the same subject in a different place.)	To show or to suggest the passage of time. To condense narrative. To advance the story. Films: *Rocky; 127 Hours; The Fall; What Dreams May Come; Shaun of the Dead New Moon; Lucy; Creed*
Emptying the shot (The standard tool for compressing time is to allow the subject to leave the frame.)	To shorten the actual time taken to complete the activity. While the subject is out of shot, the viewer will accept that greater distance has been traveled than is realistically possible. Off-screen action is very powerful because it allows you to compress time while keeping the audience's attention focused on the main subject and moving the story forward. Films: *Psycho; Back to the Future; Forrest Gump*
Cutaways (Another standard tool for compressing time is to provide appropriate cutaways.)	To shorten the actual time taken to complete the activity. Films: *Kick-Ass; Batman; Saw*
Jump cuts (A sequence of at least two shots that does not produce the illusion of continuous reality.)	To impart that time has elapsed between the shots. Films: *Breathless; Requiem for a Dream; The Limey; Lost River*

The use of time in visual storytelling is presented throughout all stages of making a film, from conception to completion. The time can be either visually explicit - temporally manifested or narratively implicit - narratively temporally manifested. To depict the time and alter the passage of time on screen is one of the most powerful directorial tools. It is up to you to choose the right technique. Film renders time through covert and overt manifestation of time. Covert manifestation on time is scripted. Audience's perception of time is elicited based on the move-ment of the narrative, with hardly any connection to the visual narrative. To give outward manifestation of time, a director can use graphics (newspapers, diary); symbols (clock, calendar, seasonal changes, sunrise, sunset); aging process (dis-playing biological, chemical, and physical processes of aging; altering character's hair, altering makeup and wardrobe; aging actor through make-up; aging charac-ter by casting more actors for the same character); indication through costume (establishing time period), indication through production design (establishing time period); time-lapse (transition from day to night, seasonal changes, moving clouds, moving traffic, moving shadows, sunset, sunrise, crowds, growing plants, construction projects); montage, punctuations (transitions, fades, dissolves, su-perimpositions, split screen, cuts, match cuts - cutting between two objects that look similar, jump cuts); and editing. It is imperative that you master the visual grammar of film. Whether you master it from books or from hands-on experience does not really matter. What matters is your ability to apply your theoretical knowledge when it is needed.

CHAPTER 5:
CONTROLLING SPACE

This chapter discusses methodology and visual strategy for creating the illusion of a 3D (three-dimensional) space on a 2D (two-dimensional) surface of a film screen. The first element that makes up a film shot is the frame. The area within the frame is made up of positive and negative space. The main subject depicted in a shot is a positive space, and the area, which surrounds the main subject is negative space. The both, positive space and negative space create an optical space. A space refers to the arrangement of objects within a shot.

The film screen is a 2D surface, without real depth. The director arranges objects within a shot, to create an illusion of a three-dimensional world on a two-dimensional screen surface, with the idea of what the *final shot* will look like.

In *The Psychology of Art and the Evolution of the Conscious Brain*, Robert L. Solso describes how we see a 3D World with a 2D Eye:

> *We human animals are two-dimensional visual creatures seemingly trapped in a three-dimensional world by the geometry of the retina. Nevertheless, the brain interprets two-dimensional visual images as having three dimensions by use of contextual cues and knowledge of the world as gained through a lifetime of experience.* (Solso, Robert L., The Psychology of Art and the Evolution of the Conscious Brain, A Bradford Book; 2003, ISBN-10: 0262693321)

In film, a three-dimensional world is recorded by a camera, then projected on a two-dimensional screen, and then interpreted as a three-dimensional world by the brain. The illusion of reality created on the screen is perceived by our consciousness as reality. And that's what we aim to do when we design a shot for a film, we create the illusion of reality. The more acceptable the fictional world of the characters is, the more believable the illusion of reality is.

The proficiency in mastering controlling of the space will help you in following areas:

- Mimic, re-create, manipulate, and modify the real word in film.
- Interpret the spatial world through a visual media.
- Provide a constant orientation to the setting.
- Effect the audience's perception of the space and time.
- Manipulate the audience's emotional response.

- Control the pace and rhythm of the film, and all its rhythmic components.
- Effectively use the economy in blocking and staging shots (blocking in depth = fewer shots).

5.1. FLAT SPACE

A *Flat Space* does not accentuate the illusion of a three-dimensional world on a two-dimensional screen surface. The illusion of depth is unintentionally or purposely suppressed. There is a loss of realism, but it can enhance other desired story or dramatic elements, like confusion, suspense, and uncertainty, but also calmness, ease, and peace. Using the extreme flatness creates a special style, which is an essential part of directors' style. Check out the work of film directors Jean-Luc *Godard (Contempt)*, and Wes Anderson *(The Grand Budapest Hotel)*.

5.1.1. STAGING ON LINE (Flat Staging)

Blocking is performers' placement and movement in relation to a position from which a shot is filmed (camera set-up). Blocking reflects characters' relationships, needs, wants, emotions, and the obstacles they are facing. Blocking also reflects the audience's desire to get closer to characters, to understand characters' emotions better, or simply to get more information. Staging is transferring blocking into acting, along with other major design components like costume design, production design, set design, make-up, lighting design and sound design. Sometimes the term blocking is used interchangeably with the term staging, meaning how the performers are placed and moved, and how they are arranged within a frame.

Staging on line requires blocking performers along the X-axis. (X-axis runs horizontally from left to right.) On-line staging, or flat staging, is the visual look achieved by combining minimal depth with central perspective. The performers are shot in either full frontal or profile with the camera horizontally perpendicular to the background at all times. Scenes tend to employ symmetrical camera set-ups and can touch on a wide variety of emotions, not just amplified emotions and situations in a comedy. (Frontal plane - a two-dimensional flat surface passing horizontally through the frame from side to side - across the screen, at a right angle to the camera axis, closest to the viewer.)

Strategy for creating a Flat Space:
- Staging on the same frontal two-dimensional plane
- Creating a shallow depth of field

- Moving camera parallel, pan, zoom in/out
- Moving performers parallel to the picture plane – across the screen
- Not-overlapping performers or objects (Staging performers next to each other)

Benefit:
- It emphasizes the lightness of the story (comedy)
- It creates a special visual look (essential part of director's style)
- It has a huge impact on the mood of the film and how the viewer feels while watching the story unfold (creates a special feeling)

Scene 5.1.1.a.

Full Frontal Staging - Single
- Gives the audience a clear associative perspective and central character.
- Allows the audience to get into the mindset of the character (subjective treatment).
- Can heighten tension, when intercut with action shots.

Scene 5.1.1.b.

Full Frontal Staging - Double
- Has no central character or the central character is left ambiguous.
- Distances the audience from the action (objective treatment).
- Distances the characters from each other.

Scene 5.1.1.c.

Profile Staging – Single
- It gives the audience a clear associative perspective.
- It has the potential of weakening character perspective, like a wide shot, or OTS shot.

Scene 5.1.1.d.

Profile Staging – Double
- It can boost conflict between two characters.

- It can also bring two characters closer together.

Scene 5.1.1.e.

Extreme Flat Staging
- It places characters directly in front of a flat backdrop.
- It can create a feeling of safety/comfort.
- It can also create a feeling of extreme discomfort.

5.1.2. MOVING CAMERA (parallel, pan, zoom in/out)

The camera moves sideways along a straight line, which is parallel to the staging line. (**Scene 5.1.2.**) The camera can also zoom in, or zoom out. A zoom is not a move, the camera doesn't change position, the camera is not moving in a physical space, so there is no change in perspective within a shot, as far the foreground and background go. The camera can also pan, either following the subject or reveling the information.

Scene 5.1.2.

A two shot (two characters within one shot) consisting of two single shots, when the separation is achieved by a camera move, and not by the cut.

5.1.3. MOVING ACTORS
(Parallel movement of an actor to the picture plane)

The performer moves parallel to the picture plane - across the screen. The camera is fixed on a tripod and remains at a constant position, or the camera is fixed on a tripod and pans; or the camera is moving sideways, parallel to the performer, like in the situation pictured below.

Scene 5.1.3.

It increases the emotional intensity, interest, or suspense, and uncertainty, since the audience does not see the place she is walking in, or the object she is walking toward. It suggests that she is moving toward her goal; it implies that she is in pursuit of a goal essential to her motivations.

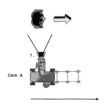 

5.1.4. SHALLOW DEPTH OF FIELD (Shallow Focus)

The depth of field refers to the area of the shot that is in focus. If only a small area of the shot is in focus, there is a shallow depth of field, also called shallow focus. Unimportant visual elements are discarded in defocused part of the shot, leaving only the most important elements in focus.

When you are designing a "shot space" (optical space), you often think about the space around the character - negative space. When a space is empty, the natural human inclination is to fill the space. But filling the space with too many objects can ironically distract attention away from the character, you want the audience to be focused on. This captures the essence and power of something the art and design calls a power of negative space. The amount of negative space often determines why the audience likes or dislikes something depicted in a shot. Things that are busy, noisy, and crowded are very distracting for the audience. The space around the character creates and enhances the desired effect. The space around the character makes the character noticeable. So, the power of negative space can be simplified in the idea that less is often more. Removing things around the character, or eliminating things around the character through a shallow depth of field, or through staging in depth, or by rim light, helps you to cut out everything, what can compete with the character, and by doing that, it will give the character more attention. I will be talking more about a deep immersion into the character's psyche using long lenses and a shallow depth of field in CHAPTER 9: Character perspective.

Scene 5.1.4.

5.2. DEEP SPACE

A *Deep Space* gives the illusion of a three-dimensional world rendered on a two-dimensional screen surface.

5.2.1. STAGING IN DEPTH (Staging along the Z-axis)

Staging in depth requires blocking performers along the Z-axis. (Z-axis runs from the foreground to the background.) It creates the sense of 3D space.

Strategy for creating a Deep Space:
- Staging in depth
- Creating a deep depth of field
- Moving camera toward or away from performers
- Moving performers toward or away from the camera
- Overlapping performers or objects

Benefit:
- It establishes the geography of a scene
- It helps the audience to understand geometry of the scene
- It gives depth and a sense of dynamics
- It creates a 3D experience
- It creates a clear associative point for the audience emphasizing the hieratic positioning of the performers
- It allows the audience to get into the mindset of the character (character blocked in a full frontal shot closer to the camera)
- It creates the feeling of real not staged situation (everything is happening in front of the camera)
- It eliminates cuts and selectively emphasizes dramatic elements within one shot
- It can change the size of a shot by moving performers along the Z-axis
- It adds the contrast and increases the emotional intensity of the scene through physical action
- It allows to control the pace and rhythm of a shot by movement of performers, or/and by movement of camera

5.2.2. MOVING CAMERA (toward or away from actors)

The camera is moving forward (**dolly in**) (**Scene 5.2.2.a.**) or backward (**Dolly Back**), toward or away from the subject.

Scene 5.2.2.a.

It satisfies the audience's desire to get closer to the character.

Cam A

1. Cam A	2. Cam A

3. Cam A   **4. Cam A**

Scene 5.2.2.b.

The camera can also move toward or away from the subject, while the subject is also moving either toward or away from the camera.

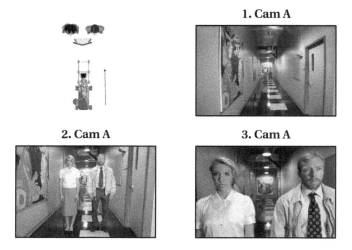

The camera can also move with the subject, keeping the subject at the same distance from the camera. It satisfies the need for inner subjectivity, and it also emphasizes the connection between characters and the audience.

5.2.3. MOVING ACTORS (toward or away from camera)

The performer(s) move toward or away from the camera, while the camera is fixed on a tripod and remains in a constant position (**Scene 5.2.3.a.** and **Scene 5.2.3.b.**)

Scene 5.2.3.a.

It fosters intimacy with a character.

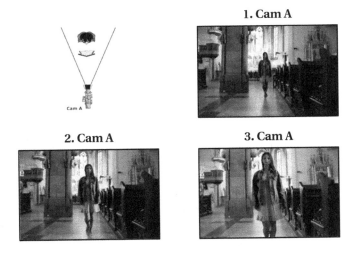

Scene 5.2.3.b.

It fosters emotional attachment to characters.

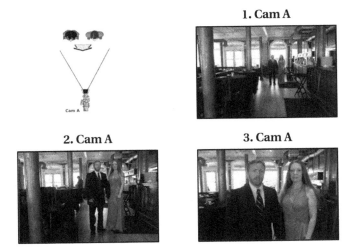

The camera can also be mounted on a wheeled-platform and can dolly in, or Dolly Back, while performers are moving toward or away from the camera.

5.2.4. DEEP DEPTH OF FIELD (Deep Focus)

Scene 5.2.4.

As I already said in the subchapter 5.1.4. SHALLOW DEPTH OF FIELD, "*the depth of field refers to the area of the shot that is in focus.*" If most of the area of the shot is in focus, there is a deep depth of field, also called deep focus. Deep focus is used, when the shot is meant to have the foreground, middle ground and background in focus at the same time. The foreground of a composition is the visual plane that appears closest to the viewer, while the background is the plane in a composition perceived furthest from the viewer. The middle ground is the visual plane located between both the foreground and background. Deep focus is achieved with large amounts of light and small aperture - the opening in a lens that admits the light. A general rule: The shorter the focal length, the more depth of field. The focal length of the lens is the distance between the lens and the image sensor when the subject is in focus. The further away from the subject, the more depth of field. That being said, the selection of lens, f-stop (the *f-stop* setting determines how much light is allowed to enter the lens), distance to the subject, the amount of light, and also the camera sensor size influences the depth of field.

The illusion of deep focus can also be achieved by using the split-focus diopter when it is possible to have one plane in focus in one part of the picture, and a different plane in focus in the other part of the picture, and all subjects from front to back are in focus. The lens can focus on a plane in the background and the diopter on a foreground.

The illusion of deep focus can also be achieved by compositing two pictures together.

Having everything in focus will help the audience understand the subject's environment better. From a dramatic perspective, a deep focus shot keeps all characters in tense conformation.

Another reason for you to have a busy, visually nosy background is, when you want to externalize - visualize the character's madness and insanity, or you want to indicate that the character had lost control of his actions, or he/she is losing his/her mind, or the character is consumed by surrounding environment.

Using a deep depth of field creates a special style (directors Jean Renoir, Orson Welles, Claude Lelouch, Andrzej Wajda), which is an essential part of director's style.

Scene 5.2.4.a.   **Scene 5.2.4.b.**   **Scene 5.2.4.c.**

5.2.5. SELECTIVE FOCUS - SHALLOW DEPTH OF FIELD
(one plane in focus; shifting the focal plane - pulling focus, racking focus)

Scene 5.2.5.a.

When shooting a scene with selective focus, the shot is meant to have a specific character in focus. This won't help to create depth, but it will help guide the audience's eyes to what the director wants. Having the opportunity to direct the audiences' eyes exactly where the director wants is a big advantage since no other elements in the frame will be distracting the audience, and they can feel more connected to the particular character - that being said, it fosters intimacy with a character. Even though it does not create depth, it still gives the sense of depth and a sense of dynamics and creates a 3D experience, just because the situation is blocked along the Z-axis.

Scene 5.2.5.b.

Selective focus can also be used to reveal objects or subjects in frame, which were previously out of focus. This can also be used to change the interest of the audience from one subject to the other or to change a character perspective. It allows shifting attention between planes, either through physical movement along the lens axis (the Z-axis) or through pulling/racking focus, without the axial cut. It directs the viewer's attention to one element of a shot through a restricted depth of field - shallow focus – only one plane is in focus. (The focus pull/rack – the change of the focus of the lens during a shot.) It allows the audience to get into the mindset of the character.

5.2.6. PLANER STAGING (exploiting two or all three separate planes simultaneously – foreground, middle-ground, background with wide depth of focus, or with narrow depth of focus)

Scene 5.2.6.

A planer staging is often used as a technique to have the action and reaction within one shot or to focus audience's attention on the most significant aspect of a shot without having to use an analytic cut or reaction shot. It satisfies the need for inner subjectivity between characters depicted in a shot, and at the same time, it helps the audience to feel more connected to a particular character. It can be done by keeping foreground and background in focus at the same time (**Scene 5.2.6.a.**), or it can be done by selective focus (**Scene 5.2.6.b.**).

Scene 5.2.6.a.	Scene 5.2.6.b.

Scene 5.2.6.c.

A planer staging can be used for externalizing the structure of the dramatic time of the story by exploiting all three planes – foreground, middle-ground, background, where the present is playing in the foreground and middle ground, and past is playing in the background alongside each other. It can externalize character's memories in one shot without illustrating them in a separate shot. This is a very interesting visual approach for rendering flashbacks without breaking spatial and temporal continuity. Chain of events split over two time periods is not played back to back, like in an epic approach, but simultaneously. The attempt to preserve space and time in two time periods is a ruling principle. Present and past are spatially and temporally coherent, they interfere.

Scene 5.2.6.d.

A planer staging can be used for visualizing character's thoughts, or projection of character's thinking, or modification of reality as a result of character's thinking, by exploiting two planes – foreground and background, where the reality is playing in foreground and a projection of character's thoughts are playing in background alongside each other (2. Cam B: steering wheel in foreground - reality, the girl standing at the porch in background - character's imagination.)

1. Cam A

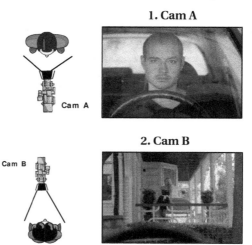

Cam A

2. Cam B

Cam B

Controlling space in film, real and optical, goes hands in hand with blocking. Blocking is performers' placement and movement in relation to the camera set-up. You will learn more about blocking in the following CHAPTER 6: BLOCKING STRATEGIES. When you've finished studying both chapters, then you can proceed to the next step – practicing this directorial concept in II. STUDIO – BLOCKING IN DEPTH. Information related to this studio can be found in PART II: STUDIOS – DIRECTING EXERCISES.

CHAPTER 6:
BLOCKING STRATEGIES

Blocking is one of the most important things a director does and has to be really good at. I remember, when I started teaching these skills at a college in the USA, my new graduate students, who were just about to graduate, told me that over their entire study nobody even touched the basics of blocking effectively. Because of that, I have decided to spend extra time in classes explaining different strategies for blocking.

Technical proficiency is the ability to perform the fundamental techniques of blocking for narrative purposes. Try to master them. The novice student-directors will be able to integrate and implement the newly acquired knowledge, and skills into their work and more advanced directors will develop and build upon previously acquired skills.

The focus of this chapter is *"blocking and staging principles," "staging styles,"* and *"staging-editing patterns."* All this will help you to determine how to line-up a shot, where to put the camera, how to frame performers, and overall how to design shots. At first glance, it seems like the focus is now on technical aspects with the purpose of mastering "technical" proficiency in blocking. However, the goal is to emphasize the role of the director as he moves from form to content, with a concentration on skillfully and creatively using the tools of filmmaking to direct the audience's attention to drama, emotions and all other critical aspects of the scene. At the end of the day, that's all that matters.

Examples I will use in this chapter for demonstrating different styles and patterns of blocking are mostly dialogue situations in which characters are either sitting or standing. I have purposely decided to use situations, where no movement or just a little movement by the performers is involved because it will be much easier for you to grasp all the different blocking techniques before applying them to situations, where the characters move around.

Blocking and staging methods

- Staging and blocking individually shot by shot

- Staging and blocking the entire scene

Basic blocking and staging principles

- On the line

- In depth

Staging style

- Shot-reverse shot pattern

- Shots based on the "inner montage"

- Integral shot (scene shot, sequence shot)

Staging - editing pattern

- Approaching and receding pattern (traditional style)

- Accompanying the emotions pattern (non-traditional style)

Continuity contributes to a film's success more than any other cinematic device. The position of performers, movement of performers, screen direction of performers, and the look of performers must be carefully blocked for continuity purposes. Any change in position, movement, screen direction, and look must be shown directly or indirectly, and it must not occur between shots.

Screen direction (Characters are looking or moving from left to right or right to left.):

1. *Constant screen direction* - Established screen direction is maintained throughout a scene.
    a) May be used to show the special relationship between characters
    b) May be used to show progression of movement in consecutive shots
    c) May be used to suggest the continuous journey of the hero
    d) May be used to maintain constant direction in the following scene

2. *Contrasting screen direction*
    a) May be used to show opposing subjects talking, or moving toward or away each other
    b) May be used to show the same subject going and returning
    c) May be used to map geography of the movement
    d) May be used for the time lapse purposes
    e) May be used for connecting two subsequent scenes

3. *Fluid/alternation of screen direction* - Screen direction is not maintained throughout a scene, and viewers are oriented as to where characters are in relation to one another. Space is not oriented only on one side of the line, which subsequently brings dynamism to an

otherwise static scene, like a dialogue scene, where a group of people is seated around a table.

4. *Neutral screen direction* (There is no horizontal screen direction, characters are moving toward, or away from a camera.)
    a) May be used to slow down or speed up the physical movement
    b) May be used to intercut two shots in which the *screen direction* is reversed

Basically, two different strategies can be employed for blocking the two-character scene, or multiple character scene. Either blocking performers across the frame, that means along the X-axis, so-called *"blocking on line,"* or blocking performers along the Z-axis, called *"blocking in depth."*

6.1. BLOCKING ON LINE (flat staging)

Again: *"Blocking is performers' placement and movement in relation to the camera set-up."* Staging on line creates blocking, where performers are blocked along the X-axis. (X-axis runs horizontally from left to right.) Performers can face each other (**Scene 6.1.a.**), they can be placed side by side (**Scene 6.1.b.** and **Scene 6.1.c.**), or blocked with their backs to each other (**Scene 6.1.d.**). But it does not inevitably mean that performers have to be shot on the same frontal two-dimensional plane all the way throughout a scene. The performers can be shot/seen from three or more different camera set-ups, where cameras are angled, and shoot either external reverse shots (**Scene 6.1.a.: Cam B,** and **Cam C**), or internal reverse shots (**Scene 6.1.e. Cam B,** and **Cam C**), or parallel reverse shots (**Scene 6.1.f.: Cam B,** and **Cam C**) or combination of all of them (**Scene 6.1.g.**) But basic blocking of performers remains same – on line.

Scene 6.1.a.   **Scene 6.1.b.**

Scene 6.1.c.   **Scene 6.1.d.**

Scene 6.1.a.   **1. Cam A**

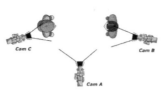   

2. Cam B   **3. Cam C**

Scene 6.1.e.   **1. Cam A**

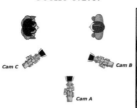   

2. Cam B   3. Cam C

Scene 6.1.f.   1. Cam A

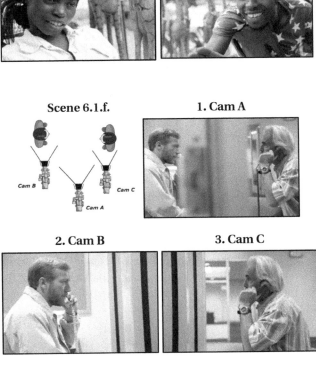

2. Cam B   3. Cam C

Scene 6.1.g.   1. Cam A

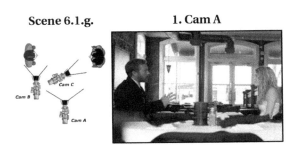

2. Cam B   **3. Cam C**

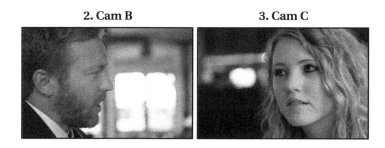

6.2. BLOCKING IN DEPTH (deep staging/depth staging/staging in depth)

Staging in depth creates more interesting blocking. (Blocking performers along the Z-axis. The Z-axis runs from the foreground to the background.) It can be done with a *Deep Focus* - when the lens on the camera has a deep depth of field (**Scene 6.2.a.** and **Scene 6.2.b.**); or the split-focus diopter is used (**Scene 6.2.c.**), when it is possible to have one plane in focus in one part of the picture, and a different plane in focus in the other part of the picture, and all subjects from front to back are in focus); or it can be done with a *Shallow Focus* - **Scene 6.2.d.** and **Scene 6.2.e.**, when the lens on the camera has a shallow depth of field and only one plane is in focus, and rack or pull focus is needed from front to back, or from back to front to bring another subject in focus.

Scene 6.2.a.   **Scene 6.2.b.**   **Scene 6.2.c.**

Scene 6.2.d.   **Scene 6.2.e.**

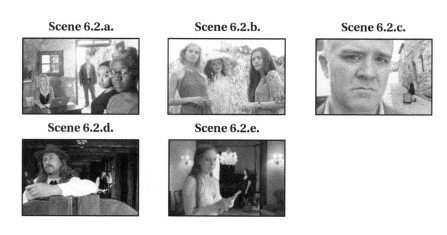

6.3. SHOT-REVERSE SHOT PATTERN

A standard pattern for shooting and editing a dialogue scene is a *"shot - reverse shot pattern."* Film theorist and film historian David Bordwell defines it as a film technique *"where one character is shown looking (often off-screen) at another character, and then the other character is shown looking "back" at the first character. Since the characters are shown facing in opposite directions, the viewer unconsciously assumes that they are looking at each other."* (Bordwell, D.; Thompson, K., *Film Art: An Introduction.* New York: McGraw-Hill Education, 2006) The players are looking in the oppressed direction, in both shots, in a shot and in a reverse shot. The illusion that they are looking at each other works, because of converging eyesights in both consecutive shots.

Shot - the reverse shot pattern is a typical Hollywood style of shooting, when a scene is shot from a variety of angles and distances, using different shot sizes, contributing to invisible editing. (Shooting coverage.) Camera positions chart below: Performers are blocked for the cross shoot - the technique for filming interactions between two or more characters in which the camera shoots alternately one or the other character in roughly the same camera angle from opposite positions/directions, with the character farthest from the camera set-up.

Camera positions chart:

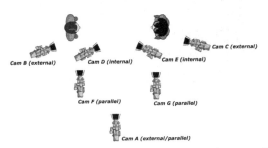

Triangular camera positions can be applied for blocking on line **Scene 6.3.a.,** and **Scene 6.3.b.** or blocking in depth **Scene 6.3.c.,** and **Scene 6.3.d.**

Scene 6.3.a.

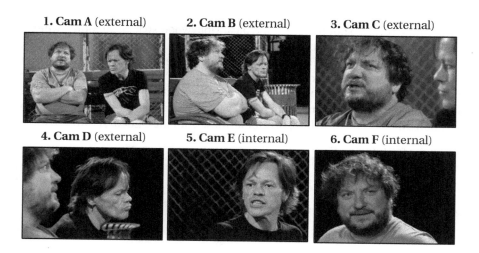

1. Cam A (external)   **2. Cam B** (external)   **3. Cam C** (external)

4. Cam D (external)   **5. Cam E** (internal)   **6. Cam F** (internal)

Scene 6.3.b.

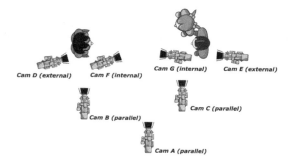

1. Cam A (external)   **2. Cam B** (parallel)

3. Cam C (parallel)   **4. Cam D** (external)

5. Cam E (external)   **6. Cam F** (internal)   **7. Cam G (internal)**

Scene 6.3.c.

1. Cam A (external)   **7. Cam G** (internal)

Scene 6.3.d.

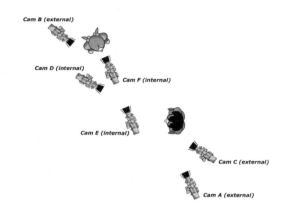

1. Cam A (external)   **2. Cam B** (external)

3. Cam C (external)   **4. Cam D** (internal)

5. Cam E (internal)   **6. Cam F** (internal)

   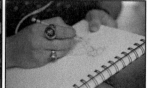

6.4. APPROACHING AND RECEDING PATTERN

The one widely used approach by all filmmakers all over the world is the *"approaching and receding pattern"* for staging and blocking a dialogue scene. And not just a dialogue scene. The characters are presented in a wide shot, proceeding with tighter shots, and then again in a wide shot. This approaching and receding pattern allows the audience to get closer to performers as the drama is arising, or when there is a need to create an intimate relationship with characters; and then constantly or gradually retreat from performers, when the story or emotional intensity drops down, or a new structural beat is nearing, or the scene is about to end. This pattern perfectly maps either story intensity or the emotional intensity of a scene. When a story gains intensity, either dramatic or emotional, the audience is "brought" closer to characters through tighter shots, and when a story declines on intensity, the audience is distanced from characters through wider shots. And then the situation can be repeated, when a following emotional beat calls for the intimacy with a character. Daniel Arion in his book *Grammar of the Film Language* says, *"This recommended peak-pattern allows the audience some emotional repose, and they can respond more fully to the really important passages."* (Arijon, D. *Grammar of the Film Language*, Silman-James Pr; 1991, ISBN-10: 187950507X) This approach may look very obvious, very conventional, but no doubts that it is a very effective pattern. With a little bit of creative effort, even a visual limitation of staging for a cross shoot purposes can be avoided.

Scene 6.4.a.

This situation shows two performers in a wide establishing shot (**Cam A**) combined with an external reverse shot (**Cam B**), combined with an internal reverse shot (**Cam C**), and then cut to a reestablishing shot (**Cam A**). And then the situation is repeated.

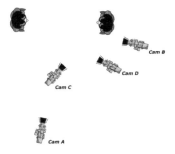

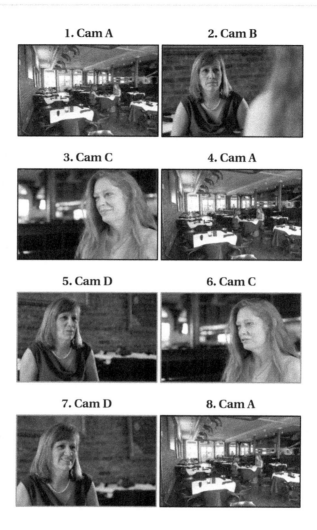

1. Cam A   2. Cam B
3. Cam C   4. Cam A
5. Cam D   6. Cam C
7. Cam D   8. Cam A

Scene 6.4.b

Receding to a wide shot can also imply the end of the scene. It can be done with a shot taken from the same camera set up as the first shot, establishing shot was taken; or it can be done with a shot taken from a new camera set up. This is a very obsolete visual architecture of the scene – to open a scene with a wide shot and to close a scene with a wide shot.

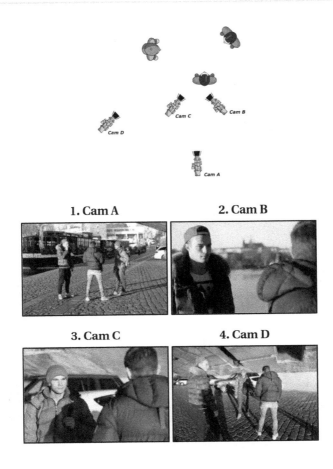

1. Cam A   2. Cam B

3. Cam C   4. Cam D

6.5. ACCOMPANYING THE EMOTIONS PATTERN

The less traditional pattern than the *"approaching and receding pattern"* for staging and blocking a dialogue or action scene is the *"accompanying the emotions pattern."* Basically, this method brings the audience closer to performers and never ever steps back from them, believing that cutting back to a wider shot would dissipate the emotion, or drama, or suspense, or tension. That being said, in order to retain the emotion on the faces of the performers (after an initial approach to performers), the camera keeps the performers in close-ups until the end of a scene, even when performers move around. Alfred Hitchcock is nicely talking about this in the book *Hitchcock by Francois Truffaut.* (Truffaut, F. *Hitchcock*, Simon & Schuster; 1985, ISBN-10: 0671604295)

Scene 6.5.a.

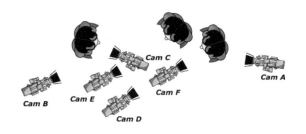

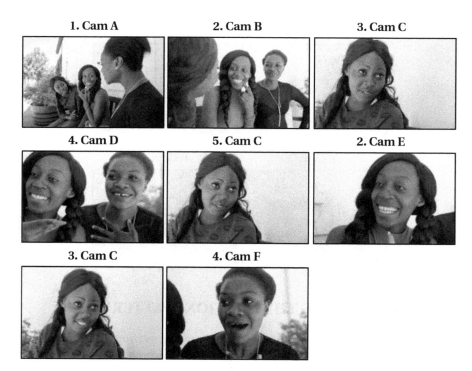

1. Cam A	2. Cam B	3. Cam C
4. Cam D	5. Cam C	2. Cam E
3. Cam C	4. Cam F	

Scene 6.5.b.

When there is a need for a tighter shot, the shot is never taken from the same camera position as a previous wider shot, but a new camera set up is chosen for a new shot, which is always closer to the eyesight of the player. And that's the rule: when the camera moves in, to do a single shot of one performer or the other, the apparent position of the unseen, off-camera performer must be corrected to maintain the apparent relationship between them. That being said, the eye-line in a single shot is slightly closer to the lens than in a two-shot, or in an OTS shot. Another reason for getting closer to the eye-line: every shot designed between 45-degree shot and straight on shot strengthens the intimacy with a character, and helps the audience to be aligned with a character. There is a simple rule of thumb that can be applied almost to all situations: it is not enough for intimacy to have just a tighter shot, it has to be more open face shot. This strategy will be discussed more in depth in CHAPTER 9: CONCEPT OF CHARACTER PERSPECTIVE.

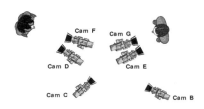

Scene 6.5.c.

The accompanying the emotions pattern can be applied to all kind of situations and not just dialogue situations. *Approaching from a distance* closer to a character is a widely-used technique. The gradual enter from afar to a character's intimate space reveals character's emotional state.

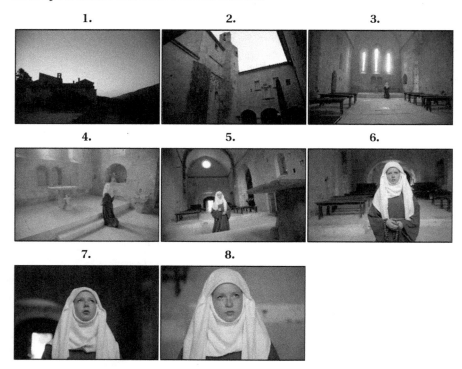

Scene 6.5.d.

The gradual enter from afar to a character's intimate space allows the audience to experience, what a character is experiencing, and that way to create an intimate connection with the character.

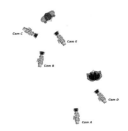

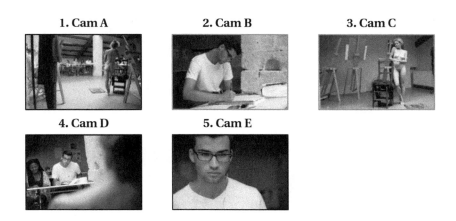

| 1. Cam A | 2. Cam B | 3. Cam C |
| 4. Cam D | 5. Cam E | |

6.6. INTEGRAL SHOT (Scene shot/sequence shot/plan-sequence/long take)

"Scene shot/sequence shot/plan-sequence/long take" is a single uninterrupted long shot that lasts for the duration of an entire scene or sequence, usually involving complicated blocking of the camera and complicated choreography of actors.

Directors employ long takes for many reasons. Some of them just want to provoke and go to extreme; some of them do it out of bravado; for some of them it is a part of director's signature; some use non-editing-driven visual narration, or totally resign on employing any editing at all. But some directors just simply record the action; or apply a home-video approach of shooting. The avant-garde approach or ambitious experimentation can be a driven force for long takes as well. Long takes can also be a result of improvisation during shooting.

But undeniable "beauty" and "power" of long takes lies in a fact that it looks like the reality captured in front of the camera is not constructed (fragmented), but it is real, emphasizing authentic unstructured footage. The attempt to preserve space and time as much as possible is the mantra in designing the long take. On the top of it, the "time" captured in a long take looks longer than the "real time." In Chapter 4: MANIPULATING FILM TIME, I said that the ability to deal with *"dramatic time," "screening time,"* and *"psychological time"* is a part of the visual literacy of a director, and you as a storyteller, you have to master all the time-manipulation techniques. Different situations call for different strategies of time manipulation. The time-expanding effect and time-compressing effect can be achieved by using long takes as well. In CHAPTER 17: II. STUDIO – BLOCKING IN

DEPTH you will learn, how to utilize this great tool – to eliminate the cut and selectively emphasize dramatic elements within one scene shot.

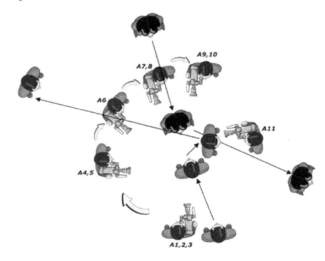

A10 **A11**

Blocking a scene is one of the hardest parts of the director's job during shooting. Sometimes a physical layout of the room dictates blocking; sometimes actors show you what they want, which might alter your original idea about blocking; sometimes you will figure out the camera placements based on actors' need to move; sometimes your Director of Photography will bring amazing ideas for blocking.

When I was preparing the film *Aphrodite*, I had in mind a Director of Photography I wanted to work with. When I finally met him and explained my vision and the actor I wanted to cast for one of the principal characters, he said that he cannot do it -- that he cannot look at that particular face through a viewfinder over 30 days of shooting. You have to understand, it was not his antagonistic state toward the actor, but his aesthetic preferences and his desire to work with unknown actors. He possessed an authentic, almost documentary-like approach to a fictional material. Of course, I was shocked and unprepared to deal with this kind of rejection. But I was also impressed with his honesty and integrity. The principal photography was approaching very fast, and I did not have a DP. Producers began to panic. Out of desperation, I hired a DP, for whom I had a respect and admiration, but felt that he is not the best choice for that film. How wrong I was! I can attribute the visual look, and the whole success of that film to him, Mr. Alojz Hanúsek. Having a shot list will help you during the blocking process, but *Aphrodite* was the first time I did not have it. I did not apply the habitual level of detailed scrutiny to a shot design in advance. The blocking was not forethought. It was done on the film set as a result of a collaboration with the DP. I was instinctively responding to physicalities of actors I cast and the characteristics of shooting locations. The actors were blocked in certain configurations in space, helping the audience to understand a relationship and characterization. That was an amazing and easy going creative collaboration, which captures the brilliance of a single individual. He helped me capture the soul of the story, which is a story not only of friendship between a boy and a horse, but amity as such, value of true relationships, search for mutual understanding, a story about heroes that do not assert themselves by strength, but by inner values and ethics of their attitudes in any situation in their lives.

Be flexible and open-minded. You will not lose connection with the scene when you reconstruct it during blocking. You firmly hold the director's reins in your hands, because you did your homework – you know, what the scene is about, you know, which character dominates the scene, and you know, how you want the audience to feel. So, changing the original plan for blocking will not work against your concept. The way the audience understands the story and their emotional involvement can be accomplished in many different ways, and not just the way you come up with, while you have been sitting at your desk. At the end of the day, what matters most is creativity. Apply your imagination.

When you have finished surveying this chapter and CHAPTER 5: CONTROLLING SPACE, return to the beginning and read it again in more detail. When you've finished studying both chapters, then you can proceed to the next step – practicing this directorial concept in II. STUDIO – BLOCKING IN DEPTH. Information related to this studio can be found in PART II: STUDIOS – DIRECTING EXERCISES.

CHAPTER 7:
MULTIPLE-CHARACTER SCENE

When characters interact in a scene, the characters can occupy the same screen position and maintain the same screen direction throughout the scene, or characters can vary their screen position and screen direction throughout the scene. Situations can be staged and blocked employing a traditional approach to defining space for the theatrical performance that means in the "box set," which is a set that utilizes three walls to enclose the stage area; or situations can be staged and blocked employing a less traditional approach, where the set utilizes all four walls. Summarizing this: All situations can be staged and blocked with an open proscenium, or with a closed proscenium, that means with or without the fourth wall of the "box set." The rule of thumb here is: the "open box" results in a more objective treatment (the viewers are treated as observers of situation); the "closed box" results in a more subjective treatment (the viewers are treated as participants of situation); the sameness of screen direction brings steadiness to the scene; the alternation of screen direction brings dynamism to the scene. That being said, the dynamism is directly proportional to the alternation, like everything in this world. Take advantage of this axiom and employ it in your blocking strategies.

7.1. SAFETY OF THREE WALLS - FIXEDNESS IN SCREEN DIRECTION

This is the variant, which gives each character a steady screen direction throughout a scene. The case pictured below (**Scene 7.1.**) portrays the situation, where three characters occupy same screen position and maintain the same screen direction.

Scene 7.1.

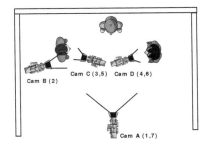

1. Cam A   **2. Cam B**   **3. Cam C**

4. Cam D   **5. Cam C**   **6. Cam D**

7. Cam A

7.2. SAFETY OF THREE WALLS - ALTERNATION OF THE SCREEN DIRECTION

This is the variant, which does not give all characters a steady screen direction throughout a scene. The alternation of screen direction brings dynamism to the scene, even though the scene is still shot in the "open box" - with an open proscenium. As you already know from the previous subchapter, the "open box" results in a more objective treatment, because the viewers are treated as observers of the situation, and not as participants of situation. But anyway, this case is the less conservative solution as the scene **7.1.**, because it brings the alternation of screen direction of performers.

The cases pictured below (**Scene 7.2.a.** and **Scene 7.2.b.**) portray situation, where two main characters occupy same screen position, and maintain the same screen direction throughout a scene, and the position of the third character results to opposite screen direction at least in one shot, without causing a disorienting effect, because the point of interest is set between two main characters, who maintain the same screen direction.

Scene 7.2.a.

The shot - **Cam B** and the reverse shot - **Cam C** results in the same screen direction of both main players (the Wife and the Man), while the third player's position (observer – the Husband) results in an opposite screen direction: The Husband occupies left lateral side of the frame in the shot – **Cam B**, and right lateral side of the frame in the shot – **Cam C**. The Husband's screen direction alters from shot to shot, what brings dynamism to the scene. By the way, the **Cam C** is not over the line, because the line is running between the Wife and the Man upstage, so all three cameras stay on one side of the line, what ensures the continuity. There is often involved some misunderstanding that the line runs between two characters closest to a camera, what would be in this case between the Husband and the Man downstage. But the line runs between characters, who interact that means in our case between the Wife and the Man upstage.

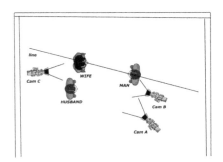

1. Cam A	2. Cam B	3. Cam C

Scene 7.2.b.

In this case, the Girl's screen direction alters from shot to shot, what brings dynamism to the scene. The line is running between the two men upstage, who maintain the same screen direction from shot to shot. But still, the "open box" makes feel the audience that they are just observing the situation.

1. Cam A   **2. Cam B**

7.3. CHALLENGING THE FOURTH WALL - FIXEDNESS IN SCREEN DIRECTION

When characters are deployed in a triangle, there are three lines of interest, where one line predominates the other two lines. The characters can either occupy same screen position and maintain the same screen direction; or characters do not have to occupy same screen position, and do not have to maintain the same screen direction. The case pictured here below portrays a situation, where three characters occupy the same screen position and maintain the same screen direction. In comparison with the scene **7.1.** in the subchapter 7.1. SAFETY OF THREE WALLS - FIXEDNESS in screen direction, this one gives you more decent, clean, single shots when all three characters interact; not to mention that you will successfully break the fourth wall. On top of it all, you will maintain the same screen direction for all characters involved, if that's what you want. That means, the situation is staged and blocked with a closed proscenium, that means with the fourth wall of the "box set." The rule of thumb here is: the "closed box" results in a more subjective treatment. The viewers are treated more as participants of the situation, and not as observers like it was in scene **7.1.** But the sameness of screen direction preserves steadiness, exactly like in scene **7.1.**

Scene 7.3.

Let's suppose you are the director of this piece craving to stage this situation in 360° space while maintaining the same screen direction of all involved characters:

So far, the situation was "covered" from all three cameras – **Cam A, Cam B, Cam C.** If the Woman has some important dialogue with the Boy, you can create another camera set-up (**Cam D**) to get a decent full-faced OTS or a single shot of the Woman talking to the Boy. (**4. Cam D** - establishing a new line, the 2nd line). Both characters maintain the same screen direction as in the shots taken from **Cam A, Cam B,** and **Cam C,** but this shot (**4. Cam D**) will finally reveal the fourth wall. (The solid wall in the floor plan below.) Now when you are about to shoot the

Woman's turn back to the Man from Cam D, you will end up with a shot over the original line (the 1st line running between the Man and the Woman). So, the shot would show the Woman not looking in Man's direction, but looking away from him – in the opposite screen direction. Their eye lines would not match. This problem can be remedied easily and has a very simple solution. Just shoot the Woman's turn to the Man from **Cam B** or **Cam A**, what are two camera set-ups on the original side of the line, the 1st line. The graph shows that **Camera A** was used for the Woman's turn to the Man. (Reestablishing the original line.) You can apply the same strategic plan for the couple - the Man and the Boy. If the Man has some important dialogue with the Boy, you can create another camera set-up (**Cam F**) to get a decent full-faced OTS shot (**7. Cam F** - establishing a new line, the 3rd line) or a single shot (**9. Cam F**) of the Man talking to the Boy. Both characters will occupy the same screen direction they have maintained in **Cam A, Cam B,** and **Cam C**; but like the shot taken from **Cam D**, this shot taken from **Cam F** will reveal the fourth wall. (The solid wall in the floor plan below.) When you are about to shoot the Man's turn back to the Woman from **Cam F**, you will end up with a shot over the original line running between the man and the Woman. So, the shot would show the Man not looking in the Woman's direction, but looking away from her in the opposite screen direction. Their eye lines would not match. This problem can be remedied easily and has a very simple solution. Just shoot the Man's turn to the Woman from **Cam C** or **Cam A**, what are two camera set-ups on the original side of the line, the 1st line. (Reestablishing the original line.)

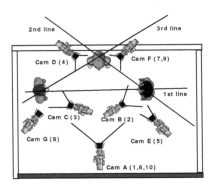

1. Cam A

2. Cam B

3. Cam C

4. Cam D   5. Cam E   6. Cam A

7. Cam F   8. Cam G   9. Cam F

10. Cam A

7.4. Challenging the fourth wall - ALTERNATION OF THE SCREEN DIRECTION (through a visual anchor)

The situation is staged and blocked with a closed proscenium, that means with the fourth wall of the "box set." This is the variant, which does not give each character a steady screen direction throughout a scene. The alternation of a screen direction brings dynamism to the scene. The "closed box" results in a more subjective treatment. The viewers are treated more as participants of the situation, and not as observers. In comparison with the scenes pictured in the subchapter 7.1. SAFETY OF THREE WALLS, and in the subchapter 7.2. Safety of three walls - ALTERNATION OF THE SCREEN DIRECTION, and in the subchapter 7.3. Challenging the fourth wall - FIXEDNESS in screen direction, this one is more dynamic (because of the alternation of the screen direction), and brings more subjective treatment (because of the "closed box.")

Scene 7.4.

When three characters are deployed in a triangle, the dominant character – The Lawyer (character at the apex of the triangle) is placed in the frame (usually in the center), while the Wife is on the left side and the Husband is on the right side. (**1. Cam A**). The dominant character - the Lawyer (character at the apex of the triangle) remains in the same place in the frame of the reverse shot - in the center (**2.**

Cam B), while the position of the others two characters results in an opposite screen direction for them in the reverse shot, on the opposite side of the screen. The Husband is on the left side (he was on the right), and the Wife is on the right side (she was on the left). The Lawyer is a visual anchor, an important tool that orients and guides the audience within the space. Screen direction of the Man and the Wife is not maintained throughout a scene, and viewers are oriented as to where characters are in relation to one another.

1. Cam A   **2. Cam B**

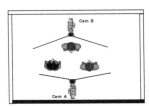 

7.5. BLOCKING IN 360-DEGREE SPACE - ALTERNATION OF THE SCREEN DIRECTION

FLUID SCREEN DIRECTION / ALTERNATION OF SCREEN DIRECTION - Screen direction is not maintained throughout a scene, and viewers are oriented as to where characters are in relation to one another. Space is not oriented on only one side of the line, which subsequently brings dynamism to an otherwise static scene, like a dialogue scene where a group of people is seated around a table. The situation is staged and blocked with a closed proscenium, that means with the fourth wall of the "box set."

The case pictured below portrays a situation where three characters do not occupy the same screen position and do not maintain the same screen direction. Continuity is assured, so a disorienting effect is out of the question, and the audience is constantly oriented as to where the players are in spatial relation to one another at all times.

The rule of thumb here is: the "closed box" results in a more subjective treatment; the alternation of screen direction brings dynamism to the scene. That being said, the dynamism is directly proportional to the alternation. It is the most challenging solution, but the permissible solution, and feasible solution.

Scene 7.5.

Variant, which does not give each character a steady screen direction.

When characters are deployed in a triangle, you have three lines of interest, where one line prevails over the other two lines.

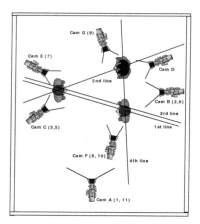

1. Cam A1

The establishing, side angle shot. The Bartender is talking to the Man over the bar. The line (1st line) is running between the Bartender and the Man. When the Bartender turns toward the Woman upstage, the Bartender creates a new line (2nd line) by his eyesight, which runs between him and the Woman.

1. Cam A2

The new line (2nd line) running between the Bartender and the Woman was established by the Bartender's eyesight.

2. Cam B

The Bartender looking from L-R at the Woman preserves original look from the previous shot (**Cam A**) maintaining the same screen direction, as well as the Woman. The shot is taken from the camera set up close to a new line (2nd line). Since the Man is included into the shot, his position resulted in opposite screen direction, as was in the shot taken from **Cam A**. He was on the right side of the frame in **Cam A**, and now he is on left side.

3. Cam C

The reverse shot of the Woman taken from close to the new line (2nd line).

4. Cam D

The reverse shot of the Bartender taken from close to the new line (2nd line).

5. Cam C

A clean single shot of the Woman taken from close to the new line (2nd line).

6. Cam B

The reverse shot of the Bartender taken from close to the new line (2nd line). The Woman preserves original look from the previous shot (**Cam C**). The Bartender now turns to the Man on Left as scene progresses and a new line (3rd line) is established between the Bartender and the Man.

7. Cam E1

The reverse shot of the Man taken from close to the new line (3rd line). When the Man later turns toward the Woman off screen, he will create a new line (4th line) by his eyesight, which runs between him and the Woman off screen.

7. Cam E2

The new line (4th line) running between the Man and the Woman off screen was established by the Man's eyesight. The Man looking to the left (from R-L) implies the Woman off screen listening and looking back to him from L-R.

8. Cam F

The reverse shot of the Woman taken from close to the new line (4th line). The Man looking from R-L at the Woman preserves original look from the previous shot (**Cam E2**) maintaining the same screen direction, and the Woman is from L-R toward him, because her position from L-R was implied by Man's look from the previous shot (**Cam E2**).

9. Cam G

The reverse shot of the Man taken from close to the new line (4th line).

10. Cam F

The reverse shot of the Woman taken from close to the new line (4th line).

11. Cam A

The whole situation can be reestablished by side angle shot, which established the situation at the beginning of the scene. The Man preserves the original screen direction from the previous shot (**Cam F**).

Don't let a multiple character scene intimidate you. First, you have to do your homework – create a verbal storyboard, then a shot list, and then diagram a scene on a paper. On the diagram outline each character's position and movement as called for in a scene description, parenthetical instruction, and by deeper emotions, and by the need of reveling characters' thoughts and emotions through action. Arranging and placing characters in a certain configuration in space should reflect everything mentioned above. And then get up from your desk, and walk it. Remember, you direct the audiences focus and emotional experience, you interpret the text, you are not plainly recording the text. If you don't get the result that you want, don't get discouraged and give up. Everything you do fails all the time. Exercise, and keep up good courage. Blocking a scene with actors and crew takes practice. You will be surprised by how well and how fast things can work out, and how comfortable you will become in blocking.

When you have finished surveying this chapter read the following CHAPTER 8: DEMYSTIFYING THE 180-DEGREE RULE (Crossing the Line). When you've finished studying both chapters, then you can proceed to the next step – practicing this directorial concept in III. STUDIO – BLOCKING IN 360-DEGREE SPACE. Information related to this studio can be found in PART II: STUDIOS – DIRECTING EXERCISES.

CHAPTER 8:
DEMYSTIFYING THE 180-DEGREE RULE
– CROSSING THE LINE

(crossing the axis, breaking the 180-degree rule, breaking the fourth wall, 360-degree space)

Anyone who has studied filmmaking learned in the first lecture about a cinematic technique that you have to obey the 180-degree rule, otherwise, you disorient the audience. If you are a rule-follower, no explanation is necessary. If you're a rule-breaker, no explanation is possible. In this chapter, you will learn how to benefit from intentionally violating this rule and how to "legally" cross the line. If you are risk averse, and rather worship invisible film technique, and sticking to standard filmmaking approaches makes you feel safer and more secure, this chapter, and the III. STUDIO - BLOCKING IN 360-DEGREE SPACE, is exactly what you need because it will teach you how to break the 180-degree rule legally. If you lean more toward the "aggressive" risk profile and have enough courage to dare to take risks, and you want to reject conventional visual and narrative codes and favor an indirect and oblique presentation, this chapter will definitely help you, because it challenges the 180-degree rule. If you want to learn more about your attitude toward the invisible film technique, take the quiz "invisible technique" in PART V. of this book.

180-DEGREE RULE

Continuity contributes to a film's success more than any other cinematic device. Position, movement, screen direction, and the look of the performers must be carefully blocked for continuity purposes. A very helpful concept for accomplishing this is the 180-degree rule. The 180-degree rule is based on an imaginary line running between two points. Following the 180-degree rule means choosing one side of the line (working area) and shooting all shots from that side. As a matter of convention, all camera set-ups are chosen on one side of the line throughout a scene. Every shot taken from one side of the line will be consistent with another shot taken from this side of the line, and in doing this, the continuity will be secured. Contrasting screen direction is used to show opposing characters talking to each other or moving toward or away from each other when only one character is seen onscreen at a time (single shot). This implies that the main reason to follow this rule is to keep the audience oriented.

Scene 8.a.

Below is a simple two-character scene in which a boyfriend is taking photos of his girlfriend. The line is running between the boyfriend and the girlfriend. All shots are taken from one side of the line.

1. Cam A	2. Cam B	3. Cam C

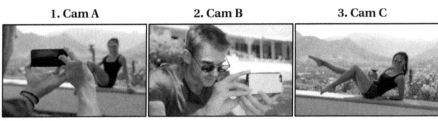

Scene 8.b.

Below is a simple two-character scene in which an artist is sketching a nude model during a life drawing session. The line is running between the artist and the model. All shots are taken from one side of the line.

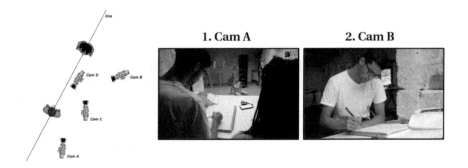

1. Cam A	2. Cam B

3.Cam C　　　　**4. Cam D**

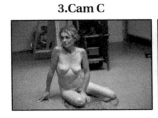

Rules draw somewhat rigid boundaries. This chapter aims to demystify the 180-degree rule. If the dramatic necessities and a need for an emotional truth require violation of the rules to the advantage of your story, then disobedience is a way to achieve excellent creative results. Don't be trapped by the rules and don't be terrified and intimidated by these rules, mostly by the 180-degree rule.

Shifting audience's perspective from a spectator to a participant:

This chapter will also teach you, how to establish a subjective manner of treatment. The staging in 360-degree space facilitates the switch in audience's perspective, from being just an observer to being a participant, assuming that the observer keeps an emotional distance from the story, and from the character, while the participant becomes more invested in the story and characters. The observer "treats" the story, like it is a film, while the participant "treats" a story like it is a reality, and he/she can get "lost" in a story. Even though the issue of identifying with a character is questionable (the film is not a reality but the illusion of reality), when you block a situation in 360-degree space, it will help you to manipulate viewers to identify with characters and suppress their critical approach.

I am listing in this chapter different techniques that can be used to cross the line effectively. The listed samples will not teach you how to ignore this rule, but how to cross the line for the benefit of your film legally. The ten strategies listed here are "legal" strategies for crossing the line.

Benefits of crossing the line and staging in 360-degree space:

1. Establishing a subjective manner of treatment:
   > You prepare the scene in 360-degrees. Also, the audience is treated as a participant, and not as an observer of the situation.

2. Favoring the character:
   a. It favors one character at the expense of another by switching screen direction. Thus, you align the audience with the character on the left side. (Favoring the left side of the frame

is discussed in chapter 12. Psycho-Physiological regularities in Left-Right/Right-left orientation.)

    b.   It visually represents the emotional shift between the characters.

    c.   It marks a shift in power between the characters.

3.   Breaking the stage's fourth wall: staging and blocking a situation with a closed proscenium, with the fourth wall of the "box set:"

    a.   It breaks the visual limitation of shooting just from one direction.

    b.   It establishes space in the scene.

    c.   It reveals information: storytelling information, dramatic information, emotional information, and point of interest on the fourth wall.

    d.   It redirects the focus to the new stimuli.

4.   Compressing time: advancing the story forward:

    a.   John talks to Britt. A switch to the opposite side of the line indicates that the audience did not witness everything. Therefore, at the edge of the cut, there is information the audience did not witness.

5.   Adding physical, psychological, and emotional dynamism and energy to the scene:

    a.   Mapping changes in physical action.

    b.   Mapping emotional intensity.

    c.   Mapping emotional beats.

    d.   Mapping changes in character feelings, motivations and insights.

    e.   Mapping changes in character's objectives.

6.   Causing a disorienting effect for dramatic purposes:

    a.   Two shooters in a gunfight (traditional quick draw fight) – you can cross the line to confuse the audience in regards to who is the villain or the hero, or who first draws the revolver or fires the first shot.

    b.   This can also be used to disorient the viewer in congruence with the character's disorientation or to show confusion in the mind of one of the characters.

8.1. CROSSING THE LINE WITH A CAMERA MOVE

A camera visibly crosses (dolly, pan, crane) the line during a shot and shoots the rest of the shot from the other side of the line. The camera can move from one side of the line of sight between two players to the other side without confusion in one continuous take. Once a camera has crossed the line and "settled" on the other side of the line, the rest of the scene can be shot from the other side of the line.

Scene 8.1.a.

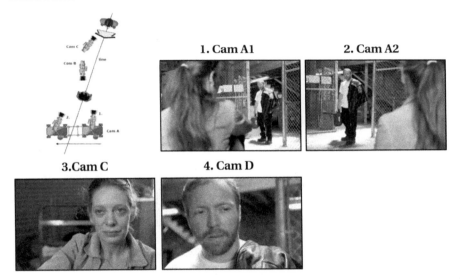

1. Cam A1   2. Cam A2   3. Cam C   4. Cam D

Scene 8.1.b.

Below is a two-character scene in which a wife is meeting the mother of her late husband for the first time over the fresh gravesite. The mother, our antagonist, was against the marriage of her late son. Our hero, the wife, initiates a reconciliation. The overall movement of the hero's journey is from left to right. But when up against the strong antagonist, the hero is moving from right to left. Right to left movement also induces discomfort, which is representative of the wife's emotional state in this scene. The mother is framed on the left lateral side of the frame at the very beginning of the scene because the left side evokes power and dominance. As the two women reach a resolution, the frame should adjust to represent the emotional shift visually. As the wife advances into the left side of the frame, the mother retreats to the right, marking a shift in power between the characters. I am rewarding the wife's endeavor by crossing the line and placing her on the left side of the frame. This is the end of the first episode of the TV Series entitled *Mountain Rangers*. I directed entire first season. The full series was aired in Slovakia in 1998. (You will learn more about left and right field process in CHAPTER 12. Psycho-Physiological regularities in Left-Right/Right-left orientation.)

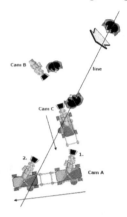

1. Cam A1	1. Cam A2	1. Cam A3

2. Cam B	3. Cam A2	3. Cam C2

Scene 8.1.c.

In this case, a camera is crossing the line between performers, not behind them, like it was in **Scene 8.1.a.** and **Scene 8.1.b.**

The first part of the scene is shot on one side of the line: shot #1 (**Cam A**) and shot #2 (**Cam B**) and beginning of the shot #3. During the shot #3, the camera is visibly crossing (dollying across) the line, landing on the other side of the line, and the second part of the scene is shot from the other side of the line: shot #4 (**Cam D**), shot #5 (**Cam E**) and shot #6 (**Cam D**).

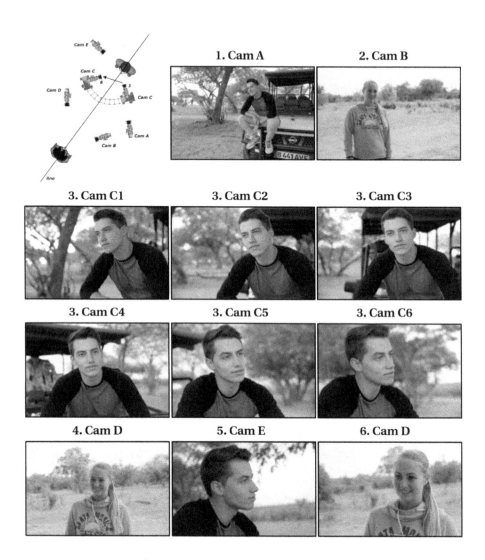

8.2. CROSSING THE LINE WITH A SIGHT OF PLAYER

The player establishes a new character *Off-Screen* (so far unseen character) by his sight. This can be used to introduce a new character; or present an opposing viewpoint of the action in a scene; or to alter the character perspective in a scene by switching the audience's attention to a new character; or changing visual perspective of the action and the spatial orientation established in the opening of the scene.

Scene 8.2.a.

The player establishes a new character *Off-Screen* (so far unseen character) by his sight. In this particular case, the camera does not cross the line. Even the player's eyesight does not cross the camera axis. The player's eyesight just establishes a new line, which is closer to a camera set-up, as was the original line. This is the first step, how to comprehend that the player's eyesight can establish a character off-screen.

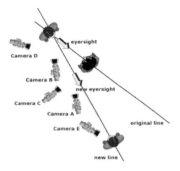

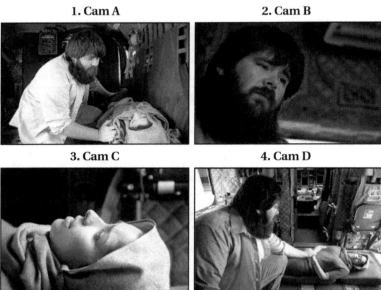

| 1. Cam A | 2. Cam B |
| 3. Cam C | 4. Cam D |

5. Cam B   **6. Cam E**

Scene 8.2.b.

This is the case when the player establishes a new line of action by her sight, and the player's eyesight crosses the camera axis. The change is happening in one shot: **Cam D**. Since her eyesight crosses a camera axis, consequently she will be seen in a few following shots in opposite screen direction as was the screen direction established in her establishing shots. Since the audience saw the change of the screen direction of the player, it will allow them to comprehend the change visually.

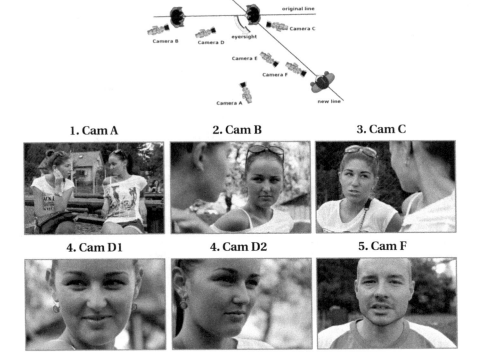

1. Cam A   **2. Cam B**   **3. Cam C**

4. Cam D1   **4. Cam D2**   **5. Cam F**

6. Cam A   **7. Cam F**

Scene 8.2.c.

The player's eyesight crosses the camera axis. This is a specific situation similar to the one when the line crosses the camera axis, described in the subchapter 8.10. CROSSING THE LINE BY CROSSING THE CAMERA AXIS. This can be used, when the player follows the movement of an *Off-Screen* character, who moves across the screen but *Off-Screen*. The player's eyesight keeps the audience oriented, where the *Off-Screen* character is. Consequently, the player will be seen at the end of the shot in the opposite screen direction, as was his direction at the beginning of the shot. The Off-Screen character could be shown before this shot looking from R-L to the player seen in the shot, and after this shot, the Off-Screen character could be shown looking back to the player from L-R.

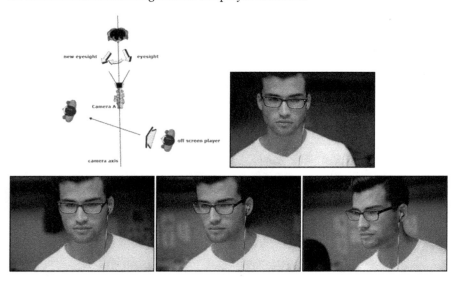

8.3. CROSSING THE LINE WITH A NEUTRAL SHOT – NON-DIRECTIONAL SHOT (shot with a neutral direction)

Do not forget that studying how to cross the line not only equips you with the mechanical skills and dexterity to do so, but it will help you with your creativity and composition skills. I don't want you to abide by a set of guidelines, I want you to expand your artistic abilities. A combination of technical ability and artistic skill is essential for every film director. Your artistic and creative mind will gradually take complete advantage of familiarity with all expressive tools of cinema. Please review again the benefits of crossing the line and staging in 360-degree space listed at the beginning of this chapter.

Neutral Shot – Non-directional Shot – this is an absolutely neutral shot because it is a shot with a neutral direction. This shot (**4. Cam D**) can be used between two shots (**1. Cam A** and **5. Cam E**) from opposite sides of the line.

Scene 8.3.

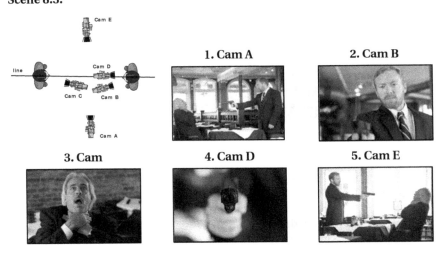

1. Cam A

2. Cam B

3. Cam

4. Cam D

5. Cam E

8.4. CROSSING THE LINE WITH A NEUTRAL SHOT – WIDE SHOT

Neutral shot – Wide Shot – This is a wide shot where it is very hard to tell the screen direction. A *neutral shot – wide shot* (usually designed as a high-angle aerial shot looking down) is not an absolutely neutral shot, like shot **4. Cam D** in **Scene 8.3.**, because it is not a non-directional shot (**2. Cam B**). But since there is no evident screen direction, this shot can be used between two shots (**1. Cam A** and **3. Cam C**) from opposite sides of the line.

1. Cam A

2. Cam B   **3. Cam C**

8.5. CROSSING THE LINE BY INTERCUTTING THE HEAD-ON SHOT AND TAIL-AWAY SHOT

The *Head-on Shot* is a shot in which the character(s) is facing the camera or moving toward the camera. It can be a non-directional shot, but it can also be an angled shot, a shot taken with the camera pointed obliquely at the subject. The *Tail-away Shot* is a shot in which the character(s) is facing away from the camera or moving away from the camera. It can be a non-directional shot, but it can also be an angled shot. Intercutting the head-on shot and the tail-away shot results in the opposite screen direction of both players, but it does not produce distraction; the continuity of the scene is not disrupted. Instead, it's the other way around, it keeps the audience oriented. (**Scene 8.5.a.** and **Scene 8.5.b.** and **Scene 8.5.c.**) Directional continuity is not important because the travel is generally neutral. There are no contrasting screen directions in two subsequent shots, even though both shots do not have to be non-directional shots.

You can use the head-on shot for opening a scene since you bring a moving character(s) from a distance toward the audience. You can use the tail-away shot for closing a scene when a character(s) is moving away from the camera. The head-on shot and tail-away shot with moving characters along the Z-axis increases or decreases their size, either fostering intimacy with characters (moving toward a camera) or, conversely, swallowing characters in its environment (moving away from a camera). Since staging along the Z-axis creates depth and makes shots three-dimensional, it produces a bigger emotional impact on the audience, because it creates an instant alignment with a character(s) or instant distance.

Scene 8.5.a.

Scene 8.5.b.

Scene 8.5.c.

8.6. CROSSING THE LINE BY SHOOTING AN IN-BETWEEN SHOT ON THE LINE

In-between Shot on the Line – this is a shot where a performer is looking directly into the camera, not off camera. (The sight line of a player is aligned with the camera axis.) It is recommended in a two-character scene to pair up a single shot (a shot of one performer) looking directly into the camera with another single shot of another performer looking directly into the camera, and, thereafter, to shoot a two-shot (a shot of two performers) from opposite sides of the line.

In a two-character scene, two single shots on the line back to back can be followed by a shot taken from the opposite sides of the line. That being said, in the **Scene 8.6.a.**, shots in-between on the line (**2. Cam B** and **3. Cam C**) can be used between two shots (**1. Cam A** and **4. Cam D**) from opposite sides of the line. The same strategy is applied for **Scene 8.6.b.** and **Scene 8.6.c.**

8.6.a.

| 1. Cam A | 2. Cam B |
| 3. Cam C | 4. Cam D |

Scene 8.6.b.

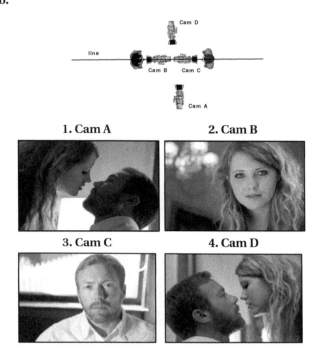

1. Cam A   2. Cam B

3. Cam C   4. Cam D

Scene 8.6.c.

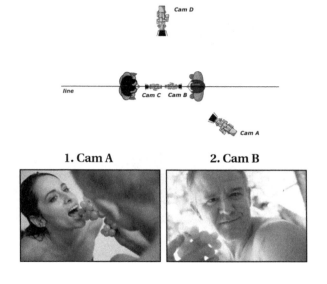

1. Cam A   2. Cam B

3. Cam C   4. Cam D

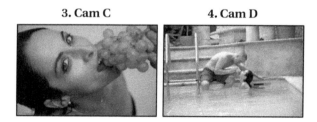

Scene 8.6.d.

In a two-character scene, after taking two single shots on the line back to back, you can choose whatever side of the line as a working area for shooting an establishing shot or for shooting the rest of the scene.

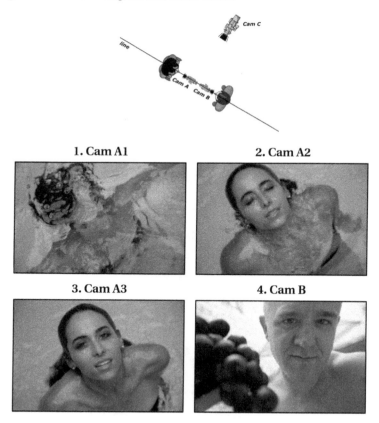

1. Cam A1   2. Cam A2

3. Cam A3   4. Cam B

5. Cam A   **6. Cam C**

8.7. CROSSING THE LINE WITH A BRIDGE SHOT (CUT-AWAY SHOT)

Bridge Shot (Cut Away Shot) – this is a shot that directs the audience's attention away from the principal action on the line. A bridge shot makes the audience forget the sense of screen direction in the last shot so a new camera set-up can be chosen over the line. Therefore, when returning to the principal action after a bridge shot, an opposite screen direction does not seem unnatural. A bridge shot can be a POV shot **(Scene 8.7.a.** and **Scene 8.7.b.)**, a CU of a prop **(Scene 8.7.d.)**, or a wide shot **(Scene 8.7.c.)**. Actually, it can be whatever; even a sequence filmed elsewhere or a subplot can be considered a bridge shot, or flashbacks, or flash-forwards. A bridge shot can be related to the principal action **(Scene 8.7.a.** and **Scene 8.7.b.** and **Scene 8.7.d.),** and it does not have to be related to the principal action or to the geography of the scene **(Scene 8.7.c.).** Usually, a bridge shot introduces a new element(s) related to a scene or story, illustrates new information, explains, suggests the passage of time, changes a narrative perspective, or changes a character perspective. Many times, a bridge shot is used in editing when a problem of continuity occurs or, the other way around, when a temporal or spatial discontinuity is desired.

"Bridge shot" and "cut away shot" basically mean the same thing and are often used interchangeably. The etymology of the term "bridge shot" refers to its origin – to provide a bridge over the line. To bridge the line, two shots are joined together through a "bridge shot."

Scene 8.7.a.

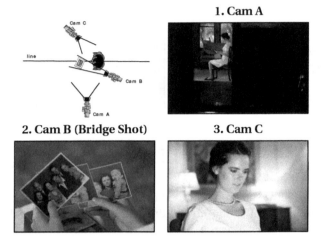

1. Cam A

2. Cam B (Bridge Shot)

3. Cam C

Scene 8.7.b.

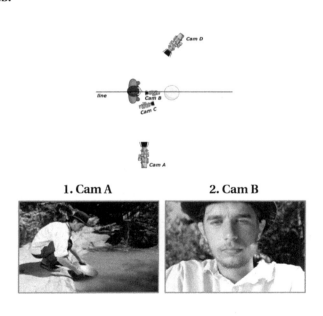

1. Cam A

2. Cam B

3. Cam C (Bridge Shot) **4. Cam D**

Scene 8.7.c.

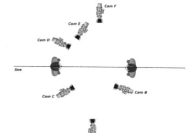

1. Cam A

2. Cam B **3. Cam C**

4. (Bridge Shot) **5. Cam D**

6. Cam E **7. Cam F**

Scene 8.7.d.

1. Cam A

2. Cam B (Bridge Shot)   3. Cam C

8.8. CROSSING THE LINE BY KEEPING BOTH PLAYERS IN FRAME

This is probably the most difficult situation to comprehend in theory, but it works in practice very well. You have been taught and trained that "*every shot taken from one side of the line will be consistent with another shot taken from this side of the line, and by doing this, the continuity will be secured.*" At first glance, the following strategy (shooting the subsequent shot from the other side of the line) contradicts the 180-degree rule. It does, but only in theory.

Crossing the line by keeping both players in frame strategy is seen a lot in two feature films I directed, *Fallacies of our Traditional Morale* (1989), and *From Morning till Dawn* (1990). This strategy - crossing the line by keeping both players in frame - was not a knowledge-based execution of the strategy. It was more the evidence-based strategy. No doubts that it needed the practical skills necessary to implement a practice like this, but still, it was a more intuitive process for me than the rational one. When you use this strategy, the audience is still correctly oriented (even though the reverse shot results in the opposite screen direction for both players), because the audience is constantly informed where the players are in relation to one another, because they see both players in a shot and in a reverse shot.

It can be done during master **(Scene 8.8.a.)**, OTS **(Scene 8.8.b.)**, 50/50 **(Scene 8.8.c.)**, and OTS CU **(Scene 8.8.d.** and **Scene 8.8.e.)** shots. But the rule of thumb here is: both players have to be seen in a shot and reverse shot, otherwise, this strategy will not work! If you cross the line cutting from a two-shot to a single shot over the line, you will cause a disorienting effect.

Scene 8.8.a.

In an establishing scene, "jumping" over the line will establish the scene immediately in a 360-degree space.

Scene 8.8.b.

In an inciting incident scene, fulcrum point scene, or revelation scene, "jumping" over the line will deepen the mystery and add ambiguity.

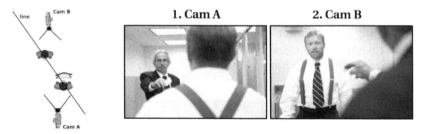

Scene 8.8.c.

In an argument scene, "jumping" over the line will increase the contrast and highlight the conflict in an otherwise static scene.

Scene 8.8.d.

In a dialogue scene, "jumping" over the line can externalize characters' confusion or disorientation.

Scene 8.8.e.

In a flirting scene, "jumping" over the line will emphasize the continuum of emotions, the sameness of goals for both characters since both characters are framed on the same side of the frame.

8.9. MONTAGE SEQUENCE

Montage Sequence is a series of short shots edited together to:

-   portray or show a passage of time
-   portray or show a time lapse
-   suggest that more time has passed
-   impart that time has elapsed between the shots
-   shorten the actual time taken to complete the activity
-   condense narrative
-   advance the story forward
-   create symbolic meaning

This is the widely used conventional approach by all filmmakers all over the world when they want to show character's progress, who is engaged in sports training **(Scene 8.9.)** or studying. At the end of the *"Montage Sequence"* a long-time period is compressed into a short *"Montage Sequence,"* and the hero is prepared for his task.

What organizes and keeps all shots together is the idea or emotion, and not the spacious orientation, two or three-dimensional. There is a heavy emphasis on isolated images rather than the continuity of a flow of images. Spatial and temporal discontinuity is acceptable. Discontinuous editing is used to fracture spatial coherence. The content of the whole sequence is more important than the content of individual images, and still, the sequence delivers a coherent message. That being said, there is no need to follow the 180-degree rule to make the audience understand what's going on in a *"Montage Sequence."* The other way around, the alternation of images, the ignorance of continuity of time and place, self-contained, isolated images, shots without apparent spatial and time connection can give the audience the rapid progression of the events or story. (Also refer to the Chapter 4: MANIPULATING FILM TIME, specifically to the COMPRESSED TIME segment.)

Scene 8.9.

8.10. CROSSING THE LINE BY CROSSING THE CAMERA AXIS

When players move, the line of action moves with them. A player's movement can result in the switching of their screen position within a shot. One player can even be outside of the shot, but it does not mean that the camera has crossed the line; in fact, the line has crossed the camera axis. The alternation of screen direction brings dynamism to the scene and breaks the sameness of screen direction, the sameness which brings steadiness to the scene. It is a very powerful tool often used to add contrast and dynamism to a scene and to highlight the tension or conflict. Refer to the CHAPTER 7: MULTIPLE-CHARACTER SCENE.

Scene 8.10.a.

| 1. Cam A | 2. Cam A | 3. Cam A |

8.11. CROSSING THE LINE TO CAUSE A DISORIENTING EFFECT, SPATIAL DISORIENTATION, OR CHARACTER'S DISORIENTATION

So far, I have covered in this chapter situations of how to cross the line without confusing the audience, where the players are in relationship to each other. In this subchapter, I will be talking about how to cross the line to cause a disorienting effect for dramatic effect purposely.

Scene 8.11.a.

In the scene below, two shooters are in a gunfight - a traditional quick draw fight. You can cross the line to confuse the audience with regard to who is the villain or the hero, who first draws the revolver, who first fires a shot, or who gets killed.

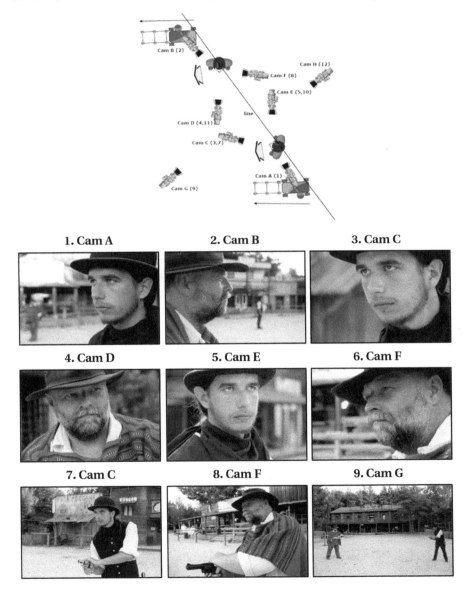

1. Cam A   2. Cam B   3. Cam C

4. Cam D   5. Cam E   6. Cam F

7. Cam C   8. Cam F   9. Cam G

10. Cam E   **11. Cam D**   **12. Cam H**

Scene 8.11.b.

In the scene below, a distressed, confused, and puzzled man wants to pay a local guy for helping him to bring his fatally injured wife to an air ambulance and transporting her to a hospital, where she is expected to recover. This is the situation when you can cross the line in order to disorient the viewer in congruence with the character's disorientation or to show confusion in the mind of one of the characters.

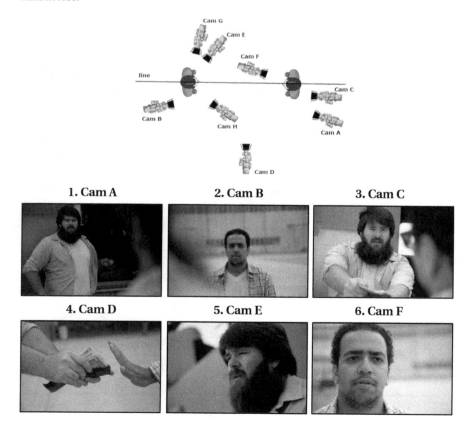

1. Cam A   **2. Cam B**   **3. Cam C**

4. Cam D   **5. Cam E**   **6. Cam F**

7. Cam C **8. Cam G** **9. Cam H**

10. Cam E **11. Cam F** **12. Cam E**

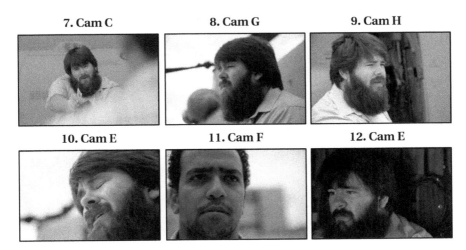

Challenging conventional wisdom, even ignoring the scholasticism can develop into a tree that will bear good fruits. Experiment, apply your curiosity to filmmaking, harness your rebelliousness toward authority, question academic rules. Reaping the fruits of your curiosity and experimentation can be really sweet.

When you have finished surveying this chapter and CHAPTER 7: MULTIPLE-CHARACTER SCENE, return to the beginning and read it again in more detail. When you've finished studying both chapters, then you can proceed to the next step – practicing this directorial concept in III. STUDIO – BLOCKING IN 360-DEGREE SPACE. Information related to this studio can be found in PART II: STUDIOS – DIRECTING EXERCISES.

CHAPTER 9:
CONCEPT OF CHARACTER PERSPECTIVE

Intro

The Greeks created gods in the image of humans. Their gods had many human qualities, such as beauty, wisdom, and power, and sometimes human weaknesses such as greed, hatred, jealousy, and uncontrollable anger. The gods were highly emotional and behaved inconsistently and sometimes immorally. Zeus, the god of the sky and ruler of the Olympian gods, was rarely faithful to Hera, the queen of the gods and his faithful wife. Hera was one of the fairest goddesses on Mount Olympus, but on the other hand, she was known to be jealous and vengeful towards people or gods who hurt or crossed her. However, because Hera couldn't hurt Zeus, since he was the god of the sky, and she was the protector of marriage, she pursued and tortured his mistresses and his illegitimate children.

The ancient Greeks loved stories and fables like this. One favorite family activity was to gather in the house courtyard to hear those myths, stories and legends, told by the mother or father. I was always curious, how those stories were perceived by listeners. The subjective nature of perception always fascinated me. The subjective structure of vision! Of course, that each story carried the meaning, feeling, an attitude, but without any doubts, those stories could cause remarkably different reactions in different listeners. But why? Because people react in different emotional ways to different emotional impulses? Can it be controlled? I am totally convinced that it can be controlled. Within the range of medium! Storytellers have always been bound by restrictions and limitations of the medium they used for their stories. Even though our experience of stories is subjective, because of our unique nature of perception, I think that it can be controlled, manipulated, and modified by a storyteller within the limitation of the medium. The narrative, thoroughly grounded in the realities of the medium, uses the tools of manipulation. The mom or father telling those stories about Greek gods used the power of the word through oral expression, allowing listeners to feel, what they wanted them to feel. These days you have the power to make the audience laugh or cry, and feel in a certain way, using tools of emotional manipulation of visual media, as that Greek mom or father did.

You might be among those who doubt how much artistic control you have over the broad vision and its execution. Many directors rely on their instinct, intuition, improvisation, and subconscious influences. But it is your call as a director to make the audience view the character with sympathy or empathy or with contempt using the *Concept of Character Perspective*. This concept will help you to understand and use different directorial strategies creatively to elicit an emotional response in the audience or to engage the audience by portraying characters in such a way that will achieve your anticipated result.

Four factors affect the Character Perspective in a Scene:

Factor number one: Camera Treatment and Shot Design

> Understanding the story, emotional involvement, empathizing with a character, sympathizing with a character, identifying with a character, or disliking, condemning, and scorning a character is achieved by controlling the content, composition, framing and movement of the shot.

Factor number two: Narrative Structure and Flow of the Scene

> The narrative structure of the scene guides and informs. The audience's responses to a character are driven by the movement of the narrative, with hardly any connection to the visual narrative.

Factor number three: Character Per Se

> Audience's emotions and responses to a character are elicited based on the way the character is scripted, with hardly any connection to the visual narrative.

Factor number four: Storyteller's Perspective

> The storyteller's perspective guides the audience's emotional response to a character. Storyteller's Perspective for visual-storytelling purposes is as equally important as the Character's Perspective because there is a direct connection between the way a storyteller sees events and the way the story is presented. As we are studying the concept of character perspective in this chapter, we can ignore the Storyteller's perspective for now, since we will delve into it in more detail in the next chapter - CHAPTER 10: CONCEPT OF STORYTELLER'S PERSPECTIVE.

Factor number one relates to a visual narrative, which is not imprinted in the script; factors number two, and three are imprinted in the script, with hardly any connection to a visual narrative; factor number four is imprinted in the script, and it is related to a visual narrative. Since you can control the viewer's perception of a scene through visual narrative, you have to master the concept of character perspective and its execution. It's of vital importance that you grasp the concept of character perspective and *Strategies and Methodologies for Modeling a Character Perspective* in the scene. Both strategies and methodologies will help you to better articulate and communicate your ideas and help you to better control the audience's emotional responses to the story events, and to characters.

Three stages of attachment to the character:

Your goal is to create an emotional attachment between the audience and characters in your film. You want them to get emotionally involved, emotionally engaged.

Murray Smith's breakdown of the process for attachment or identification with a character asserts that there are three distinctive responses to a given character – *Recognition, Alignment, and Allegiance.* He refers to this process as a *"Structure of Sympathy"* and describes each stage as a stage, when *"the audience recognizes the character's traits based on the scene" (recognition)* or *"the audience gets to know the character based on all visual factors that make a particular character visually prominent" (alignment)* or *"the audience weighs and morally evaluates everything about the character and his/her actions." (Allegiance).* During the third stage, the audience connects emotionally or morally or ideologically with the characters. (Smith, M. *Engaging Characters: Fiction, Emotion, and the Cinema,* 1st Edition, Clarendon Press; 1995, ISBN-10: 019818347X)

Three possible models of character perspective within a scene:

As a director, you have to control and regulate the viewers' perception of events and their own emotions. The way you can do this is to engage the viewer emotionally in the scene and characters. One of the most important factors to help you determine where to put the camera and how to control and regulate the viewer's perception, and emotions is to determine whose scene it is. Typically, one character dominates the scene. The character's attitude, feelings, emotions, thoughts, perspectives, or character's unique view of the situation or world lead the scene. You may be under the false impression that the audience will view the character with sympathy or empathy or hate just because the character is scripted this way.

No doubt, the subjective perspective is striking. Make sure that you give the scene or part of the scene to the right character. Obviously, the dominant focus is on one character, but you can shift from one character to another, and at any given instant you have to be sure, who is your dominant character. Making a bad decision in this particular regard can destroy a scene.

1st Model: Consistent Character Perspective

One character is favored in a scene. A camera is associated with one character perspective.

Director's goal:

I want to enhance the audience's identification with one character.
I want to make the audience share the POV with one character.
I want the audience to empathize, sympathize, and identify with this char-
acter.
I want the audience to disdain, condemn, and scorn this character.
I want the audience to understand character's emotions, thoughts, feelings,
dilemmas, attitudes, and character's transformation.
I want the audience to be involved with story events and emotions through
one character.
I want the audience to be connected or disconnected emotionally or morally
or ideologically with one character.
I want the audience to be informed, whose identity is changing.
I want to stimulate the audiences' curiosity about the character.
I want to reorient the audience's attention to a new event.
I want to stipulate visual interest.

2nd Model: Fluid Character Perspective

Alternations of character perspective within a scene. Camera shifts character perspective. Make sure when you switch perspectives, there is a reason for it, and that your viewers will be able to follow the switch.

Director's goal:

I want to change the audience's alignment from one character to another one.
I want to mark the emotional shift between the characters.
I want to mark a shift in power between the characters.
I want to introduce a new character.
I want to render that a character makes a critical discovery.
I want to map a character's realization of things.
I want to map a character's surprise.
I want to change the interest of the audience from one character to the other.

3rd Model: Neutral Stance

The events and emotions are rendered objectively. The camera is a passive observer. The camera is an impartial, objective observer. The camera presents events from an objective point of view and does not favor any of the characters involved in a scene.

Director's goal:

I want to maintain a neutral stance.

I want to render a situation from an observer's POV - from third-person POV.
I want to keep a respective distance.
I don't want to favor one character over another one.
I don't want to judge characters.
I want to have an unclear character perspective.
I want to treat viewers more objectively.
I want to distance the audience from characters and purposely discourage the audience from getting involved with characters.
I want the audience to witness something unknown to the characters objectively.
I don't want the audience to be connected emotionally or morally or ideologically with the characters.
I want to integrate distance and voyeurism into a visual narrative.

The first two models described above, *Consistent Character Perspective* and *Fluid Character Perspective,* are subjective treatments because they engage the audience more emotionally with a scene and with the character(s). The third model, *Neutral Stance,* is a more objective treatment because it distances the audience from the character(s). However, this model is suitable for action scenes, situations in which you want to distance the audience from the character or purposely discourage the audience from getting involved emotionally with the characters. This model is also suitable for situations when you want to pick up the narrative pace.

Shift in a Character Perspective:

You need to get an audience's attention in order to alert them that what they are about to see will be rendered or seen from another character's perspective; or that what they are about to see is more important than what they have seen up to this point, and it is a pivotal moment in the scene or story; or that this is the critical moment when a character is about to discover something or make a decision that will alter his or her journey; or this is the moment of *tragic irony,* when the audience recognizes something unknown to the character.

A change in *"Character Perspective,"* but also mapping the *"Pivotal Beat"* (a beat, when the story changes direction), mapping *"Pivotal Moment"* of a scene (an important moment in which the action of the scene takes a significant turn, or something really important to the outcome of the scene happens), mapping the *"Fulcrum Point"* (a pivot point which plays a central role in the story, when the story makes a major change in direction), mapping the *"Emotional Turn"* (character's emotional shift or change caused by story events), mapping a change of identity of the character, and mapping raise in *"Dramatic Intensity"* (all element of forces that heighten tension) can be visually rendered in a number of ways via a change in the visual pattern or change in rhythm:

Change in a visual pattern:

- Instantaneous proximity to the characters (moving camera closer to the character or action, Zoom in, cut on same camera axis).
- Shift from wider shots to tighter shots (using close-ups).
- Shift from regular/obvious camera angels to spectacular ones (using low angle, high angle, dutch angle shots).
- Shift from Static Shots to Moving Shots.
- Shift from an Objective Visual Treatment to a Subjective Visual Treatment.

Change in rhythm:

- Shift from stationary staging and blocking to blocking in movement.
- Shift from a slow narrative pace to a fast narrative pace.
- Modification in pictorial rhythm.
- Modification in editorial rhythm.

The Director's Choices:

Dramatic and emotional emphasis on visual storytelling can be achieved in various ways through critical director's choices. These choices include the *Mood and Tone* of the scene, *Emotional Meaning* of the Scene, and *Character Perspective*. To establish an intimate relationship between the audience and the character or to simply align the audience with one character or another, or to distance the audience from a character, each choice must be carefully planned.

A director makes critical choices in designing each scene, and the decision about Character perspective is one of the most important that a director makes. As I already said, *the character's attitude, feelings, emotions, thoughts, perspectives, or unique view of the situation or world lead the scene.* The narrative, emotional, and psychological importance of a character can be achieved by emphasizing his/her visual dominance within the shot, within the scene, within the film.

Decide:

- *Whose scene is it?*
- *Whose subjectivity is important?*
- *Who should the audience associate with?*
- *Who do you want to be focused on?*
- *Whose head does the audience have to be in to understand the scene, to understand what character is feeling, to understand the plot?*

Decide and Execute:

- *With whose perspective is the camera associated?*
- *Which character does the camera privilege?*
- *Whose perspective guides the audience?*

Character Perspective affects:

- *The audience's perception of the character.*
- *The audience's emotional involvement.*
- *The impact of the story.*
- *The audience's understanding of a story.*
- *The emotional meaning.*

Even though the audience's attention can be split, at any given instant you have to be clear whose scene it is. You can give viewers opportunity to see one character (let's say the main/principal/major character) through the other's character eyes (let's say a secondary/supporting/minor character), but only because you want to make them feel what your (main) character feels. The viewers' ability to empathize with the other (secondary) character can help you accentuate the main character's feelings.

Camera placement, shot design and sound create the subjective perspective. Do not merely render a scene, do not record, do not document, do not mechanically reflect rather than interpret a scene from a character's perspective. You will not only achieve a striking emotional impact on the viewers' perception, by involving them emotionally, but you will also set up an "emotional goal" for each scene.

Director's goal:

I want to make them empathize with a hero.
I want to make them hate this character.
I want to make them cry, laugh.
I want to make them understand the character's concern.
I want to make them feel sadness.
I want to make them feel passion.
I want to get them sexually excited.

You will learn more about the emotional manipulation in CHAPTER 11: EMOTIONAL MANIPULATION/EMOTIONAL DESIGN.

Your task is to transport the audience to the inner life of the character. The film renders the subjective state of a character/inner state of mind through:

- Visual means of film:
  - Outer manifestations of action (physically transforming the internal to the external).
  - Visualization of the "inner state of mind" by illustration.
  - Camera treatment (overall visual design, camera angle, size of shot, composition, framing, time).
  - Shot design (explicit and implicit meaning, staging and blocking).
  - Other visually expressive means of film (lighting, production design, costume design, make-up, graphic design, different visual components).

- Oral means of film:
  - Dialogue
  - Dialog revelation (externalizing feelings through the dialog)
  - Voice-over narration
  - Interior monologue
  - Soliloquy
  - Sound design

Methodology and visual strategy for rendering a scene based on character perspective:

As you already know, one of the four factors that influences character perspective in a scene is *Camera Treatment* and *Shot Design*. The character's attitude, feelings, emotions, thoughts, perspectives, or character's unique view of the situation is physicalized through a shot design. The way the audience understands the story, their emotional involvement, and whether they empathize, sympathize and identify with a character or whether they dislike, condemn, and scorn a character is achieved by controlling composition. The composition is a deliberate arrangement and organization of all visual elements in a specific location of a shot, and relation of all visual elements to the rest of the elements in a shot. To captivate the audience's attention, you have to create an eye-catching point of interest. The eye-catching point of interest emphasizes the most important part of the shot. The eye-catching point of interest can be created by visual attraction, or by setting a graphic focus, or by giving the object principality through a visual prominence.

Research shows that our everyday conscious experience of the visual world is fundamentally shaped by the interaction of overt visual attention and object awareness. Our narrow field of view limits the amount of data we can acquire at any single glance, and it is considered the focus of our attention, both visual and cognitive. Attention is defined as *the process by which we select a subset from all of the available information, for further processing.* When you are directing, you are targeting this behavioral and cognitive process by selectively concentrating the audience on a specific aspect of information, while simultaneously you want them to ignore or suppress other perceivable information.

Great Polish film director Andrzej Wajda said, *"Cinema consists of drawing the audience's attention to the significant elements and eliminating the superfluous."*

What are the means we use to do this?

1. *Framing, which eliminates from the start what we don't want to show the audience.*
2. *Lighting, which leaves in darkness or shadow whatever might distract the audience's attention from the subject.*
3. *The movement of the camera, which, by heading toward the essential, will sweep aside the superfluous as it goes."*

(Wajda, A. *WAJDA ON FILM: A MASTER'S NOTES*, 3rd edition, ACROBAT BOOKS; 2015, ISBN-10: 0918226295)

You will learn in this chapter how to give principality to an important character through pictorial dominance. In this part of the chapter you will learn, how to clearly determine and specify all visual factors you can use for emphasizing a character's narrative dominance, externalizing a character's emotional state, or manifesting a character's thought process, or drawing the audience's attention to a character's unique view of the world, or simply showing how a character views the situation around him/her. Here I postulate factors and visual elements that can help you visually articulate the character's perspective within a scene. The list is based on how the eye responds to visual stimulus, how graphic aspects carry the meaning, how composition suggests the character's inner state of mind, how visual design indirectly indicates something about the character, how visuals represent the character, how visual elements create visual conflict, how visuals create symbols and how the audience can decode them, how colors symbolize emotions, how to utilize lines and shapes for rendering a character's dilemmas and choices, how to suggest an emotional arc or changes of the character by visual means of film, and how to overall communicate ideas and interpret them through visual aspects of the shot. When all the visual elements are combined, the full impact of the film experience will be interpreted by the audience.

If you are looking for a "crash course," all below-listed factors, which determine visual prominence/dominance/importance of character, may help, but it is not to be used as a substitute for the hard work that is necessary. Knowledge alone is not useful. Secondly, what you say to viewers is not as important as how they will interpret it. The examples below will make you think there is no way this can work. It all depends on the visual execution of these different strategies in order to attain the desired results. However, there are also examples of different visual solutions for rendering a character's perspective in a scene that will make sense on paper, but when you go out and use them, you may find that you fail each time. There is a reason for this. Filmmaking is not an exact science! There are other factors outside your control that can affect an outcome, so it's best not to be disappointed when you don't get the desired results at first. If you believe a certain approach isn't going to work, do not give up. Refine your methods, experiment with your approach in different ways, and monitor the differing results when you do certain things differently. But don't forget: the concept of character perspective is one of the most important directorial tools!

Benefit of the Concept of Character Perspective:

For One-character Scenes:
- Establishing a subjective manner of treatment.
- Aligning the audience with a character.
- Articulating the emotional focus of the scene.
- Physicalizing and externalizing the character's emotions, thoughts, feelings, dilemmas, and attitudes.
- Signaling a transition to memories and reminiscences of a character.
- Visualizing narrator's/director's attitudinal point of view (judgments).
- Accommodating the audience's ability to understand a story.

For Two-character and Multiple-character Scenes:
- Establishing a subjective manner of treatment.
- Articulating a point of interest for the audience (associative point).
- Favoring one character over another.
- Visualizing a character's emotional attachment to or distance from another character.
- Visualizing emotional transitions.
- Visualizing emotional and dramatic twists, turning points, fulcrum points, and pivotal moments.
- Visualizing a character's transformation.
- Mapping emotional beats.
- Emphasizing the dramatic and emotional intensity of a story.

9.1. FRAME COMPOSITION (positioning a character within the frame, negative space, camera angle, shot composition)

One of the most effective ways of communicating the narrative, emotional, and psychological importance of a character to the audience is through a *Frame Composition:*

- Positioning object within the frame: central symmetrical composition; the proximity to the frame – leading space/looking space, negative space, static composition, dynamic composition
- Vertical camera angles: eye-level shot, low angle, high angle, Dutch angle, birds-eye view
- Horizontal camera angles: straight-on shot, semi-profile shot, profile shot
- Open-frame composition, closed-frame composition, single shot, two-shot, group shot
- Isolation of a character: wide shot vs. close up (CU)

Scene 9.1.a.

Symmetrical positioning of characters within the frame for the sake of setting focus creates a balanced composition.

Scene 9.1.b.

The dynamic asymmetrical positioning of characters within the frame creates an unbalance/attraction of imbalance/dissonance in the composition/dynamism in the relationship of the character and the frame edge/negative space. A character near the frame edge has more attraction than a character in the center. In the subchapter 5.1.4. SHALLOW DEPTH OF FIELD, I said, *"The amount of negative space often determines why the audience likes or dislikes something depicted in a shot. The space around the character creates and enhances the desired effect."* Giving a character plenty of negative space behind his/her head does not bring the simplicity and calmness into the shot that negative space usually does, but it will increase the contrast and desired attachment to the character. At the same time, it has to be said that a busy background can externalize a character's mental or emotional state – overburden, tiredness, weariness.

Scene 9.1.c.

A spectacular shot/disorienting shot/unfamiliar perspective can be used to externalize a character's internal state.

 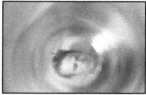 

Vertical Camera Angle specifically means the angle between the camera and the subject. It can be *an Eye-level Shot, Low Angle Shot, High Angle Shot, Dutch Angle Shot,* and *Birds-eye View Shot.* The vertical camera angle makes an indirect comment on the importance of the character.

Scene 9.1.d.

Eye-level Shot – even though the eye-level shot is generally considered a neutral shot as far as character importance and emotional impact goes, it is often used to convey straightforwardness.

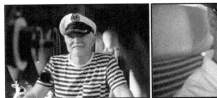

Scene 9.1.e.

Low Angle Shot – makes a character look superior, dominant, and powerful, and it is usually used to suggest authority, pride, and advantage over other characters.

Scene 9.1.f.

High Angle Shot – makes a character look inferior, helpless and defenseless, submissive, deficient, belittled, and it is usually used to diminish the importance of a character.

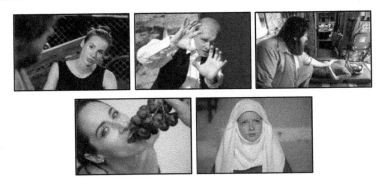

Scene 9.1.g.

Dutch Angle Shot – suggests imbalance and instability, and it is usually used to convey anxiety or chaos.

Scene 9.1.h.

Birds-eye View Shot – suggests insignificance, and it is usually used to convey a scale of a scene – spatial size from an omniscient point of view.

Horizontal Camera Angle specifically means the angle between the camera and the performer's eyesight. It can be a *Straight-on Shot, Semi-profile Shot,* or *Profile Shot.* The audience can align itself more with the character who is in a *Straight-on shot/Full-face Shot/Full-frontal Shot/Frontal View/Head-on Shot* "(**Scene 9.1.i.**). *Profile Shot* weakens the character's importance or makes him/her look more aggressive (**Scene 9.1.k.**). *Semi-profile Shot/Three-quarter angle/45-degree angle* (**Scene 9.1.j.**) demarcates the border between the subjective and objective treatment.

Scene 9.1.i.

Straight-on Shot

Scene 9.1.j.

Semi-profile Shot

Scene 9.1.k.

Profile Shot

Shots can be categorized in a number of ways. One of them is by number of characters.

Single Shot - has a single performer in the composition of the frame. Spatial separation can indicate physical, mental or emotional isolation of the character. Often designed as an *Open frame composition,* when a shot extends out and beyond the shot frame.

Two Shot - has two performers in the composition of the frame. Most frequent shot in mainstream films contains action and reaction. Often designed as a *Closed frame composition,* when both performers are closed within a border and do not go beyond the edge of the shot frame. (Self-contained shot.) Used to show the emotional attachment or distance between characters.

Three Shot - has three performers in the composition of the frame. A comedy genre template shot.

Group Shot - has a group of performers within a shot, when a group of people are interacting. It allows an actions scenes or dialogue scenes to be played out without changes in a camera position.

Isolation of a character depicted through the size of a shot can be accomplished in two different ways. The most "scholastic" approach is to depict isolation through a wide shot, where the character is literally lost in a shot.

Another approach, more sophisticated and most likely more intellectual, is to use CUs for visualizing a character's isolation. The graphic focus on a detail of something a character is concentrated on or occupied with gives a sense of a character's emotional or intellectual attachment to the object. It can also be used to depict a "state of public solitude" the character is in.

When you want to externalize the emotional distance between characters within a shot frame, you can do it photographically employing the features of camera lenses. Two characters within a shot can be gradually distanced by a focal length.

9.2. PHYSICAL SIZE (size of shot; CU of props; physical size in a two and group shot)

Character's emotions, the mental state of the character, and the expression of emotions can be explicitly or implicitly conveyed through a *Size of Shot*. A size of shot can also provide a character with specific properties: psychological nature, social traits, and historical and cultural influences. Emotional, moral, ethical, regional or societal alignment with the character is explicit through the size of the shot. The size of shot invokes emotional responses as admiration or contempt, sympathy or apathy, love or hatred. That being said, the size of shot "colors" the viewer's affective relation to the character. Size of shot directly establishes the character's importance within a scene. There are conventions in film and television industry which assign names and guidelines to common types of shots, framing and picture composition. The exact terminology varies, but the basic principles are the same.

(CU – Close Up; MS – Medium Shot; MFS – Medium Full Shot; FS – Full Shot)

(XCU – Extreme Close Up; CU – Close Up; FCU – Full Close Up; WCU – Wide Close Up)

A CU can be used to increase emotional impact on viewers and for creating intimacy. The CU satisfies the need for inner subjectivity and emphasizes the connection between the character and the audience. The CU is a gateway to a character's soul.

CU

XCU

In a two-character scene or multiple-character scene, a character in a tighter shot (a shot in which the subject appears to be very close to the camera, as in a CU) dominates in size, and is favored over a character(s) in wider shot (a shot in which the subject appears to be far from the camera, as in a full shot or long shot): **Scene 9.2.a.** and **Scene 9.2.b.**

Scene 9.2.a.

1. Cam A

2. Cam B   **3. Cam C**

Scene 9.2.b.

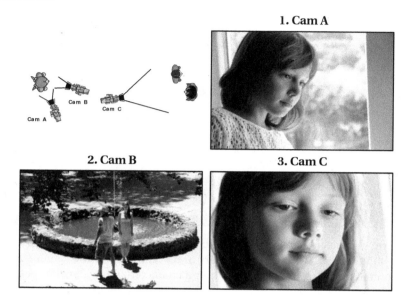

1. Cam A

2. Cam B

3. Cam C

Scene 9.2.c.

Blocking a character in a full shot weakens his importance.

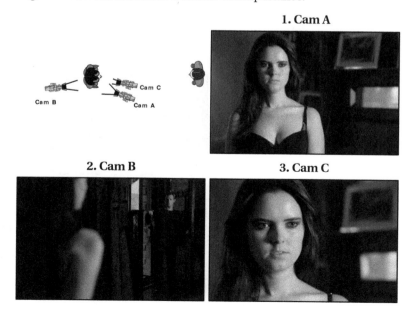

1. Cam A

2. Cam B

3. Cam C

Staging strategies for two/multiple character shots - a larger foreground character in contrast with a smaller background character implies the importance of the larger foreground character. (**9.2.d.** and **9.2.e.** and **9.2.f.**)

Scene 9.2.d.	Scene 9.2.e.	Scene 9.2.f.

Scene 9.2.g.

Changing a character's size by her movement within the frame along the Z-axis – moving closer builds involvement.

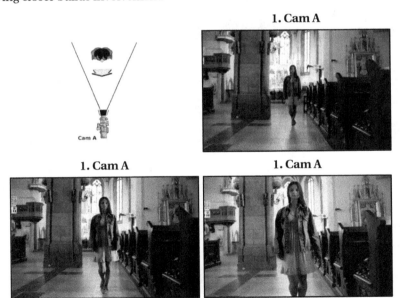

1. Cam A

1. Cam A

1. Cam A

CU of a prop puts the audience in the head of the character. The CU of a prop is a gateway to the emotional and mental world of the character. (**Scene 9.2.h., Scene 9.2.i., Scene 9.2.j.**) In the previous subchapter, 9.1. FRAME COMPOSITION, I said, *"The graphic focus on a detail of something a character is concentrated on or occupied with gives a sense of a character's emotional or intellectual at-*

tachment to the object. It can also depict a "state of public solitude" the character is in.

Scene 9.2.h.

Scene 9.2.i.

Scene 9.2.j.

9.3. DEPTH OF FIELD (unequal size of characters within the frame; selective focus; pulling the focus; exploiting all three planes, zoom in/zoom out)

The *Depth of Field* refers to the area of the shot that is in focus. If only a small area of the shot is in focus, there is a shallow depth of field, also called shallow focus. Unimportant visual elements are discarded in the defocused part of the shot, leaving only the most important visual elements in focus.

When you are designing a "shot space," you often think about the space around the character. When space is empty, the natural human inclination is to fill the space. But filling the space with too many objects can ironically distract attention away from the character you want the audience to be focused on. This captures the essence and power of something art and design call negative space. The amount of negative space often determines why the audience likes or dislikes something depicted in a shot. Things that are busy, noisy, or crowded are very distracting for the audience. The space around the character creates and enhances the desired effect. The space around the character makes him/her noticeable. So, the power of negative space can be simplified in the idea that less is often more. Removing things around the character, or eliminating things around the character through a shallow depth of field, staging in depth, or by rim light, helps you to cut out everything that can compete with the character. Doing that will give the character more attention.

The depth of field plays a significant role in designing a shot for the purposes of character perspective because it gives you the ability to selectively focus on a character while keeping the foreground and background out of focus. To be able to separate the character from the background and foreground allows you to immerse the audience in the character's psyche.

Scene 9.3.a.

Unequal size of characters within the frame.

The fore placement of one character over another gives that character prominence. This creates a clear associative point for the audience, emphasizing the hierarchic positioning of the performers – larger foreground character in contrast with smaller background characters implies the importance of the larger foreground character. His/her visual prominence is fortified by the focus. This strategy allows the audience to get into the mindset of the character.

Scene 9.3.b.

Selective focus.

When shooting a scene with selective focus, the shot is meant to have a specific character in focus. This won't help to create depth, but it will help guide the audience's eyes to what the director wants. Having the opportunity to direct the audience's eyes exactly where the director wants is a big advantage since no other elements in the frame will be distracting the audience and they can feel more connected to the particular character. That being said, it fosters intimacy with a character.

Scene 9.3.c.

Pulling or racking the focus

Focus Pull/Rack refers to the change of the focus of the lens during a shot. This directs the viewer's attention to one character through a restricted depth of field, such as shallow focus or when only one plane is in focus. It allows attention to shift between planes along the lens axis (the Z-axis) by pulling/racking focus without the axial cut. That means it eliminates cuts and selectively emphasizes one or another character within one shot. Pulling or racking the focus is used to reveal a character in the frame, who was previously out of focus. This will help to change the interest of the audience from one character to the other.

Scene 9.3.d.

Exploiting two or all three planes – foreground, middle-ground, background.

Having everything in focus will help the audience understand the character's environment better. From a dramatic perspective, a deep-focus shot keeps all characters in a tense confrontation. The audience is able to see how characters in one part of the frame react to what is going on in other parts of the frame. Another reason for you to have a busy, visually noisy background is to externalize interior states – to visualize the character's madness and insanity or to indicate that the character lost control of his actions, or he is losing his mind or is consumed by the surrounding environment.

As far as planar staging, which can be used for visualizing a character's thoughts, projecting of a character's thinking, or modifying reality as a result of character's thinking by exploiting all three planes, please refer back to the CHAPTER 5: CONTROLLING SPACE, section PLANER STAGING. Externalizing character's memories in one shot without illustrating them in a separate shot, is another advantage of exploiting all three planes at the same time – foreground, middle-ground, and background.

Scene 9.3.e.

Zoom in/Zoom out.

When a story gains intensity, either dramatic or emotional, or a situation calls for intimacy with a character, the audience is "brought" instantaneously closer to a character through zoom in, and when a story declines in intensity, the audience is instantaneously distanced from a character through zoom out.

Commonly today, filmmakers use a variation of zoom shots, push-in shots, and hidden zoom shots in order to give the same effect of emphasizing a character within a shot. A push-in shot uses a normal or long lens to push into the scene and to get close to a character. Sometimes, filmmakers use a technique referred to as "hiding the zoom," which is a combination of a push-in that transitions seamlessly into a zoom to create an even closer view of the character.

This technique was incredibly popular in the 1970s, but it was a period when using zoom lenses was considered a very amateurish approach. The great director Wim Wenders *(Paris, Texas)* worked on Michelangelo Antonioni's film *Beyond the Clouds* as a sort of assistant when he was already established as a great director with a number of films.

> *I had always refused* to *shoot anything with a zoom lens. It was forbidden. (…) Much to my horror, Antonioni shot virtually everything with a zoom lens. And I was impressed by the result at times.*

This experience softened some of his dogmatic and rigid ideas that he used to have about directing. Similarly, another guru director, Bernardo Bertolucci *(Last Tango in Paris)*, for many years looked on the zoom as an instrument of the devil. These days, however, he has a more peaceful relationship with zoom. (Trirard, L. *Moviemakers' Master Class: Private Lessons from the World's Foremost Director.* New York: Farber and Farber, 2006).

9.4. LENSES (Normal lenses, Long lenses, Wide lenses/Fisheye)

In his textbook *Cinematography: Theory and Practice,* author Blain Brown states that *"Cinematic technique means the methods and practices we use to add additional layers of meaning, nuance and emotional context to shots and scenes in addition to their objective content. The lens is one of the primary tools in achieving these means."* (Brown, B.: *Moviemakers' Cinematography: Theory and Practice,* New York and London: Focal Press, Taylor & Francis Group, 2012.) Brown goes on to write that the lens is what the director uses to put the audience in the world of the film and is the barrier in which the characters are able to move.

Camera lenses are one of the most important creative tools in the filmmaking process. Above all else, you have to make yourself familiar with the different types of lenses and how to best utilize their properties. The film is a visual art form, and therefore a director must be able to properly use lenses to tell a story with images and not just rely on the power of dialogue. However, a director should not allow the camera lenses to distract from the story or the actors' performance.

Camera lenses reflect the world of characters. And because of that, they are one of the most important devices that play a significant role in designing a shot for the purposes of character perspective.

"Standard/Normal Lens" - Normal lenses render perspective similarly to the way our eyes see perspective, however, they do not take in an angle of view similar to our eyes. Because normal lenses create an image with a perspective similar to what our eyes see, height, distance, speed, changes in apparent sizes of objects and people at different distances from the camera, all look natural. Normal lenses do not have extreme depth of field, and under usual lighting conditions, they cause the background behind an image to be slightly out of focus.

"Wide Lens" - A wide-angle lens has a short focal length, which exaggerates distances in front of the camera. This causes objects to seem farther away than they actually are. These lenses are called "wide-angle" because they take in a broad view of the scene in front of them. Wide-angle lenses are commonly used for establishing shots because of the great panoramic images that they produce. Due to their short focal length, these lenses have a great depth of field; when they are focused on a subject, the background and much of the foreground are also in focus. Their great depth of field also makes camera movement easier because they do not need to change focus when moving through space where the action is taking place. Their wide angle of view also helps diminish any imperfection in camera movement, creating moves that appear very smooth.

"Wide Lens" (Vistas and Establishing Shots) – Establishes exterior locations to help the audience understand the world that the characters are in helps describe emotions.

"Wide Engle Lens" – *delivers a great Depth of Field to an image (Foreground, middle-ground and background are in focus simultaneously.)* The audience is able to see how characters in one part of the frame react to what is going on in other parts of the frame.

"Fisheye Lens" – Short focal length lenses exaggerate perspective by causing parallel lines in the scene to converge quicker than we would normally see with our eyes. This holds true with all objects, making a building appear taller than it actually is; or making a person appear taller when shot from a low angle with a wide lens. Perspective makes near objects seem larger and far objects seem smaller. Car-mounted cameras using wide lenses accentuate the speed the car is going, making high-speed chases appear faster. These lenses can also distort the face when used for close-ups, causing the subjects face to bulge or bloat and appears grotesque – this can be used to enhance emotion or help build uneasiness between the audience and the particular character, it puts the audience in the character's frame of mind. Generally, a Fisheye Lens shows how the character sees the event or how the character experiences the world around him; externalizing character's feeling, emotions, mental process, the inner state of mind.

"Telephoto Lens/Long Lens" – Brings distant objects closer. It compresses space, making objects appear to be on the same horizontal plane. Exaggerates movement toward or away from the camera. Long focal length lenses take in a narrow angle of view and magnify a small portion of the scene in front of the camera. These lenses allow to pick out details within a scene and isolate them. The depth of field in long lenses is incredibly shallow, throwing backgrounds progressively out of focus as the focal lengths increase. This shallow depth of field gives a director the ability to selectively focus on subjects while keeping the background out of focus and less distracting. Using long lenses can enhance the effect of rack-focusing, helping to draw the viewers' attention from the background to foreground or vice versa. Long focal length lenses distort perspective lines so that they appear to converge farther away than our eyes see, causing objects to change size much more slowly than we anticipate them to – this can cause subjects to appear almost suspended in space. Another great effect of the long lens is the compression of space – this causes subjects to appear closer together than they actually are, making a crowd appear almost claustrophobic or heightening the effect in dramatic or emotional interactions between characters. When used in a close-up, long lenses flatten the subject's facial features. *Long Lens* - separation of the character from the background and foreground - a deep immersion into the character's psyche.

"Prop Lenses within a scene" – reflects objects. Distorts objects and images. It is used for illustrating a character's state of mind.

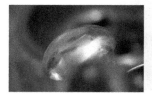  

"Shooting Through Objects" - Shooting through objects such as pane of glass, curtains, or water, to put the audience in the character's mind, or to foreshadow events, or to foreshadow character's decision.

 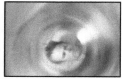

"Selective Focus - Shallow Depth of Field". When using shallow depth of field, only part of the image is in focus, drawing the attention to whatever that portion may be. It is very common to use shallow depth of field to make a character stand out from the background and draw the attention to him/her only, opposed to allowing the entire frame to be in focus, which would cause the audience slight confusion as to what they ought to focus on. Utilizing shallow depth of focus allows a director to choose and emphasis exactly what he/she wants the audience to pay attention to.

"Deep Depth of Field/Deep Focus" - A deep depth of field creates an image in which nearly everything in the frame is in sharp focus. Deep focus shots are commonly used to emphasize the scale of a scene, as well as to allow the audience to see more of what is going on in a scene. Most, if not all, establishing shots are deep focus shots in order to give the audience a full understanding of where the characters are and what is going on.

"Soft Focus" (Focus Throw, Defocus) - Soft focus occurs when everything within the frame is out of focus. Often, soft focus is considered a mistake, however, it can be used to create unique effects or disorientation or hallucination of a character, or it can be used to show POV shot from a character, who is drunk or disoriented. The unsettling effect of a soft-focus shot evokes non-ordinary, usually unstable mental state of the character, or the subjective experience she is going through, or when she is about to realize something. Sometimes a soft-focus shot is used as a transition between shots.

9.5. LINES (converging lines; vanishing point; frame within the frame; surface divisions)

Lines in a shot can create shapes and imply direction. They can be literal or implied. They can be straight or sharp, vertical, horizontal, or diagonal, and they can convey a different meaning. In designing a shot, they are often used to deliberately guide eyes to the most important information in a composition, to a specific character or to divide a shot into segments and emphasize or suppress a character.

Scene 9.5.a.

Converging Lines – converging lines lead attention to the character in the distance.

Scene 9.5.b.

Vanishing Point – attraction of the vanishing point. Gaze is attracted to the *vanishing point* area in a shot or out of the shot. It is used for articulating a point of interest for the audience by placing characters in that area of the shot.

Scene 9.5.c.

Surface Divisions (one character) – isolation of a character or physicalizing characters' emotional distance. Surface divisions can help you to direct the eye of the viewer to a specific area of the shot occupied by the character.

Scene 9.5.d

Surface Divisions (one character) – separation of a character.

Surface divisions can help you to comment on a character's emotional or mental state.

Scene 9.5.e.

Frame within the Frame – frames the main character in a doorway or window. A frame within the frame provides a sense of depth since it gives added depth to the shot. It also directs the attention of the viewer to a part of the composition emphasizing the main character by enclosing her/him within a secondary frame – contracting the shot size and producing a less dynamic image. It can also emphasize the voyeuristic feeling.

Scene 9.5.f.

Frame within the Frame can also produce a dynamic image. Sloping lines within the frame produce a more dynamic composition.

Surface Divisions (two frames within one frame). When two separated frames are joined in one frame, the formal balance disappears. It creates an image where two images are visually integrated into one and do not fight each other for attention (**Scene 9.5.g.**). It can also be used to create a divided interest, where two images fight each other for attention since both characters are equally important and none dominates in the attraction (**Scene 9.5.h.**). Competing areas of interest within a shot frame can create ambiguity in the viewer's mind as to which character is principal and thus is a way to control the viewer's emotional response. But a frame within the frame, where two characters are physically separated is mostly used for creating disconnection or highlighting differences or similarities between two characters (**Scene 9.5.i.** and **Scene 9.5.j.**). The distinct separation of the two characters in **Scene 9.5.j.** is emphasized by color separation and light separation. The color palette of the characters' costumes helps the audience subconsciously distinguish differences between the two characters. The female character is dressed in warm colors; the male character is dressed in cold colors, the female character is illuminated by the warm light, and the male character is illuminated by cold light.

Scene 9.5.g.   **Scene 9.5.h.**

Scene 9.5.i.   **Scene 9.5.j.**

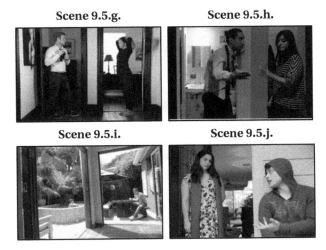

Scene 9.5.k.

The Dirty Frame – frames the main character in the background, in focus, and other objects or people in the foreground, out of focus, emphasizing the voyeuristic illusion. Integrating elements of *voyeurism* into a visual narrative can be a central visual element for creating a feeling that characters are observed from a distance or that the audience is "peeping" into the life of the characters.

9.6. OTS (OTS shot; pseudo-POV shot)

In this subchapter, I will discuss the importance of the OTS shot (*Over the Shoulder Shot*) and all its phenomena:

- Usefulness in articulating a point of interest.
- Cheesiness when overused – lack of impact.
- Shooting standard coverage – *"dump-truck" directing* (American cinematographer Gordon Willis's expression, meaning shooting a ton of footage and letting the editor craft the film. Refer back to the *CHAPTER 3: CONCEPT OF VISUAL UNITS,* segment *Coverage vs. Shot-by-Shot Style.)*
- Unrealistic situation of having two people standing opposite one another and talking.

Scene 9.6.a.

OTS shot (*Over the Shoulder Shot*) directs the audience's attention to the character who faces the camera.

Scene 9.6.b.

Generally, the character, who does not face the camera is weakened by the OTS. This factor can be utilized in designing a scene for the purposes of character perspective, by favoring one character to the detriment of another, in a two-shot. In a two-character scene, a character in a single shot is favored by the camera, and a character in an OTS shot (with his back toward the camera) is weakened by the camera.

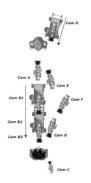

1. Cam A

2. Cam B1

2. Cam B2

2. Cam B3

3. Cam C

4. Cam D

5. Cam E

6. Cam F

7. Cam E

8. Cam D1

8. Cam D2

4. Cam G

Scene 9.6.c.

Too many OTS shots automatically result in an objective treatment and distance the audience from both characters. (**Scene 9.6.c.** and **Scene 9.6.d.**) It is often a result of employing a standardized style of shooting a film using coverage, where not every shot is carefully planned out. (Please refer back to the *CHAPTER 3: CONCEPT OF VISUAL UNITS*, section *Coverage vs. Shot-by-Shot Style.*) But when you want to distance the audience from characters or purposely discourage the audience from getting involved with characters, this strategy might work for you. This treatment results in an emotional response in which the audience just observes characters. It is like a two-party consent between characters and the audience when the audience enjoys watching/observing characters. Distance and voyeurism are integrated into a visual narrative.

The OTS can also be used, when you want to withhold the identity of the character, by not showing his or her face. Or, if there is no need to show the character's face. This technique can apply a lost or changed identity of a character, who does not want to be known or whose identity is changing. The lack of identity can make a character unknowable, but it can also make the character more interesting to the audience because it stimulates curiosity. This technique can help you to create a mysterious character like a spy, an eavesdropper, killer, psychopath, character who is looking back on his/her life, a doctor who is informing the main character that she is dying of malignant tumor, or the first person anonymous narrator - something like a first-person pseudo-limited perspective: everything is seen through the eyes of the character of the story, even audience can see him/her, but only his/her back.

Scene 9.6.c

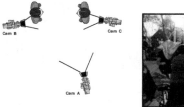 

1. Cam A

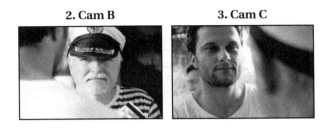

2. Cam B   **3. Cam C**

Scene 9.6.d.

1. Cam A

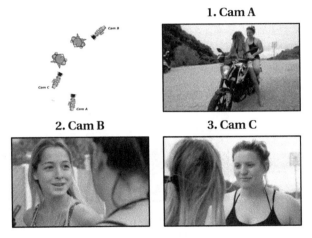

2. Cam B   **3. Cam C**

In the subchapter 9.2. PHYSICAL SIZE, I said that *the CU satisfies the need for inner subjectivity and emphasizes the connection between the character and audience and that the CU is a gateway to a character's soul.* There is another shot that conveys character subjectivity – the POV (point-of-view) shot. The POV shot enables the viewer to see virtually what character sees - real or imaginary. (More discussed in the following subchapter 9.7. POV SHOT). The Pseudo-POV shot uses an over the shoulder shot when a character who belongs a POV shot is a part of the shot.

Both shots (POV and Pseudo-POV) allow the audience to see what a character sees, but the POV shot is a more subjective shot, while the Pseudo-POV shot is more objective, offering a voyeuristic feeling. It is up to you to decide which shot gives the audience a bigger identification with a character, POV or Pseudo-POV, or to what extent you want to integrate voyeurism into a visual narration. To summarize, when the OTS shot is designed as a Pseudo-POV shot, it does not weaken a character's perspective, as I said earlier, but it fortifies a perspective of the character who is seen in a single shot before or after an OTS shot (**Scene 9.6.e., 9.6.f., and 9.6.g.**)

Scene 9.6.e.

Scene 9.6.f.

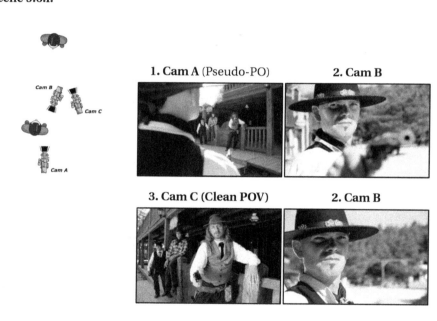

Scene 9.6.g.

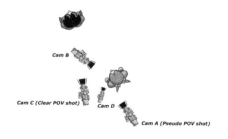

1. Cam A (Pseudo-POV)   **2. Cam B**   **3. Cam C** (Clear POV)

4. Cam D   **5. Cam B**   **6. Cam A** (Pseudo-POV)

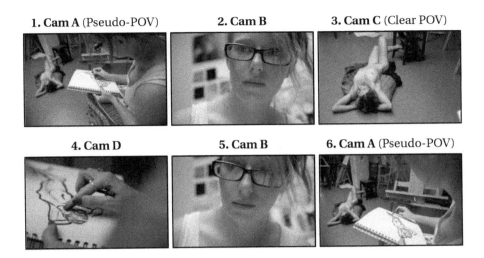

9.7. POV SHOT

POV shot (a point-of-view shot) shows how the character sees the situation (real or imaginary); a POV shot explains the emotional, mental, and psychological state of the character and establishes and re-establishes a character's identity.

One would think that a POV shot is the most powerful tool to get in the character's head. It appears that we have been misunderstanding the concept of the POV shot and its impact on the audience for years. There is widespread confusion about what and how much can be conveyed through a POV shot. Things seemed to get worse when video games rendering the viewpoint of the player's character arrived. Some young filmmakers with years of gaming experience think that the most subjective treatment in a film can be achieved through a POV shot.

Whether you are a complete game geek or a novice, you know what I am trying to imply here. There are video games where the main character is seen through the perspective of another character, and there are video games where the player is the hero. In the first type of video games, the player is still in full control of the main character, able to move the main character, but all the action is seen through the "boss's" perspective. But in the second type of video games, the person playing the game is the hero, and action is seen through the eyes of the player and not through a character within the game itself, such as is the case, typically, with first-person shooter games. The "first-person shooter" video games inspired live-action first-person-shooter feature films. The world's first POV action movie is *Hardcore Henry*, directed by Russian film director Ilya Naishuller, released in 2016. The feature film shot fully in first-person POV, is nothing new. *Lady in the Lake*, directed by American film and television actor, director, and producer Robert Montgomery in 1947, was the first feature film to show the scene exactly the way a character sees it.

The first-person concept may work in video games, but it does not work in a feature film since the film is not interactive. The audience does not feel like the protagonist in these films, only like someone tied to the protagonist's back. There is no way to feel like the protagonist because the passive screen experience of the protagonist's perspective does not replicate a personal POV. It does not make the audience feel what they want to feel or what they should feel, or, better said, how a director would like them to feel. These films look like watching someone else experiencing the events pictured in the film. Now I am nearing the biggest problems of these films. Since we are watching someone else experience, we need to see his/her reaction to what he/she is going through. We need to see the protagonist, or the "player," being involved in the action from a third-person perspective in order to understand how he/she feels about his/her experience. The POV shot has to be coupled with the reaction shot of the character who belongs to the POV shot. Deprived of seeing the character's reaction, we have no clue how the character feels about what he/she sees.

In his textbook *Making Movies Work,* author John Boorstin states:

> *The POV puts us in the scene, but it doesn't put us in the hero's head, it puts us in his shoes, and unless something pretty spectacular is going on that is not a very thrilling place to be.* (Boorstin, J. *Making Movies Work: Thinking Like a Filmmaker.* Los Angeles: Silman-James Press, 1995)

All scenes pictured below portray situations where subjective POV shots are interspersed with objective shots of characters who belongs the POV shots. In POV shots, we see what the character sees (**Scene 9.7.a.** and **Scene 9.7.b.**), explain why the character feels a certain way (**Scene 9.7.c.**), show important story element (**Scene 9.7.d.**), or picture impulses that cause the character to react a certain way (**Scene 9.7.e.**). To summarize, POV shots render either perceptual subjectivity (the audience sees what the character sees) or mental subjectivity (the audience sees what the character is dreaming, recalling, thinking, fantasizing). Whatever the case may be, in order to get the audience inside the head of the character and activate their emotional responses, it is not enough to show, what the character sees, you need to show how the character reacts on what he/she sees, real or imaginative.

Scene 9.7.a.

Scene 9.7.b.

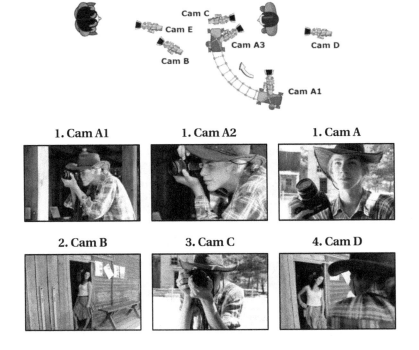

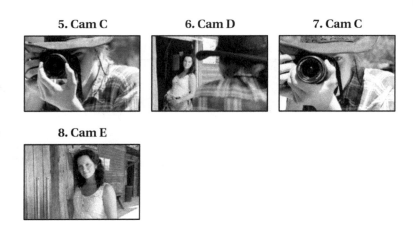

5. Cam C   6. Cam D   7. Cam C

8. Cam E

Scene 9.7.c.

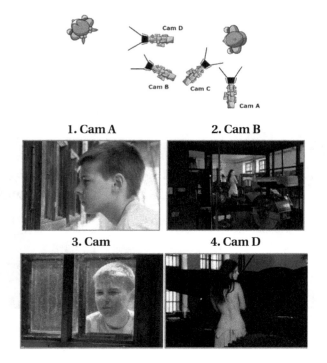

1. Cam A   2. Cam B

3. Cam   4. Cam D

Scene 9.7.d.

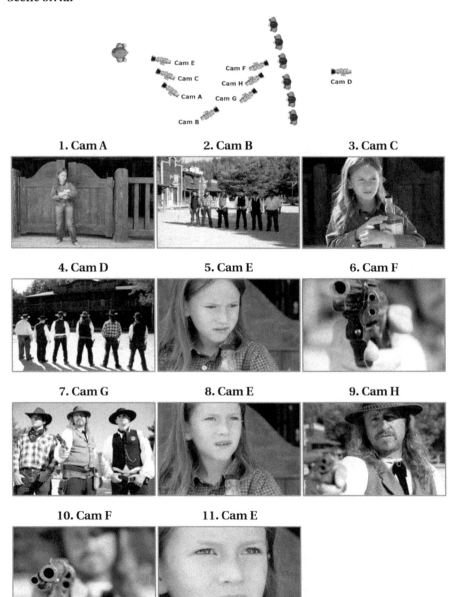

Scene 9.7.e.

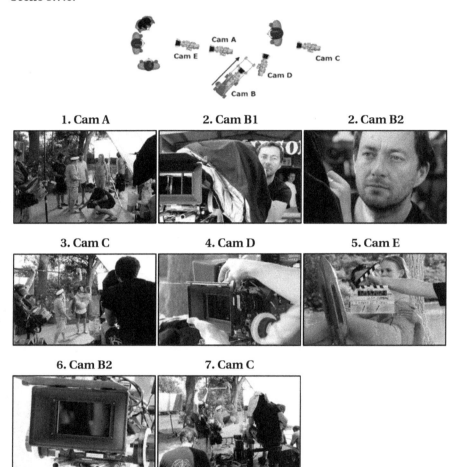

5.8. LIGHTING (accent lighting; silhouettes; low-key lighting; high-key lighting)

The lighting design influences how the story and characters are perceived by the audience. Lighting, in general, belongs to one of the critical directorial choices, which will affect the audience's perception of the whole story, and affect how the audience feels about the character.

Portrayal of a character through lighting:

- Controlling how the charter is depicted through lighting.
- Controlling how the charter is viewed by the audience.
- Controlling how the charter is perceived by the audience.

Besides these complexities, lighting design forms part of the overall visual look of the film, enhances the expressive potential of the film, and contributes to a unity of the film. In this subchapter three topics will be discussed: How to give principality to the main character by light, how to convey the emotional meaning of a scene, and how to convey character's interiority by lighting design.

"Accent lighting"

Lighting for emphasizing the character – point of interest is visually articulated by light: light = important, dark = unimportant.

Adding background accents to the shot can add extra depth and texture to each shot, which is the element indirectly linked to a character perspective because it contributes to the illusion of reality.

"High-key lighting" over lights the subject and reduces contrast. It can convey a happy mood, positive emotions of a character.

"Low-key lighting" intensifies the contrast in an image. The tone is darker, it can portray drama and tension.

"Brightness"

Even though the high-key and low-key lighting refer to a shot's overall brightness, a part of the shot can be illuminated differently to affect the audience's attention; and affect how they perceive a character. Minimal visual information can bring the mystery and suppress the character. On the other hand, human depth perception reflects forced perspective, when a "brighter is nearer." The light is a focal point. A boy in the shot below appears closer than he actually is. The use of lines and light give him prominence. The distinct separation of the two girls, in the scene below, is emphasized by a light separation. The light helps the audience subconsciously distinguish differences between the two girls, the forced perspective (light precedes position) articulates the point of interest for the audience - the red hair girl.

"Silhouettes"

Silhouettes add mystery to characters since the details of characters are partly or completely obscured.

"Rim light" (backlight, hair light) lights the subject from the back and produces a rim on the edges of the subject. This lighting pulls the character off the background, it separates the character from the background and makes her dominant within a shot.

9.9. CAMERA MOVEMENT (dolly in; tracking shot; rotation; handheld camera; shaky shot; vertigo shot)

Another approach used widely by filmmakers all over the world to communicate the narrative, emotional, and psychological importance of a character to the audience is through *Camera Movement. Camera movement* suggests the subjective perspective of the character, reveals off-screen space related to the character, punctuates changes in the character's feeling, indicates the change in character perspective, it stimulates the audience's curiosity, and allows the viewer to witness something unknown to the character objectively.

A camera can move anywhere along the XYZ axis: *Dolly In, Dolly Back, Trucking, Panning, Tilting, Pedestal up, Pedestal down, Handheld Shooting, Crane/Jib Shooting, Floating Camera, Drone Shots, Steadicam Shooting, Zooming in, Zooming out.* Moving shots are very engaging, and they basically serve to further the effectiveness of visual storytelling. Here is what you can convey through a camera move in correlation to character perspective:

- Directing the audience's attention to the specific character.
- Increasing/decreasing the importance of the character.
- Revealing what the character is looking at off-screen.
- Revealing something unknown to the character, real or imaginary.
- Shifting the character's perspective.
- Favoring one character over another character – crossing the line, introducing a new subject of interest, or revealing new information related to the character
- Expressing the character's excitement.
- Externalizing the character's interiority.
- Indicating that a character is about to make a critical discovery.
- Indicating that a character is about to realize something.
- Mapping a character's surprise.
- Visualizing character's dreams, fantasy, hallucination, on unconscious thoughts, urges, and memories.

Scene 9.9.a.

Dolly In – creating emotional intimacy with a character by approaching closer to the character. This technique brings the audience really close to the character, concentrating on her reactions, emotions, and feelings.

1. Cam A1   **1. Cam A2**

1. Cam A3   **1. Cam A4**

Scene 9.9.b.

Dolly In – This can be used for getting closer to the character's insight by implying how the character feels about another character; visualizing that the character is about to make a critical discovery; portraying a character's realization about another character; revealing secrets about the character; signaling an association launched by seeing another character; signaling transition to memories; or just increasing the audience's interest about the character.

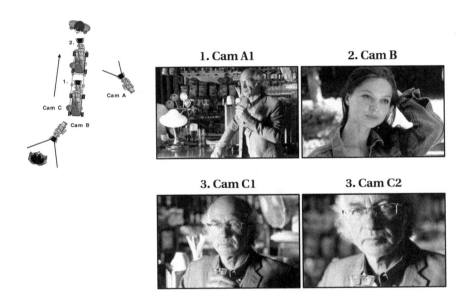

1. Cam A1 **2. Cam B**
3. Cam C1 **3. Cam C2**

Scene 9.9.c.

Rotation – An overhead 360-degree rotation, pointed straight down, connotes love or romance. Rotation around the character can be used to externalize a character's unbalanced state of mind.

Scene 9.9.e.

Dolly Counter Zoom (Vertigo Shot) – the camera lens zooms out while the camera dollies towards the characters, so the characters remain the same size relative to the rest of the shot. Or the camera dollies further away from the characters while the zoom is adjusted, so the characters' size remains the same. During the shot, there is a continuous perspective distortion, mostly noticeable in the background. The foreground remains stable, while the background expands backwards. This effect creates a visual equivalent of the disorientation congruent with the character's disorientation. If it is used as a POV shot, it can indicate that a character is intoxicated, strung out, or just about to lose consciousness.

1. Cam A1

1. Cam A2

9.10. COLOR

In this subchapter, I address the organic function of colors by investigating their role in engaging the audience with characters.

Colors provide information that helps the audience to understand the physical world of the characters and also influence how viewers feel about characters.

The role of colors:

- Colors convey information. The information the color provides can be literal or symbolic.
- Colors evoke emotional responses in viewers. The emotional effect of color is used to make viewers feel a specific way.
- Colors symbolize meanings.
- Colors create composition. Arranging colors in harmonious or contrasting ways is part of the shot design and part of a story structure. A shift of color from one scene to another can convey a change in time, establish a new time period, map a complicated story structure (flashbacks, flash-forwards, memories, reminiscences, retrograde time), convey a change in mood, or indicate a shift in a character's state of mind.

Choosing the right color requires understanding the psychology of colors, how the hue, tint, tone and shade influences the feelings that color conveys. You have to familiarize yourself with the basics of color theory and how to choose the most effective color schemes. Even though there is no universal validity for the role of colors for a general audience, or socio-demographic groups, or ethnic groups, or cultural groups (since colors are associated with the various cultures, religions, and traditions around the world), you use the colors to captivate the audience's attention, to evoke different feelings, and to communicate your ideas and thoughts.

Normal Colors

Emphasizing certain colors for an emotional and psychological effect.

Black – unhappiness, sadness, remorse, mourning, death, mystery, anonymity, elegance, style, sexuality and seduction. White – purity, innocence, simplicity, cleanliness, peace, youth. Red – passion, desire, love, speed, strength.

Omitting some colors

Removal of color from a scene or from the whole film will enhance or intensify emotional reactions. It can also emphasize that particular color later on in the story by bringing it back to the story.

Color Distortion

Color distortion is used to manifest a character's feelings visually, emotions, thought processes, internal states of mind, or special/unique views of the world. *Color Distortion,* or *Coloring* a scene with a specific color, can indicate the madness in a character's mind or the ambiguity of demonic characters. Generally, color distortion is used to elicit stronger emotional reactions.

Color Meaning

Colors can provoke specific emotional and physiological reactions, and most of the audience will react predictably to certain colors. Even though colors have specific symbolic meaning, often these associations are cultural or traditional, only sometimes universal. It is highly typical, for example, for white to be associated with innocence, purity, life, afterlife, and happiness in Western cultures, but mourning or death and loss in Eastern cultures.

5.11. COSTUME

The costume is one of the director's expressive tools for telling a story. Costume denotes status of the character or geographical location; costume can indicate where a character originates from; costume gives information about the period or specific season; it provides information about ethical profile, marriage, or family, or the function of a character with regards to the protagonist; costume reflects a character's personality; it shows how the character wishes to be perceived, as opposed to how the character really is; it stipulates visual interest; and it can be used for many other things. Besides these complexities, costume forms part of the overall visual look of the film and contributes to a unity of the film. A costume's, color, shape, silhouette, and texture can put an emphasis on the audience's emphatic views of a character and can help the audience to be aligned with a character a director wants them to be aligned with.

Coding Characters

Style, shape of the costume, decoration, cut of the fabric, the layers of clothing, and color in costume can identify characters and/or give them prominence. *Color Coding* establishes a character and makes her memorable for the audience. By giving a character a specific color motif, the audience can associate that specific color with that specific character and tell the characters apart. Predominant colors of the costume can help the character to stand apart.

Character development

Changes in the costume color of a character over time can externalize a character's state or map the change a character undergoes during the course of a story – character development. A gradual progression of colors in the costume of the brunette girl (from warm colors to cool colors), maps her shift from happiness to sadness. Costume conveys any shifting emotions of the character.

Mood

Warm colors convey happiness and safety.

Warm saturated colors can be used to create intimacy and excitement.

Cool colors suggest sadness and danger.

Forced Perspective

Warm colors appear closer, because they have a tendency to advance. Red emits the longest visual wavelength of all. When one character has precedence of place and another of color, the color gives the background girl prominence.

Cool colors appear farther because they have a tendency to feel like they are receding, backing away.

Forced perspective can be made in bright colors as well. *Bright* colors appear closer.

Texture

Giving principality to the main character can be attained by the attraction of texture. A character in a costume with lots of texture looks closer.

A character with a little texture looks farther away, even though she is blocked closer to a camera.

9.12. VISUAL WEIGHT (throwing off the balance – positioning characters)

The dramatic and emotional content of a shot affects how the audience perceives the character. Learning to manipulate and control the content of the shot will enhance your storytelling skills. Among other things, you have to control the balance of a shot. Balance is determined by the *Visual Weight*, which is conditioned by a position of visual elements in the frame. Since, in a shot design, visual elements have different weights, they can help to create visual hierarchy, symmetry/asymmetry, harmony/discord, and balance/unbalance. Giving principality to the main character can be attained by balancing and unbalancing masses.

Factors that affect the visual weight are:

>   Color, Contrast, Lightness/Darkness, Size, Mass, Texture, Density, Complexity, Direction, Symmetry/Asymmetry

Visual weight is heavily linked to symmetry. To accomplish symmetry and balance in a shot design, objects must appear equal in visual weight. But using a more dynamic composition can help you with a character's perspective in a scene. We are conditioned to notice what is different. Giving principality to the main character can be attained by the attraction of "abnormality." Any object set off the balance will grab attention. To draw attention to one character and suppress the other one, you need to purposely throw off balance and create a visual hierarchy so that the focus will shift or attention will be maintained on the character you want. That being said, a character in the center (**9.12.a. – Cam B** and **9.12.b. – Cam B**) has less weight than one at the edge of the composition, (**9.12.a. – Cam A** and **9.12.b. – Cam A**) and does not dominate in attraction; a character that is bigger than another or occupies a bigger portion of the shot is naturally heavier (**9.12.c**) and dominates in attraction; a character higher in the frame is heavier than a character framed in the lower part of the frame (**9.12.d**) and dominates in attraction; a character in a costume with saturated and brighter colors will draw more attention than a character in a costume with darker and low-saturated colors. Brighter colors generally call attention to the subject. (**9.12.e**).

9.12.a.

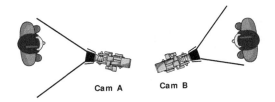

Cam A   Cam B

1. Cam A   **2. Cam B**

9.12.b.

1. Cam A   **2. Cam B**

9.12.c.

9.12.d.

9.12.e.

9.13. DISTORTED IMAGE

Another effective way of communicating the narrative, emotional, and psychological importance of a character, and his/her interiority to the audience, can be accomplished through a *Distorted Image*.

In *Natural Distortion*, visual features of the image are distorted through the organic element of the scene. You can use natural distortion for the purposes of externalizing the inner thoughts and emotions of a character, for externalizing an inner world of the character, to show the character's world becoming unstable, and to put emphasis on character perspective and how that character views the world, either clearly or distorted. It can also be used to alter the audience's perception of the character.

Shooting through objects like glass windows is perhaps the most effective way to manipulate perspective within a scene – either manipulating or confusing the audience's perception of a character; or externalizing the character's perspective on what he sees or how he sees it. Shooting through objects such as glass, water, or plastic to put the audience in the character's mind, or to foreshadow events, is a commonly used approach. Glass, eyeglasses, bottles, door glass panes, and stained-glass windows are the most up front.

The rain on the window can be reflected on a character's face (shadows cast by the raindrops), or you can shoot through the raindrops on the window, so it looks like a character is shedding tears. Similar effect can be achieved in a shower.

Either you are prudish or sort of a boundary-less person or you don't want to challenge some of the community's standards of modesty; or you obey the film rating regimes; or you want to protect vulnerable members of the community such as children, from the harm which would otherwise flow from film scenes that deal with nudity and sex; or you just want to follow the standards of shooting formulaic sex scenes in the most generic way; there are situations when you don't want to show a naked body in a lovemaking scene, or a naked body of the person in a shower, so you decide to shoot it either through misted glass, or sheer curtains, or windows, or doorways. It can add tantalizing carnality, and voyeurism. You don't have to be sexually explicit, and still, you can create feverish chemistry of a steamy encounter, with an erotic charge. A scene will have a sex appeal, without outright graphic sexiness, and they will induce the audience's erotic imagination. But remember, no nudity in a film scene, but the possibility of sex can be sexier than the sexual act itself.

Fabric Curtain, Air Curtain, and Prop Lenses within a scene distort objects and images. Shooting through these can be used for illustrating a character's state of mind.

Fog (smoke and other particles) can give off different atmospheres within a scene that can put an emphasis on the audience's emphatic views of a character in their surroundings, i.e., a child walking through a foggy forest that is hard to see in will invoke a much stronger response in an audience than seeing a child walking through a clear forest.

Duplicated Images of a character in a mirror can be used to emphasize the duality of a character as well as the inner-turmoil, or it might indicate schizophrenia.

Time-lapse Photography is utilized to show or to suggest the passage of time in a character's development, or to emphasize the drug-induced perception of reality by the character.

Artificial Distortion

Direct appeals to the viewer to feel emotion can be archived by shooting through Plexiglas, prisms, and crystals. Lenses choices affect the audience's emotional response. Lens distortion (during shooting): ultra-wide angle lens distortion/fish-eye lens distortion (significant amount of barrel distortion), barrel distortion (straight lines bend outward from the center of the image), pincushion distortion (straight lines bend/"pinch" inward from the center of the image), mustache distortion (mixture of barrel and pincushion distortion), tailored lens distortion (traditional fish-eye distortion with a high resolution throughout the image), night vision Astroscope lenses adapted to a full frame camera (unique swirly bokeh), split diopter lenses/split focus diopters (puts objects near and far into focus). Lens distortion (during postproduction): adding lens flares, light hits, fog, and shimmer.

Visual features of the image can be distorted artificially during shooting using painted mirrors, paintbrushes, and large panes of glass. Visual features of the image can be distorted artificially during postproduction through the developing process, push-developing (over-processing), transferring footage over different media, the bleach bypass – desaturation, increasing contrast – for intensifying the drama and characters' emotions, or to engender specific feelings. There's a real renaissance in using celluloid for filming. The properties of celluloid (the grain structure, exposure latitude of the film, shallower depth of filed, unlimited colors, to name a few) help directors to realize their creative intent. The decision to shoot on celluloid is mostly justified by aesthetics: a look and texture of film; a desire to remain true to the look and feel of the period setting; the decision to simulate the look of a specific period or era. The critically acclaimed film releases in 2016/2017 being shot on celluloid: *La La Land* (Dir. Damien Chazelle), *Dunkirk* (Dir. Christopher Nolan), *The Post* (Dir. Steven Spielberg), *Call Me by Your Name* (Dir. Luca Guadagnino), *The Florida Project* (Dir. Sean Baker), *Battle of the Sexes* (Dir. Jonathan Dayton and Valerie Faris), *Phantom Thread* (Dir: Paul Thomas Anderson).

> *"The properties of celluloid and a traditional film education continue to build an acute awareness of the potential of the medium of film as a creative tool. Many know of the values of film acquisition – crew discipline, unlimited color, large exposure latitude, and proven archival properties."*
> Jacob Dodd. "Joining Celluloid: The Art of Film Editing" *https://james riverfilm.wordpress.com/2017/01/30/joining-celluloid-the-art-of-film-editing/. Accessed January 15, 2018.*

Color Distortion

There are so many different techniques and tricks that you can use to create unique effects for effecting the audience's emotional response. You use specific colors to captivate the audience's attention or evoke different feelings in the viewer. Commonly used techniques in visual storytelling is a color distortion during shooting or color grading during postproduction to visually manifest a character's feelings, emotions, thought processes, the internal state of mind, or special/unique view of the world. It can also indicate that a character is intoxicated. I have already mentioned in the subchapter 9.10. COLOR that *"Color Distortion or Coloring a scene with a specific color can indicate the madness in a character's mind, or the ambiguity of demonic characters. Generally, a Color Distortion is used to elicit stronger emotional reactions."*

Conclusion:

As a director, you have to specify all visual factors clearly you will use for emphasizing a character's narrative dominance, or externalizing a character's emotional state, or manifesting a character's thought process, or drawing attention to a character's unique view of the world, or simply showing how a character views the situation around him/her. There are some factors and some visual elements that you must consider in designing your scene, depending on the look and feel you are trying to achieve. A visual weight, depth of field, lines, frame within the frame, colour-coding, and distorted image, can be used, when you want to give prominence to the character in visual representation, or when you want to appeal to the viewers' emotions. Try to employ as many factors and visual elements as you can. Which method you employ depends upon what you will try to accomplish with your scene in terms of character perspective, as well as how you want the audience to feel about the character. The perception of a character influences the audience's cinematic experience.

The concept of character perspective is one of the most important directorial concept, which is surprisingly easy to learn, and easy to tackle. The translation of new knowledge into improved directing skills will be seen in your work immediately. It still surprises me that this concept is dismissed by film scholars. Even film veterans devote to this concept very little time in film classes. Already Francois Truffaut *(The 400 Blows)*, French film director, pointed out, that *"this technique of telling a story according to a "point of view" has been familiar to novelists since Henry James and Marcel Proust, but has been remarkably neglected by filmmakers, even those who collected Academy Awards while "Notorious," "Rear Window" and "Psycho" were gripping audiences around the world, but never receiving the slightest consideration from critics or Festival juries.* I am offering this chapter for bridging the gap between studying this particular concept and practice.

When you have finished surveying this chapter, return to the beginning and read it again in more detail. Then you can proceed to the next step – practicing this directorial concept in IV. STUDIO – MODELING CHARACTER PERSPECTIVE. Information related to this studio can be found in PART II: STUDIOS – DIRECTING EXERCISES.

CHAPTER 10:
CONCEPT OF STORYTELLER'S PERSPECTIVE

Intro

This chapter does not strive to make you theoretically efficient in narrative theory or film theory studies, and this chapter does not require extensive theoretical knowledge about the fundamentals of film analysis in order to comprehend the topic. This chapter just points out the importance of *Storyteller's Perspective* for overall narrative purposes and visual-storytelling purposes. This chapter strives to provide the most effective, efficient, state-of-the-art training to help student-directors make their films consistent, unified, more efficient, and more effective. It is imperative that directors master this concept because it will provide them with total creative control over the narrative. Awareness about the storyteller's perspective helps the director to translate that perspective from screenplay to screen, and also helps to articulate the manner of narrative treatment. Needless to say, the more you know about this concept, the more efficient your work will be. A lack of proper knowledge and lack of efficient training is one of the first things noticed in narrative – broken narrative.

I have already pointed out in this book the importance of the storyteller's perspective for film narrative when I introduced you to the concept of character perspective in CHAPTER 9: CONCEPT OF CHARACTER PERSPECTIVE, where I said: *"Storyteller's perspective for visual-storytelling purposes is as equally important as the character's perspective, because there is a direct connection between the way a storyteller sees events and the way the story is presented."*

First and foremost, it should be said that the storyteller's perspective is imprinted in the script, and it is not something you should "artificially" bring into the script when you conceptualize a film. Of course, there will be instances when you want to change a narrator because you think that the subjective treatment would suit the story better than the objective treatment, you think that a more highly involved narrator would shed a more interesting light on the theme, or you think that a more highly involved narrator would be able to engage the audience into the story more actively. When the film turns out to be broken all the way through, you will tend to add the voiceover narration, later on, believing that by doing this, you will add consistency and continuity to the narration and save the film. That being said, there will be situations when you will be challenging scripted story-teller's perspective.

So, why should you care about storyteller's perspective, when it is already "imprinted" in the script? In essence, you, as a director, have to care about it because you have to transform the storyteller's perspective from the screenplay to the screen and you have to also decide on a narrative treatment.

Director's Job

A director's job is to interpret a written storyteller's perspective to the screen, remaining faithful to the style and form of the original perspective. It is an active job to ensure nothing is "lost in translation." A director, however, is permitted an artistic license in order to overcome the limitations of a written perspective or heighten the impact of the story by modifying the original perspective. The freedom to create artwork entitles him/her to make adjustments.

Interpretation of written storyteller's perspective involves:

1. Transforming scripted storyteller's perspective to the screen:
   You have to transform (translate) the storyteller's perspective to the screen. The story events and characters in a screenplay are presented the way a storyteller sees them and judges them.

2. Formulating narrative treatment:
   You have to decide on a narrative treatment. Storyteller's perspective implies a narrative treatment (subjective or objective), and narrative treatment indicates a visual treatment. Storyteller's perspective also implies a character perspective (consistent, fluid, or neutral stance).

Storyteller's perspective affects the audience's responses to the story events and characters. The audience's responses are influenced by how much the narrator knows, and how objective or subjective he/she is (the storytellers' gender tend to be somewhat problematic in the anonymous narrative), that being said, overall by narrator's attitudes. You are a director, and it is up to you to determine what kind of storyteller's perspective will be employed and which point of view will be employed to help the audience better understand the story, purposely mislead the audience, or withhold or reveal something about characters and story events. Think how a chosen storyteller's perspective affects an overall film in terms of the genre's narrative conventions, subjectivity, reliability, and the audience's expectations. You won't know what's best for you until you've tried it, so start practicing! Exercise your creative control over the storyteller's perspective!

The best place to start practicing this directorial concept is the directing exercise: V. STUDIO – ALTERNATION IN STORYTELLER'S PERSPECTIVE. Before proceeding further and starting working on the V. STUDIO, please read up through this chapter. To retain and apply the knowledge described in this chapter will help you with this hands-on directing exercise and with all films you will be directing in the future.

Even though the film narrator is different than the literary narrator, since the *Film Language* is not a linguistic semiotic system, but different semiotic systems combining verbal and nonverbal communication, we can still recognize in film narration different viewpoints/perspectives like in literature: first-person perspective, second-person perspective, and third-person perspective.

Concept of Storyteller's Perspective

First-person Perspective

A. **Limited**

The story is told as if the character is telling it directly. The major pronoun here is "I." Film reproduces the first-person vision of the world as seen through the eyes of the character of the story, who is at the same time a narrator of the story. (Dir. Robert Montgomery: *The Lady in the Lake*; Dir. Andrej Sokurov: *Russian Ark*; Dir: Julian Schnabel: *The Diving Bell and the Butterfly*; Dir. Ilya Naishuller: *Hardcore Henry.*)

B. **Extended**

The camera shows the character involved in the action from a third-person perspective. The *character is* reflecting on his/her past, and the character's voiceover provides the audience with a first-person commentary. The protagonist, a character within the story, is a narrator – the first-person narrator, the autobiographical narrator, who reports things from the perceptual point of view of his/her younger self. The narrator is older and wiser for his/her experiences. (Dir. Milos Forman: *Amadeus*; Dir. Martha Coolidge: *Rambling Rose*; Dir. Clint Eastwood: *Million Dollar Baby*; Dir. Adrian Lyne: *Lolita*; Dir. Sam Mendes: *Jarhead*)

Second-person Perspective

A. **Voice Narrator**

The voice of the narrator is directly addressing the viewers. The story is told as if it is happening to the viewer. The major pronoun here is "you." (commercials, instructional films, interactive media, public service announcements...)

B. **Camera Narrator**

a.   The character directly addresses the viewers through the camera. (Dir. Jean-Luc Godard: *Breathless*)

b. When the camera is established as a character in the scene, the audience feels (or should feel) that the camera is speaking directly to them from a second-person perspective. (The camera creates a point of view for the audience that is somewhere between first and second person.)

Third-person Perspective

The story is told through an all-knowing narrator (omniscient), or a narrator whose knowledge is limited to one character, either major or minor (limited omniscient). The major pronoun here is "he/she." The actions of characters are rendered from the observer's point of view. The narrator can disclose everything that the character thinks or feels, he/she can describe thoughts and actions of all characters, and he/she can use any narrative device. The omniscient point of view allows the audience to enter the mind of all the characters.

A. Covert Narrator

A covert narrator presents events without being part of the story; it is a virtually hidden narrator – anonymous narrator. It looks like the story is told by nobody. It is the most-used point of view in narrative films.

B. Overt Narrator

An overt narrator presents events with or without being part of the story.

a. Off-screen Narrator (Invisible)

The narrator, usually a commentator, is without personality, even without presence. He/she may comment on a situation, report on events, and express a character's feelings. He/she can be explicit and tawdry, he/she can give summaries, he/she can make fun of characters, and he/she can verbalize what characters cannot articulate for some reason, for instance, because of lack of intelligence. (Dir. Todd Field: *Little Children*; Dir. Fred Zinnemann: *The Day of the Jackal*)

b. On-screen Narrator (Visible)

Almost always a filmmaker.

- Presented visually (Dir. Woody Allen: *Sweet and Lowdown*)

- Presented visually as a character of a story while simultaneously addressing the audience (Dir. Woody Allen: *Annie Hall*; Dir. Federico Fellini: *8½*; Dir. Jane Anderson: *The Prize Winner of Defiance, Ohio*; Dir. Christoffer Boe: *Reconstruction*)

The narrative does not have to be confined to a single fixed storyteller's perspective. The narrative can be far more flexible and diverse in film than in literature. The narrative can be told with many variations in perspective, but at any given moment, you, as director, have to be clear who is telling the story. This knowledge can liberate you artistically. Be very careful of when and how you switch perspective; otherwise, you might confuse viewers. Always justify the switch. (Dir. Claude Lelouch: *A Man and a Woman*; Dir. Francois Truffaut: *The Day for Night*)

You are a storyteller. *First*, you have to learn how to tell a story, how to "speak fluently" to the audience. Of course, that first you got something to say. Only when you have something to say do people bother to watch. Now, more than ever, if you can't tell a story in a way that grabs the audience's attention, and make them emotionally invested, you may fail. Learn how to do it, and try to do it masterfully. "*You have to learn the rules of the game. And then you have to play better than anyone else.*" (Attributed to Albert Einstein, *The Theory of Relativity.*)

A good director takes his/her viewers on a journey, leaving them emotionally moved, inspired, pondered, energized, encouraged, elated, enriched, motivated, powerful, happy, relaxed. But telling your story to get your audience engaged all the way through takes practice and experience. It may take a lot of practice. Make sure you give yourself adequate time.

When you have finished surveying this chapter, return to the beginning and read in more detail. Then you can proceed to the next step – practicing this directorial concept in the V. STUDIO – ALTERNATION IN STORYTELLER'S PERSPECTIVE. Information related to this studio can be found in PART II: STUDIOS – DIRECTING EXERCISES.

CHAPTER 11:
EMOTIONAL MANIPULATION/EMOTIONAL DESIGN

Controlling viewers' feelings – how to engage viewers emotionally with characters and story events

Intro

Directors have to develop an in-depth understanding of the emotions and psychology of characters and their application in designing a film. A director has to control the design of the shot and fashion each visual element to create a strong emotional and psychological connection with the viewer.

In real life, you can find yourself in situations that elicit an overly emotional reaction you're not prepared to deal with, leaving you feeling out of control. In order to overcome this reaction in the future or even avoid it without exposing yourself to emotional stress, you might want to use some activities and relaxation techniques for stress reduction. Since you, as a director, are also exploring material for your own projects, do not throw out your emotional experience and do not even think about undertaking anger management. Try to figure out what triggers your feelings. Psychologists suggest we might be able to use behavioral and cognitive strategies to steer our emotions.

What is it about a situation that makes you feel a certain way? How do you react to certain stimuli? What does the situation mean to you in terms of emotions? How does your body react to real joy, anger, excitement, sadness, or fear? Listen to your body and communicate with your body. Learn what natural feelings and intuitions are trying to say to you. Be a guinea pig for your films. You can extremely benefit from it since you need to trigger the audience's emotions and manipulate and control them. Suffer and enjoy.

Emotional Stimuli (Triggers of Emotions) and Film

Emotions are triggered by stimuli, which start in our senses or in our minds. Emotions that start in our senses are natural responses to the world around us, and emotions that start in our minds are created consciously or unconsciously. The stimuli that come to us through our senses – sight, hearing, touch, smell, taste – are real. Since you can only see and hear the film and you can't touch, smell, and taste the film, you can employ only two out of five human senses. Limited "sensual" perception of film limits your "manipulation tools" as a director, but do not forget the viewer's mind. Emotions can also be created in mind without any real impulses. Actually, you have three pathways for how to get under the skin of your viewer – sight, hearing, and mind – and trigger their emotional responses. That means you can attack their sense of sight, their sense of hearing, and their imagination in order to trigger their emotions. You could argue that "mind's emotions" in the film are in fact triggered through sight and hearing. You are right, but thinking that you have not just two doors but three to your viewer's body might help you to understand better that you can launch a viewer's imagination and fantasy by not showing and telling them everything.

In CHAPTER 9: CONCEPT OF CHARACTER PERSPECTIVE, I said that even though the issue of identifying with a character is questionable (film is not a reality but a substitute reality), try to manipulate viewers to identify with a character and try to suppress their critical ability. Of course, not each film inclines to accept the principle of "audience identification." Some films deliberately utilize an "alienation effect" by keeping the audience aware that they are watching a substitute or even an illusion of reality, but not reality. These films constantly disrupt viewers' identification with characters for the sake of activating viewers' rational participation of events presented in the film. Viewers are bending to immerse themselves in the story emotionally and are forced to think while they are watching. After all, the rational participation creates feelings anyway. Since these films do not exclude emotions, we can also include them in our consideration of emotional manipulation.

Strategies of Emotion Regulation – Emotional Engagement

You can modify, control, and regulate the audience's emotions. Stimulus can diminish or enhance the emotional reaction. You can dramatically change how the audience sees a situation or a character based on how you manipulate their perception. Of course, that people differ in emotional intensity. Research shows that *"some people find themselves in emotional tumult even in reaction to mundane events, while others remain unperturbed under the most trying of circumstances."* Your audience consists of viewers, whose tastes in film varies, whose preferences varies, who are highly emotional people, and also unemotional people. Among your viewers will be those, who are emotionally intense, and can get excessively absorbed in the story events, but there will be viewers, who won't be influenced and emotionally moved by same story events. Who is your target audience? *Those whose feelings burn with intensity or those who are utterly cool?* Clearly defining your target audience can make all the difference when you are creating content. Having understood that viewers are driven by emotions, you have to master certain techniques to affect their perception. I am getting increasingly philosophical here, but still, be prepared that viewers that comprise your audience will emotionally differ.

The film is regarded as a highly arousing/stimulating medium. As a director, it is your responsibility to determine how to approach the situation in order to forward the story towards its completion and narrate the story in a way that the audience will be able to comprehend, thus making it possible for them to experience the film emotionally. Try to fashion each element in advance in order to create a strong emotional and psychological connection with the viewer. To accomplish this goal, you, as director, have to control the viewer's perception of fictional reality. To reach your goal, you need to manipulate the audience's emotions. You can manipulate the audience's emotions and perceptions in two different ways:

1. Passive engagement:
    The audience can simultaneously live through the character's emotions.

2. Active engagement:
    Since viewers believe that characters are in control of their actions (of course they are not), they (viewers) want to make the characters: take out their anger and their frustrations, get out from a scary or dangerous situation, realize the human quality of others they interact with, respect unconscious warnings, learn from their mistakes, enjoy happy moments in their lives, and cry and laugh.

In the meantime, I can conclude that a director has to control the audience's perception of events and emotions in the scene for the sake of engaging the audience emotionally with characters and story events. The way to engage the audience with the events and emotions of a scene is a director's first and most important critical decision in designing that scene.

Emotional Response

The immediate emotional response can be achieved in a couple of different ways. You must understand that you do not have other options; a director must use emotional triggers to elicit an emotional response.

a) By engaging viewers emotionally:
    -   Passive engagement
    -   Active engagement

b) By forcing viewers to think about what the character is feeling.

Director's Job

Film's potential to manipulate the audience to experience certain emotional responses, is an undeniable fact. The first consideration about what is shown in a film that controls how the audience will perceive the narrative should involve knowing what emotions a director wants the audience to experience at any particular time. *"The first part of the director's job is knowing what the audience should be feeling, and when. The second part is harnessing the tools to get them there"* (Sijll, J. *Cinematic Storytelling: The 100 Most Powerful Film Conventions Every Filmmaker Must Know*, 2nd edition. Michael Wiese Productions, 2005, ISBN-10: 193290705X).

Decide:

- How do you want the audience to feel?
- How can you create the feelings you want the audience to have?
- What emotion is the scene eliciting, and ultimately, what do you want to communicate to the audience?
- What elements within the scene are contributing to the particular emotional sensation you want them to feel, and how can you heighten the sensation by filmmaking means?
- What tools can you use for emphasizing and accentuating emotions?
- What tools can you use to invoke a particular emotional response?

Guidelines for Controlling Viewers' Emotions/Feelings in the Scene:

You have to decide exactly what you want the audience to feel and then fashion everything in the scene that will guide them in that direction.

1. Identify the feeling of the scene.
   First, you must know the emotional meaning of the scene, what it is that your audience should feel (happiness, sadness, fear, anger, love, jealousy, contempt, hatred). How do you want the audience to feel? What feeling do you want to engender and/or grow in the audience? (Go forward and briefly review CHAPTER 13: DIRECTORIAL-DRAMATURGICAL ANALYSIS, specifically the part where I am talking about the mood and tone of the scene. When you determine the mood and the tone, it will help you to identify the feeling of the scene.)

2. Analyze the emotional triggers.
   a) Figure out what can trigger the feeling(s) you want your audience to have (intensity of stimuli).

b) Figure out how you can accentuate triggers that will make your audience feel a certain way (intensifying the stimuli).

3. Name the emotional weight of the scene within the film. (emotional dynamic of the scene; how does the scene fit into the emotional structure of the film; when the story gains intensity, the emotional structure must do same).

4. Make a concept of how to create the feel you want the audience to have. The ways you can trigger viewer's emotional response:
   a) By portraying the source that triggers the emotional reaction.
   b) By portraying the emotional reaction of the character to the source – to the impulse.
   c) By portraying emotions. (When you see somebody crying, most likely, you will cry also.)
   d) By identifying with the character. (When you make the audience identify with a character's psychological makeup, most likely the audience also emotionally identifies with the character.)
   e) By sympathizing with the character. (When the audience is experiencing a similar feeling that the character is experiencing, the audience will respond similarly to the impulses.)
   f) By empathizing with the character. (When the audience understands a character's feelings and possess a natural ability to empathize with others, the audience will respond similarly to the impulses.)
   g) By attacking natural human emotional senses, which automatically trigger emotions – spontaneous emotional reaction. (A sudden invasion to the field of vision triggers fear; unexpected events cause spontaneous surprise; the viewer naturally reacts to disgusting things by disgust; death causes sadness; physical harm directly attacks the viewer's feelings.)
   h) By relying on emotional associations – emotional memory. (The audience might respond likewise if a character is responding to some emotional impulses. But be careful, because, for instance, the picture of a flourishing meadow evokes positive emotions only to those who do not suffer from hay fever.)
   i) By exposing the character to "negative" forces. (Film situations push the audience's buttons.)

j)   By creating dangerous or unwanted situations, the character is not aware of.

k)   By externalizing feelings through the action, dialog, voiceover narration, interior monologue, or illustration of an emotional state.

We tend to assume that everyone experiences things with similar emotional urgency. But it is not the case. Not every scene you create will resonate the same way with every viewer, and not every viewer will respond to your (emotional) manipulation similarly. Some of them won't even be affected by your manipulation (emotions just pass right through), some of them will be unemotional, and some of them will be unresponsive to your triggers, but some of them can be totally emotionally destroyed. Realize that powerful tools are at your disposal and use them appropriately. You might activate triggers that can evoke negative emotions and cause emotional wounds, even affect emotional health or death. At the same time, it must be emphasized that any emotion (even negative) when aimed at serving the main goal of the art, which is to make people better, can be applied. Use them well.

Don't forget, emotions are something that will remain in the memories of viewers even longer than the story itself.

How to make the audience emotionally invested? Try to trigger their emotions.

When you have finished surveying this chapter, return to the beginning and read in more detail. Then you can proceed to the next step – practicing this directorial concept in VI. STUDIO – EXTERNALIZING/PHYSICALIZING INNER STATE OF MIND OF CHARACTER. Information related to this studio can be found in PART II: STUDIOS – DIRECTING EXERCISES.

CHAPTER 12:
PSYCHO-PHYSIOLOGICAL REGULARITIES IN LEFT-RIGHT/RIGHT-LEFT ORIENTATION

"When I studied under Professor Lubomir Kocka, I was already an established filmmaker. Having written, directed and shot 11 feature length films (most of which won prestigious awards around the world and found distribution through majors such as Sony, Warner, Paramount etc.) I was a little skeptical when it came to taking classes. Even with all the previous professional experience I had, Professor Lubo made me look at things through a new and unique perspective. His classes were dynamic and filled with knowledge. His insights on the Psycho-physiological Regularities in Left-right/Right-left Orientation were challenging and certainly changed the way I look at directing a movie now. I can only say thank you!!"
Tristan Aronovich, Brazilian Film Director

Intro

What will be discussed in this chapter is based on my personal opinion. As a director, I don't want to establish a method of scientific investigation in film, and I don't want to discover a universal law that works for all of the arts. I am even aware that director's ability to control and regulate a viewer's responses are limited, even though I don't like it.

In my childhood, I remember how I struggled reading comic strips. To whom should I pay attention first – to the figure drawn on the right side or left side of the panel. Which speech bubble is first – who is delivering the first line, and who the next one? All confusion disappeared when my father gave me this simple advice: *"Read everything from left to right. First, pay attention to the figure drawn on the left side. First, read the speech balloon on the left side or the one placed in the highest position in the frame."* Then came elementary school, with writing essays and analyzing the structure of sentences. *"Do not forget, the newest information or the most important information in the sentence should be placed on the right side of the sentence."*

"The story character's placement in the panel and speech balloon placement in comic books contributes to the legibility of the story by employing the pattern of reading, that means from left to right." Probably that was my first rational take on a need to apply composition, visual elements, and screen direction in order to make a story progress in a readable pattern. Still, it was a more intuitive process than a rational one. Years of studying in art school, painting, drawing, and photographing, brought something else to my unconscious awareness of the lateral

sides of a frame. Even in my early films, I arranged objects in the frame intuitively and instinctively rather than rationally. The feature film I directed in 1990, *From Morning till Dawn*, written by Zuzana Križková, changed everything. I don't know where it came from, but I knew that this was the film in which each shot had to be designed based on specific psycho-physiological rules related to the left and right side of the frame. The complicated story structure, the string of flashbacks, and the introspective nature of the story led me to apply some specific rules if I wanted to be clearly understood by the audience. After a car accident, a middle age woman, who is caught between life and death, brings together a music composer and a surgeon. The film in an unusual form raises artistic statement about human loneliness, but also about the need for mutual communication and understanding. Believe me, I wanted to communicate the meaning and subtext of the story clearly. So I postulated some rules to follow and stuck with them throughout the film. Regardless of the success or failure of this particular film, since then, each film I have directed has something to do with L-R/R-L orientation of characters and other cinematic elements designed within the shot.

Rules

One statement regarding filmmaking has been quoted so many times that I don't remember to whom it has been attributed: *"The only rule in filmmaking is that there are no rules."* Frank Capra, an Italian-American film director, producer, and writer paraphrased this statement: *"There are no rules in filmmaking, only sins. And the cardinal sin is dullness."* No doubt, he is right. But by making films, studying and teaching, teaching and studying, I eventually found out that for me, there are some rules.

Although everybody tells you that there are no rules and principles for filmmaking – or if there are, they can be broken in favor of a better idea – you should learn these rules. If you don't take advantage of the opportunity to learn these rules, you will not know how to break them. Remember that some of the most spectacular films are striking because they broke some of these rules. The driving force for studying these rules can be rebellion, but it can actually be whatever: your desire to learn the filmmaking process, a desire to evolve your directing skills, the game-changing aspiration - the aspiration of setting up some principles for film language. At the same time, you could be driven by a desire for money, power, and glory. Or it might be as simple as *"Just wait, I'll show you all!"* Whatever works for you.

From history, we know that in art, some rules were formulated and widely accepted by artists and the public: balance and unity; perspective; golden rules: rule of thirds, rule of odds; rules of proportions and narration; symmetry and patterns; viewpoint; Aristotelian unities, Aristotle's seven golden rules of storytelling; firmness, commodity and delight; unisons, octaves, fourths, and fifths. Even though they have only a temporary influence, you should learn them. Why? I was not completely correct when I said that you should learn rules for the purposes of breaking them. Actually, I shouldn't formulate it that way. Even the knowledge of rules doesn't replace an invention, and the knowledge of rules does not create a film. Nevertheless, this knowledge will help you to translate and communicate your vision and ideas. After all, having more knowledge will make you better equipped for directing.

A Director's Primary Goal

You have to facilitate the audience's ability to understand and interpret the images and sounds on the screen. The viewers respond to a film and understand it by applying significant aspects of their

- Own real-life three-dimensional perceptual (visual and oral) experience.
- Own real-life personal experience and vicarious experience.
- Social, cultural, historical, and educational experience.
- Cinematic experience.
- Knowledge of codes of visual and oral conventions and styles in film.
- Temperament, emotional sensibility, psyche, morality.
- Current mood.
- Personal memory.
- Experience of the psycho-physiological circumstances under which the film is viewed.

As a film director, I know that there is a plethora of ways I can manipulate the onscreen image to impact the viewing experience and interpretation of the audience further. One such area is the onscreen placement and blocking of characters. You direct the viewer's perception. In order to maximize visual communication, you have to utilize all tools that are at your disposal, and one of them is unquestionably controlling the composition and the lateral orientation of all subjects within the frame.

The goal of this book is to help you to develop and evolve the narrative filmmaking skills and visual storytelling abilities you need to accomplish your directorial goals, to educate and train you to make professional films of high artistic level and to develop your artistic and craft skills. The main focus is the conceptualization process and methodology of

- How to communicate the idea and meaning of the scene.
- How to communicate the essence of the scene.
- How to translate abstract ideas about story, place, and character into images.
- How to effectively visually narrate the story.
- How to articulate and communicate structural elements of the story and character through staging, blocking, and camera treatment.
- How to translate the director's intent.
- How to construct a scene.
- How to manipulate and control the audience's emotional responses.

Try to envision and figure out all elements in advance. Do not leave anything to chance and concentrate on each detail. Much of a film's success, and inevitably your success, will come from such attention to detail. You will see the great difference subtleties can make. I don't want to say that there are no another approaches to directing. Even methods that are the opposite of this one, like improvisation can bring enormous success. However, those methods you don't have to learn; just grab the camera or cameras and go and shoot the film.

Psycho-physiological Regularities in Left-right/Right-left Orientation

I have very carefully chosen the "technical term" *regularity* instead of the term *rules*. Before going further with discussion, it is first necessary to comment on the notion that the term *psycho-physiological regularity* carries with it a couple of assumptions: one, that a state of physicality of outside stimulus (in this case a composition within a lateral frame) affects a person mentally without his or her contemplation of it, unconsciously rather than through the subconscious or a process; and two, that while the term *regularity* does carry with it the connotation of something "methodical, proper, constant" it is applied here as something similar to the idea of a "custom," something that works but is not law. Distilled to its essence, this concept refers to the connotations attached to a specific side of the screen. When characters occupy one side of the screen or move from one side to another, whether the audience is aware of this phenomenon or not, they are receiving subconscious information concerning the character's perspective and state of mind. If properly utilized by a visionary filmmaker, orientation and screen direction can greatly impact a film.

Over my fifteen years at Savannah College of Art and Design (SCAD), all graduate students taking my class, Directing for Film and Television, have worked on the research project: Psycho-physiological Regularities in Left-right/Right-left Orientation. The purpose of this project is to increase theoretical and practical knowledge about issues related to screen direction in the form of research and survey. Student-directors are supposed to address issues of the theoretical and practical significance of left-right/right-left orientation. Here, I am crediting all my students, named and unnamed, whose work I am using in this chapter, who took this class in the period between the fall quarter of 2002 and the spring quarter of 2017.

I read all research reports, make the student presentations of each research paper more of a learning experience for their classmates, and get all students involved in the discussion. That way, I can tell how much time and energy they have invested into the project and discover how they feel about it. For some of them, this project is an eye-opening experience, but some of them reject it from the very beginning, claiming that art is an entirely intuitive process and cannot be mastered by rules of thumb or reduced to formulas. Anyway, I don't doubt for a second that it is worth the effort, and I do believe that all of them have benefited from it in their own careers, and you will benefit from their research as well.

An enormous amount of material I possess can easily swell into an entire book, which would be titled: *Psycho-physiological Regularities in Left-right/Right-left Orientation in Shot Design*. I plan on reusing assignments and workshop handouts I've written, research papers of my former students, and some of my older works to fill its pages. Currently, I'm reevaluating the feasibility of that book. With as much material as I possess, it would take a couple of months just to go through it. However, I am totally convinced that the result will be a collection of stunning information that could end up being the most directing-altering book you will ever read. It has so much good material to offer that it will take your game to a higher level.

In this book, I endeavor to show you the essence of this topic because I regard it as necessary for evolving your directing skills before I write a new book and you get the chance to read it. So, in the meantime, let's swim in uncharted waters. The waters are uncharted because this is really something unique, something that has not yet been covered in a single published book on directing in all its wide complexity.

There are a few articles here and there; a few studies have been conducted on this topic, but not a single book has been written on it. A study conducted in 2012, "Directionality of Film Character and Camera Movement and Subsequent Spectator Interpretation," sought to understand the significance of character placement and movement on the subsequent interpretation of the spectator (Egizii, M.L., Denny, J., Neuendorf, K.A., Skalski, P.D., & Campbell. http://academic.csuohio.edu/kneuendorf/SkalskiVitae/Egizii.etal.2012.pdf. Accessed November 27, 2016.) So, the focus of this study was how a film viewer interprets lateral motion from left to right and from right to left. The results of this investigation suggest that spectators have a more negative view towards characters who engage in right-to-left movement as opposed to those who utilize left-to-right movement. This study further concluded that possible causes for such interpretations, including religion, media use, recall, psychometrics, and handedness, are responsible factors in the occurrence of this phenomenon. The findings observed from this study are significant to the argument that a character placed on the left side of the screen is more likely to be viewed as dominant, as the character-in-question's movement begins from the right side of the screen and ends on the left.

While the aforementioned study was not able to definitively pinpoint the cause of this phenomenon, several professionals have linked it to the western tradition of reading language from left to right. Blain Brown, in his book *Cinematography: Theory and Practice: Image Making for Cinematographers and Directors*, for example, argues that *"lateral organization is largely the result of cultural conditioning, due to the eye scanning pages from left to right in the process of reading."* (Brown, B. *Cinematography: Theory and Practice: Image Making for Cinematographers and Directors*. New York and London: Focal Press, Taylor & Francis Group, 2012). Overall, research and theories both support the idea that left-to-right movement evokes comfort due to normality, whereas right-to-left movement does not.

Many of my students base their research on the fact that in our culture, our eyes tend to move from left to right, which is derived from the nature of reading from left to right. Thus, this way of scanning causes us to perceive forward progression in this order. Because of that, the vast majority of students come up with the conclusion that "the left" is more important or more interesting than "the right," but that is not universal. It is no wonder that my students draw many of the same conclusions that acclaimed professionals in the film theory field have:

> *The habit of reading left to right is culturally so strong that it is claimed Western readers use the same left-to-right scan when looking at paintings, cinema and theatre. This may be a consideration when staging positions in a set up.* (Ward, P. *Picture Composition for Film and Television*, 2nd edition. Focal Press, 2001, ISBN-10: 0240516818)

> *Psychologists have told us that those of us who grew up moving eyes from left to right when we read, find it is more "comfortable" for us when a character in a film moves from left to right. When they go from right to left, a tension is created.* (Proferes, N. *Film Directing Fundamentals: See Your Film Before Shooting*, 2nd edition. Focal Press, 2005, ISBN:0240805623)

> *The placing and the movement of the subjects within a frame is also based on convention. (…) As audiences have learned to 'read' these conventions, it is necessary to be aware of them and apply them if the audience is to understand the picture for the message or story intended.* (Bowen, C. and Thomp-

son, R. *Grammar of the Shot,* 3rd edition. Focal Press; 2012, ISBN-10: 0240526015)

These are only a couple of samples I utilized to illustrate the widespread opinion that lateral organization is derived from the nature of reading, which means from left to right. Are there elements that go beyond the boundaries of cultural background and that can support the left-right/right-left orientation regardless of how one scans and perceives an image? Four of my former graduate students, Tristan Aronovich, Rick Shepardson, X.A. Medina, and Venkat D. Chunduru claim that this is not just an applied pattern of how we read. They believe that there is most likely a universal law or a universal cognitive principle that rules lateral organization and drives us to scan from left to right.

Tristan Aronovich *(Alguém Qualquer),* film director, producer, and founder and director of the Latin American Film Institute, looked into two different arguments in order to present a universal coherence for reading and perceiving the left-right/right-left orientation: that of the Earth's movement and that of brain dominance.

The first argument, without any doubts, goes beyond cultural boundaries and can easily be interpreted as universal – meaning that all human beings that inhabit Planet Earth will most certainly be impacted by the nature of such movements and obviously by the orientation of such movements. That impact could have an important subconscious structural development in the way one perceives not only an image, but rather the world and the entirety of reality around him/her.

In order to clearly understand the second argument – brain dominance – Aronovich says that it is first paramount to acquire a basic understanding of what exactly the science of brain dominance proposes and examines, and he bases his argument on Ned Herrmann's brain dominance and lateralization theories. (William Edward "Ned" Herrmann, was an American creativity researcher and author, known for his research in creative thinking and whole-brain methods.) His conclusion:

After understanding the complexities presented and analyzed by the field of Brain Dominance, one can easily realize this is yet another strong argument that supports the Left-Right/Right-Left Orientation in a universal way, regardless of cultural background – since the way the human brain works and how the brain hemispheres behave are related to its physiological and biological structure, rather than related to cultural background.

Excerpt from the paper "Psycho-physiological Regularities in Left-right/ Right-left Orientation" by Rick Shepardson, where he is questioning the traditional alphabet argument:

This approach negates a very important part of the visual process. As a result, the importance of left-right orientation in the film goes unappreciated. Upon further study, we find evidence that contradicts cultural conditioning, lateral organization in art in general, and film in particular extends far beyond how one reads. It is not only derivative of our cultural background, but perhaps even part of our genetic makeup.

Excerpt from the paper "*A Project on Screen Grammar: The Mystery and Magic of Left/Right and Top/Bottom psycho-physiological Regularities in Visual Medium*" by Venkat D. Chunduru:

The earth rotates around the sun from Left to Right. Is this cosmic design making human beings perceive everything from Left to Right including the images that we perceive on screen and text from L-R? In order for the survival and existence of the galaxy, the earth rotates in its orbit from L-R, which also indicates that the progression of time happens from L-R. The rotation of the earth in its orbit from L-R causes the sun to rise in the east and set in the west. This led to the fact that we perceive time on clocks from Left to Right. Let us imagine the first evolution of some form of existence on earth. One fine day, in search of light, the primitive man must have run toward the direction of where the sun's rays are falling on earth. If we imagine the same thing graphically on the map, we perceive it as moving from Left to Right. He is looking for something from L-R. There is a progression from L-R in his search. Later on, in the evolutionary process, it must have had a genetic impact on the humans to perceive everything from Left to Right. Finally, this theory must have something to do with human anatomy. The placement of the heart on the left side of the human body is an inexplicable truth. Clearly, there is a more unified structure to favor everything for L-R from a universal force in relation to our human bodies.

The three samples above from the work of my students demonstrate that lateral organization is rooted deep in human nature, and it extends far beyond how we read. Here, I want to quote a bigger portion from the research paper of my former student Rick Shepardson:

In the article Left and Right in Science and Art, Charles G. Gross and Marc H. Bornstein theorize that our tendency to divide the world before us in terms of left and right is a byproduct of evolution (30). (...) Because the natural world is asymmetrical, we assign order and value to that which is on the left and that which is on the right (30). (...) Somewhere down the road, we have even developed certain affinities for the left and right. There are both cultural and universal similarities in how we relate to left and right. According to studies performed by the University of Melbourne Laterality Laboratory, a majority of physiologically normal individuals exhibit a leftward attention bias known as pseudoneglect. According to Geri Jewel of the National Library of Medicine, pseudo neglect causes most of us to bisect lines slightly to the left of their true center. (...) Scientific studies of eye movement have shown that when examining a picture, the eye does not necessarily move in any direction particular to alphabetic flow. In How People Look at Pictures: Before, During, and After Scene Capture, Jason S. Babcock relates Guy T. Busswell's findings in relation to the psychology of perception of art. (...) Busswell found that no two eye patterns were the same. (...) Thus, eye movement is limited to neither right nor left...it then seems that whether the viewer reads the image from left to right or right to left likely has more to do with composition...

So, we find that whether something should be placed on the left or whether it should move to the right is not an absolute dictated solely by our alphabet. Instead, there are many factors that play into asymmetrical compositions...thus, the organization of elements within the film frame is not simply a matter of East or West. Culture may play a part, but so does the biological forces that unify us all. It is a conundrum enhanced by the collision and unity of images. (...) Inattention to the left to right/right to left paradigm could explode in your face, and undo all that you as a director have worked so hard to accomplish.

Bibliography:

- Charles G. Gross and Marc H. Bornstein: *Left and Right in Science and Art*
- Geri Jewel
- Jason S. Babcock, Marianne Lipps, and Jeff B. Pelz: *How people look at pictures before, during, and after scene capture:* Buswell revisited
- Guy T. Busswell: *How People Look at Pictures: A Study of The Psychology of Perception in Art.*

I found that the article *How Language Shapes Thoughts*, written by Lera Boroditsky and published in *Scientific American*, has a very interesting contribution to this topic:

New cognitive research suggests that language profoundly influences the way people see the world. That being said, languages shape how we understand space and time. (...) English speakers arrange time from left to right.

Hebrew speakers do it from right to left (because Hebrew is written from right to left). Pormpuraawans, we found, arranged time from east to west. That is, seated facing south, time went left to right. When facing north, right to left. When facing east, toward the body, and so on. Of course, we never told any of our participants which direction they faced. The Pormpuraawans not only knew that already, but they also spontaneously used this spatial orientation to construct their representations of time. And many other ways to organize time exist in the world's languages. In Mandarin, the future can be below and the past above. In Aymara, spoken in South America, the future is behind and the past in front. Reproduced with permission. Copyright © 2011 Scientific American, a division of Nature America, Inc. All rights reserved.

Unfortunately, the discourse of the left to right/right to left paradigm in film is often oversimplified.

Assumption

I professionally lean toward a view based on the claim that lateral orientation is a universal phenomenon. Regardless, if it's true or not, and regardless of if the theory of left-right/right-left orientation and regularities is taken into careful consideration and is woven into the visual narrative and shot design in advance, the result can be highly subjective handling of characters and viewers alike. If mishandled or ignored, vague left-right/right-left orientation may leave the viewers questioning why they didn't connect with the story, but if used to the film's advantage, the viewer will be unable to express in words how they were so deeply moved.

Studies have shown that there exists a left and right field process whereby audiences create preference and emotional connection with subject placement within the classic artwork. In other studies, conducted with mirror images, participants overwhelmingly chose the left-side image as being more favorable or appealing. Other studies have been conducted through women's groups raising questions about gender equality in relation to screen orientation. Still, other studies report that reversed images have little or no effect on viewers' ability to understand the contextual or original meaning of the work image even after reversal. However, I see the intent of directors to use left-right facing screen direction as a tool to strengthen and weaken characters and their "hero's journey."

12.1. PROTAGONIST VS. ANTAGONIST (hero against villain)

The person who is on the Left side of the frame is more important, powerful and dominant than the person, who is on the Right side of the frame. The overall movement of the Hero's journey is from Left to Right when faced with obstacles the Hero is forced towards Right to Left framing.

It is advised to place a protagonist on the Right side of the frame just before a conflict begins, so when the protagonist tries to fight with antagonist, he can move from Right to Left, because the antagonist on Left side looks more powerful, and also because the protagonist needs a process to take the placement of the antagonist in the frame.

If the protagonist is an underdog, or if he is being pursued during the film, then he can be on the Right side of the screen because he has something to prove or there is a dominant antagonist that is after him.

The screen direction may change to suggest a change in character roles and to create more tension for the impending conflict. A protagonist on the right side of the screen does not have to be weak but may face a great adversary who "dominates" most of the film. This allows a greater emotional moment when they triumph at the end and take the Left side of the frame.

When the protagonist is replaced by an antagonist on the Left, a sense of unease is created, which may be a deliberate decision for the mood of the movie or the character.

If a Hero (Protagonist) is Left of frame and Villain (Antagonist) is right of the frame, then the Anti-Hero can be on either side of the frame depending on what the director is trying to convey. Or the virtue or evilness of other characters in the scene.

Scene 12.1.

The example below renders a classical situation, where the protagonist placed on the Left side faces the antagonist placed on the Right side.

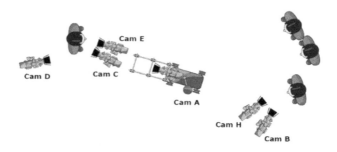

1. Cam A.1.

1. Cam A.2.

2. Cam B

3. Cam C

4. Cam D

5. Cam E

6. Cam H

7. Cam E

12.2. DOMINANT VS. SUBMISSIVE (gender dominance; age dominance; group dominance)

There stands a debate over Left-Right perception effects meaning of a visual, artistic work whether painted or on screen. Studies have been made to support both sides of the argument addressing issues ranging from gender dominance and audience preference to the perceived communication of the work. This sub-chapter will attempt to address the issue of Left-Right dominance as it relates to screen orientation in the visual medium of film narrative, more specifically to social dominance - gender dominance, age dominance, and group dominance.

A dominant character can be anyone in authoritative position or strong mind-set or having more knowledge, or extraordinary ability. A submissive character can be anyone that is struggling mentally, physically, or is in a position of being controlled or pursued or someone who willingly submits to the authority. Dominance on the Left does not always mean that the character on the Right is a weak character (it can even be a strong protagonist). Subordination does not equal weakness but rather a control, or attempt to control by authority.

Directors rely on the shot design to create a dominance of the screen. By studying films that involve the embrace of a man and a woman, it will be recognized that the person who is on the Left side of the frame will be the dominant character within the scene. There seems to be an apparent dominance within romantic relationships of classical films, and they appear to be located on the Left side of their counterpart. The message is clear: male dominance and female passivity, the model for heterosexual romantic love in films, where a female character is passive and powerless, and she is the object of desire for the male. Or Control-Male Domination vs. Female Submission in another film genre. (**12.2.a.** and **Scene 12.2.b.** and **Scene 12.2.c.**) The same mantra extends to the age dominance (**Scene 12.2.d.**) and group dominance (group-based social hierarchies: cultural, social and racial privilege, derived from cultural, social and racial stereotypes. (**Scene 12.2.e.** and **12.2.f.** and **12.2.g.**) The person who is on the Left side of the frame is more dominant than the person who is on the Right side of the frame. Such placement can be utilized to provide a symbolic representation of the power and struggle between characters, social inequality, a lack of gender equality, as well as to depict ethical dilemmas or foreshadow what is to come.

12.2.a.

Scene 12.2.b.

1. Cam A

2. Cam B   **3. Cam C**

Scene 12.2.c.

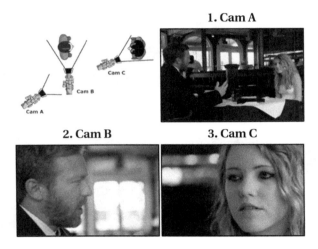

1. Cam A

2. Cam B   3. Cam C

Scene 12.2.d.

1. Cam A

Scene 12.2.e.

1. Cam A   2. Cam B

3. Cam C   **4. Cam D**

12.2.f.

12.2.g.

Despite the doctrinal acknowledgements of personal freedom, racial justice, gender justice, sexual freedom, and sexual autonomy, when it comes to addressing the excesses of hetero-normative and patriarchal sexuality, and racial inequity, and lingering inequity in male-female marriage, not too much has changed. The portrayal of male and female characters, and white and black characters, in films in a post-racial (color-ethnic-blind) era and post-feminism era (gender-related societal progress) still perpetuates same old stereotypes. Such enduring inequality is reflected in placing characters on the left and right side of the frame. Representation of political correctness, as an ideal of fairness and open-mindedness, in a post-racial era and post-feminism era, must be reflected in films. Applying "Psycho-physiological Regularities in Left-right/ Right-left Orientation" in lateral organization in regard of genders and races is a dangerous concept, because it reflects the androcentrism (male supremacy), and white supremacy (racist ideology based on the belief that white people are superior in many ways to people of other races), which is not transparent, but it is harmful, because it still mimics gender and racial inequality.

In comparison with heteronormative narrative films, there is no research or information regarding this topic in LGBT films. This topic needs additional work for a deeper understanding of the complexity of this issue. There is a need for deeper qualitative research (ethnographical, phenomenological, grounded theory, history, and ethnomethodology) and further practical applications of this concept for the depiction of lesbian, gay, bisexual and trans characters. The practical application often leads to a deeper understanding of a concept. I will challenge old ideas and conduct further research. Stay tuned! You will learn more about it in my next book - *Psycho-physiological Regularities in Left-right/Right-left Orientation in Shot Design*. It is my goal to share all new knowledge with you.

12.3. SYMPATHETIC VS. UNSYMPATHETIC

The analysis of empirical data as well as investigating the blocking of characters in practice provides evidence that supports the claim that the character looking from Left to Right, or the character on the Left side of the screen is more sympathetic. This finding can be used in practice to manipulate the viewer's perception of characters, and of the journey they are on in a given film. The audience feels more sympathetic to the characters on the Left side or looking from Left to Right, and less sympathetic to the characters on the Right side, or looking from Right to Left.

Sympathetic character inhabits frame Left, or inhabits frame Right, but looking from Left to Right, and her movement is generally Left-Right, which represents the sympathetic character overcoming of an obstacle or conflict. Conversely, unsympathetic character inhabits frame Right or at least is looking from Right to Left, and his movement is generally Right-Left to impede or obstruct the sympathetic character's progress. When the sympathetic character changes screen direction from Right to Left, it is either showing his retreat from an obstacle or him overcoming it.

Scene 12.3.

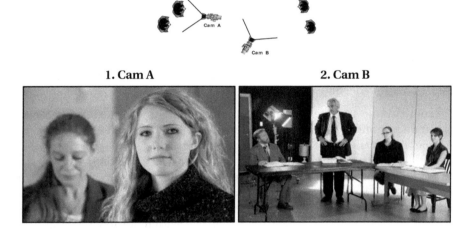

1. Cam A   **2. Cam B**

12.4. DIRECTIONALITY OF MOVEMENT

Within the theology of shot design, directors have the ability to induce different levels of comfort to help forward the narrative. It has been recognized that people will feel more comfortable if shots are based on ideologies of naturalism and regularity of everyday life. On the contrary, to cause discomfort for an audience, directors can design shots that support beliefs about evil or weakness. This assertion can be applied to the movement as well in regards to character blocking and actual camera movement. As for psychological elements of Left to Right movements, versus Right to Left movements, the comfort or discomfort of the movement is ingrained in the psyche. There are many theories as to why this is the case. Overall, research and theories both support the idea that the Left to Right movement evokes comfort (**Scene 12.4.a.**), due to normality, whereas Right to Left movement induces discomfort (**Scene 12.4.b.** and **Scene 12.4.c.**).

Scene 12.4.a.

Scene 12.4.b.

Scene 12.4.c.

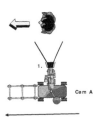 

12.5. PURSUING GOALS AND OBJECTIVES

The main character in film always has a task. The process of the task is becoming directional, Left to Right. In the process to achieve the goal/task, the hero goes from Left to Right - the hero's journey travels from Left to Right. The obstacles that push or interfere with the hero, force that character from Right to Left. Left to Right suggests moving forward/toward the hero's goal. However, there are some cases where this is not true, such as when the hero is stepping into his past (Right to Left) to confront buried trauma, or approaches from the villainous side of the frame (Right to Left also) when the hero's intentions are not true to him or herself.

Based on the idea that generally a protagonist will be placed on the Left side of the screen for dominance, that character will move from Left to Right across the screen, when in pursuit of a goal essential to his motivations as a character.

Emotional/psychological associations with a figure's position on the screen do exist, as the brain must organize and prioritize information in an image. However, the idea that Left to Right orientation = progression, and Right to Left = regression, may to seems very simplified for some of you. The rule can be intellectually challenged for greater depth in storytelling. It is already creatively used by many film directors to create hidden meanings and paradoxical associations between characters and their motives in visual narrative.

Study of neuroplasticity extensively explains how the human brain continues to evolve over the course of a lifetime. Brains are not fixed things, they continuously adapt, learn and change in structure. Even over the short course of a film, a brain can learn the rules and conventions of the film they are watching and adapt to the method of storytelling. Past research indicates that most protuberant real-world objects possess natural regularities that observers commonly assume in perceptual judgments of figural orientation and interpretation. In other words, when people study or observe forms they immediately seek a pattern.

12.6. RETURNING HOME

Basis Argument: When the character is moving from the Right to the Left of the frame, she is coming back or returning home, or she goes back to places, she has already been, or she is just leaving. A criminal is coming back to the scene of the crime; the grieving husband is revisiting a restaurant, where he proposed to his wife; she coming back to a hotel room after dinner; he is returning to his childhood village. But "*coming home*" can be meant metaphorically as well - coming to terms with something that happened in childhood, or looking for things may have been lost in traumatic childhood.

12.7. HISTORY OF THE STORY

The placement of character between the L-R/R-L fields and the way of using character's movement from Left to Right or Right to Left can determine the movement of time in conjunction with the plot. At the same time, it can bring the particular meaning, or emotion to the scene, especially to the period between the last and next scene.

If a character starts a journey, he is usually moving from the Left to the Right. However, there can be a story, where characters move from the Right to the Left at the very beginning of the film. This portrays an emotional goal for the characters because on the whole journey they are going to chase their memories in order to find themselves again.

If a character recreates the life of his dying father by remembering the stories he was constantly told as a boy, the film can start with him placed on the Right lateral side of the frame, when he launches into a flashback.

Both examples above imply the stories when the protagonist reports things from the perceptual point of view of his younger self. Flashbacks or memories are bookended with a present time, where characters in present time are depicted from Right to Left (contemplating the past), and the whole story set in past moves forward in a conventional manner, from Left to Right, because the story is moving into the future.

In a nonlinear narrative, where a character is placed on Right side in present time and in retrospectives as well, it signifies the importance of her childhood, how it has influenced her career, the role it will play in the story. She carries her past into her future, she does not leave it behind, she maintains a strong connection to childhood, but she is not moving on from the past. Past is amplified into the future, in a full circle.

12.8. FUTURE OF THE STORY

In the subchapter 12.4. PURSUING GOALS AND OBJECTIVES, I said: *"The process of the task is becoming directional, Left to Right. In the process to achieve the goal/task, the hero goes from Left to Right - the hero's journey travels from Left to Right."* Also in the subchapter 12.6. HISTORY OF THE STORY, I said: *"If a character starts a journey he is usually moving from the Left to the Right."* Summarizing – When the story moves from present time to the future, it moves from Left to Right. But Left-Right, Right-Left orientation in conjunction with a character's task and story time, can be used paradoxically. Placing the main character on Right side, instead of the Left side in a nonlinear narrative can symbolize his efforts to rewind and undo the past. Basically, a screen orientation symbolizes his efforts to rewind and undo the past. The film can establish a pattern of character's orientation Left-Right in dreams, and Right-Left in reality, symbolizing character's want to create a future in the dream world, and fix his past in reality. The paradox is that the dream world is not real, so no future can be made in it. The character is torn between the dream world and reality; in the dream world, he can be with his wife but not his children, vice versa for real world. The exception to the rule is when the character is faced with his wife, he is oriented Right-Left despite being in the dream world. She exists as a projection of his guilt about her death, so he literally looks to the past when he talks to her (although the audience is initially unaware she is dead). The character's screen orientation changes to the standard (Left-Right) only at the end, after he has dealt with his wife's memory and accomplished his goal of changing another character's mind. Begins Right-Left as he wakes up from the final dream, but soon changes to Left-Right, symbolizing his progression, fulfilled goals and completed character arc.

12.9. CHARACTER CONTEMPLATES THE PAST

While several symbolic meanings can be derived from the psycho-physiological regularities of Left and Right orientation in cinema, its implications regarding time are the most fascinating one. There are, arguably, innumerable reasons as to why the human brain subconsciously associates Left-oriented images with the past and Right oriented images with the future, at least according to the conventions of western society. For example, one reads from Left to Right, thus understanding the progression of story, and similarly time, in a linear fashion: if one stops midsentence, for instance, words to the left represent the story already told, i.e. the past; words to the right symbolize the story that is yet to unfold - that which will take place in the future. Additionally, when time moves clockwise, it travels forward from Left to Right, yet motion that moves counterclockwise journeys backward from Right to Left. This argument does not go beyond cultural boundaries, and it is heavily influenced by the viewer's cultural background, how a Western World person scans and perceives an image.

Basis Argument: When the character looks to the Left, he is thinking about the past. Furthermore, if a character is moving from the Right to the Left of the frame, he is coming back, or leaving or trying to get away from something, or he is regressing into the past or his old ways. If the antagonist tries to go to someplace, Right-Left movement works more because the antagonist's movement can be regarded as coming to the protagonist. The character that moves from the Right to the Left is related to the passive, memories, evasion, breaking away from something. Characters also look left, either leading up to a dream, memory or flashback.

In cinema, there's seems to be one constant, when relating to the past. It appears that in order to psychologically evoke the idea of reminiscing and looking back to the past, the character will look to the Left of the frame or face the Left of the frame. Psychologically we associate looking to the left of frame as looking to the past. Therefore, when directors are trying to relate this notion of reminiscing or of flashbacks, they will usually compose the shot with either eyelines moving from Right to Left, or the action within a scene moving in that direction. Alternatively, when we as an audience are transitioned back into the present, or when the character is looking towards the future, the character is usually looking towards the Right of the frame. This is a subconscious phenomenon that when not adhered to, it can create disorientation in the viewer.

In summary: History and the Past exist on the Left side, when characters are in movement leading from Right to Left specifically in and or around dream sequences and or bringing up memories from the past before flashbacks and/or searching for the truth. A character standing on the Right side of the frame facing Left is a common convention for leading to flashbacks in a film. It is a cinematic cue for memory (flashbacks) or imagination.

An interesting case can be made for nonlinear narratives since they vary by nature from the traditional structure of visual storytelling. In fact, nonlinear films can make use of Left and Right orientation in a number of ways, depending on several factors.

Scene 12.9.a.

Scene 12.9.b.

Scene 12.9.c.

Scene 12.9.d.

Scene 12.9.e.

Scene 12.9.f.

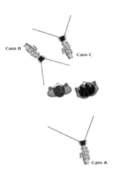

1. Cam A   **2. Cam B**

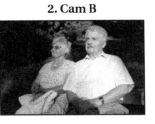

3. Cam C   **4. Cam B**

Scene 12.9.g.

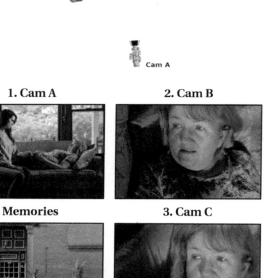

1. Cam A   **2. Cam B**

Memories   **3. Cam C**

Scene 12.9.h.

1. Cam A

(Reminiscences)

12.10. CHARACTER CONTEMPLATES THE FUTURE

This subchapter is pursuing the nature of the lateral-time paradigm, which has been introduced in the previous subchapter 12.9. CHARACTER CONTEMPLATES THE PAST that the past and future temporal concepts are spatially represented - past being located to the Left and future to the Right.

Basis Argument: When the character looks to the Right, he is thinking about the future. If the character moves from the Left to the Right side of the frame, he is trying to go to some place, he is moving into the future or moving on with his life. Characters also look Right, either leading up to the daydream, fantasies, or flash forwards.

In summary: The future and the present become on the Right side when characters are in movement leading from Left to Right. It can also imply that the character is entering into the unknown.

A flawed character who is seeking redemption looks or moves from Right to Left. A character who has been redeemed is bringing together his past and future, and he moves from Left to Right, signifying that redemption has been achieved, and he is finally able to move on with his life.

Scene 12.10.a.

Scene 12.10.b.

Scene 12.10.c.

Scene 12.10.d.

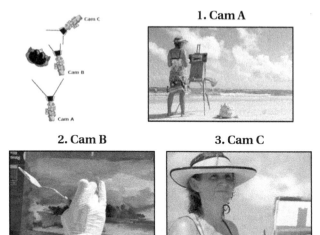

1. Cam A

2. Cam B   3. Cam C

Scene 12.10.e.

Scene 12.10.f.

Conclusion:

The film is not an exact science, and as such, it is nearly impossible to determine rigid formulas or dogmas aiming at ruling this art form or the Left-Right/Right-Left Orientation. Ned Herrmann's brain dominance theories are also not yet proven, and concrete scientific evidence and solid data remain to be catalogued. Everything is passive of interpretation and subjective analysis, and ultimately, it is the sensibility and vision of the director allied with the receptivity of the audience that shall (or not) yield to the desired artistic results. The perspective in this chapter does not represent a worldwide view of the subject. However, it is at least curious and fascinating to realize that the Left-Right/Right-Left Orientation and regularities can find support in several different arguments and hypothesis, and not only in cultural or regional theories concerning image analysis but rather in universal laws of nature.

With respect to historical, social and cultural circumstances, it appears that there are only conventions that have a tendency to change over time, as well as the audience's response to those conventions. If this is true, we should unscrupulously use those conventions. Why use less, when more is at our disposal? What is for certain is that a careless attitude towards the Left-Right/Right-Left Orientation could have disastrous results. *Inattention to the Left to Right, and Right to Left paradigm could explode in your face, and undo all that you as a director have worked so hard to accomplish.*

CHAPTER 13:
DIRECTORIAL-DRAMATURGICAL ANALYSIS

Intro

A director's principal responsibilities are to determine how to treat the story in order to usher the story towards its completion, accommodate viewers' ability to comprehend the story, and engage the audience emotionally with characters and story events. A director chooses how to tell the story, how to color it, how to choreograph it. To accomplish this goal, a director has to do his/her directorial homework: the *Directorial-Dramaturgical Analysis*.

This chapter addresses the issues of a directorial-dramaturgical analysis by examining the whole process that leads up to film pre-production and ensures the integrity of the production, and director's autonomy, providing information that helps to facilitate the director's artistic vision. The aim of a directorial-dramaturgical analysis is to examine fundamental dramaturgical and directorial mechanism for transforming a screenplay to the film, by trying to interpret the screenplay from an individual director's perspective and laying the basis for transforming his/her interpretation to the film. It is an active job, a comprehensive exploration of the context in which the screenplay resides. A director examines and evaluate objective evidence and facts of the screenplay by means of analysis, search and observation. It is a thorough analysis of the physical, political, economic, socio-cultural settings of the story; the psychological background of the characters; the various representations of the story in regards to narrative and visuals; as well as the screenplay analysis: story structure, dramatic structure, rhythm; concept, theme, scenes. Even though the objective evidence is characterized as completely unbiased, since all directors are colored by their own interests and ideals, no doubts that the analysis includes personal reflections on objective evidence and facts of the screenplay. This is a surprisingly difficult task even if the director is a writer of the screenplay. It is a creative process with the objective and academic tone within. In general, it encompasses the whole conceptualization process.

This chapter provides directors with a checklist to help them to stay organized during the conceptualization process while they analyze a script and make critical directorial choices. This chapter explains how to do a story breakdown, scene breakdown, and shot breakdown. The strategy explained here will liberate directors artistically, allowing them to harness their creativity and communicate their vision effectively.

Critical directorial choices

A director has to practice conceptual approaches and rationalize every possible step in advance when designing a film. For every film, a director makes critical choices for narrative and aesthetic purposes: choosing every element within the frame, constructing the actor's performance, and utilizing all elements of visual storytelling in order to create a story that communicates to the audience meaning and emotionality. A director's goal is to create a compositional structure in order to express his/her intention efficiently, clearly, and impressively.

One of the first critical choices a director makes, includes determining the *Mood and Tone* of the film and of each scene.

Determining the mood and tone of the scene is essential in designing it. For many, if not most, it might seem like a baffling concept to distinguish a mood and tone. At first glance, the problem appears difficult, but actually, it really isn't. First and foremost, you have to differentiate mood and atmosphere from mood and tone, because these two pairs of terms are closely related, and sometimes they are used interchangeably.

- Atmosphere:
  The dominant tone or mood of a work of art associated with a particular place: "He lived in a dark old house with a depressing atmosphere." An aesthetic quality or effect, especially a distinctive and pleasing one, associated with a particular place: "A restaurant with an Old-World atmosphere" (*English Dictionary*).

- Mood:
  A pervading impression by an observer; the general feeling or the atmosphere that a film scene creates for the viewer. Mood = Feeling of the scene. The mood is an extension of setting (*English Dictionary*).

- Tone:
  The director's feelings towards the subject (*English Dictionary*).

  Tone is a literary technique that shows the author's attitude towards the audience or reader. (…) Similar to tone is mood, which is the created atmosphere with the intention of coaxing a certain emotion from the audience and is created through setting, theme, and tone. ("Tones, Moods, and Irony in the Canterbury Tales." http://www.studymode. com/essays/Tones-Moods-And-Irony-In-The-1166673.html. Accessed December 22, 2016).

Tone is the attitude a writer has towards the subject they're writing about. It is evident in their diction, style, and opinion if they express one. Mood is the atmosphere created by the setting, and actions of people and characters in it. (http://wiki.answers.com/Q/What_is_the_tone_or_mood_in_literature. Accessed December 22, 2016)

Conclusion: A particular place/environment/location/setting has a special atmosphere → atmosphere creates a mood → and mood generates a feeling.

There is a possible contradiction between the Mood and Tone of the scene: In Homer's Odyssey (the founding epics of Greek literature) Odysseus longs to hear the seductive yet dangerous song of the sirens that lure sailors to their deaths.

MOOD Audience's feeling; the general feeling or atmosphere of the scene created within the viewer.	TONE Director's attitude/feeling towards the subject and situation/style/presentation
Nervous Uneasy Disastrous Unsettle Discomfort False	Optimistic - Cheerful - Hopeful - Giving the illusion of hope. Seductive - The more beautiful it is, the more deadly it is. Enchanting. Whimsical.

The contradiction brings a great point of how different approaches to an audience can impact the meaning of the message. Here is a perfect example of why deciding how to deliver your story to an audience is so important.

If you take the lyrics as a whole, without any of the music, they seem dark and angry, but when Johnny Cash sings the song it has a joking and light tone to it. (...) the way in which Cash sings can make a song with dark lyrics seem light.
(http://www.personal.psu.edu/sbm162/blogs/the_speaking_self/2010/01/what-about-tone.html. Accessed February 27, 2013)

Directorial-dramaturgical Analysis

The following checklist will help you to stay organized while you analyze a screenplay, conceptualize a film, and make critical directorial choices. The checklist includes the most important areas you should take into consideration when you analyze the screenplay from the director's point of view.

STORY BREAKDOWN:

- Articulate a *Vision Statement* – general statement that expresses your most important ideas
- Determine the *Historical Context* of the story
- Determine the physical, political, economic, and socio-cultural *Settings of the Story*
- Determine a *Theme (story's reason to be told), Premise, Poetic, and Style*
- Determine your *Personal Imprint*
- Determine the *Genre* – be aware of "conventions" and apply them or reject them
- Determine the *Storyteller's Perspective*
- Determine a *Visual Look*
- Analyze all *Story Elements* and *Structure Components* that can be translated into the film:

  1. *Story Structure* (Narrative structure and flow of the scenes, acts, inciting incident, turning points, plot points, tragic moments, last moment of suspense, collective action of all story elements – character actions, dialogue, a series of connected events leading to a conclusion)
  2. *Dramatic Structure* (Organization of storytelling – chronological time, non-linear time, the order of scenes, continual progression, general narrative principle/narrative position/narrative style – subjective treatment, objective treatment, change of narrative position, narrative flow)
  3. *Visual Structure*
  4. *Emotional Structure*

SCENE BREAKDOWN:

The best method of construction I've come up with is to go over a scene in my mind constantly, telling myself what I am doing as I direct. The very process of telling myself the story over and over forces me to eliminate unnecessary details. (Wajda, A. *Double Vision: My Life in Film*, 1st American edition. Henry Holt & Co., 1989, ISBN-10: 0805004513)

- Determine the *Premise of the scene*
- Determine the *Objective/Purpose/Intent of the scene* (Contribution to narration, mood, unity, and continuity.)
- Determine the *Conflict/Tension*
- Determine what's at *Stake* in the scene.

- Determine the *Payoff* for the scene
- Determine how the *Outcome* of the scene moves the story forward.
- Determine the *Climax* of the scene.
- Determine the *Space* (Different options for visual storytelling through space)
- Determine the *Tone* of the scene/director's critical choice (director's attitude/feel towards the subject and situation he/she tries to portray. What you want to portray – what emotions you want to portray.)
- Determine the *Mood* of the scene (audience's feeling: the general feeling or atmosphere of the scene created within the viewer; the feeling(s) the audience feels or thinks about when they watch the scene; what the audience will get from the emotions portrayed)
- Determine an *Emotional Meaning* of the scene and the way you are going to control viewers' feelings
- Determine how you will translate inner feelings, motivations, and insights of characters into filmable situations
- Determine the *Character Perspective*
  - Character's objective/intention/goal in the scene. What does he/she want? (Tension comes from conflicting objectives.)
  - Determine how the character's goals move the story forward
  - Character's feeling
  - Character's attitude
  - What's at stake for individual characters?
- Determine *Plot Points* (points that move the story forward)
- Determine the *Beats/Unit changes* (Where does the story change directions?)
- Determine the *Pivotal Moment* (A pivotal beat is an important beat in which the action of the scene takes a significant turn, or something really important to the outcome of the scene happens, or simply when the story changes direction. In a pivotal scene, usually a character makes a decision that alters the direction of the story. In a bigger picture, you can see the pivotal moment/pivotal beat as the *turning point* – the major plot event/moment that causes some big change and alters the route of the character in the plot.)
- Determine the *Placement* of the scene (where the scene takes place in a storyline – *"When the story structure gains intensity, the visual structure and emotional structure must do the same."*)
- Determine the *Nature* of the scene (stationary or in movement)
- Determine the basic *Blocking and Staging Principle*
- Determine the *Staging Style*
- Determine the *Staging-editing Pattern*

- Determine *Dramatic Tension, Emotional Impact, Imaginative Involvement, Aesthetic Value* (balance of masses, tonal balance, color, graphic design, optimizing the aesthetics in composition, eye-pleasing composition, information value)

SHOT BREAKDOWN:

- Determine the *Dramatic Elements* of a shot (storytelling reason for a shot, motivation, information, composition, camera angle; continuity in – content, movement, position, dialogue; change of continuity – an apparent time interval between two shots)
- Determine the *Camera Set-ups* (camera placement, framing, camera angle, lens selection, composition)
- Determine *Technical Elements* of a shot (size of shot, DOF, camera movement, color, modes of lighting, running time, position of a shot in a scene, number of subjects within a shot)
- Determine *Visual Conventions* (film language standards, placing of the subject within the frame, composition principles, well-grounded composition guidelines, various aesthetic guidelines, visual rules, rule of thirds, diagonal dominance, visual balance, tradition, regulations, genre conventions, genre codes, conventional signs, clichés, stereotypes)
- Determine the *Theatrical Element* (blocking, costume, makeup, props/set, acting choices)
- Determine the *Film Time* (compressed, expended)
  In addition, try to apply your knowledge to *Shot Design* (how to direct the viewer's attention to the line of plot using screen direction; how to direct and redirect "narrative flow" using screen direction; how to control a movement of the story using screen direction; how to manipulate dramatic time, psychological time, and screening time using shot design)

Try to skillfully and creatively use filmmaking tools to direct the audience's attention to what is substantial on the screen and to all critical aspects of the story, especially drama and emotions. Try to fashion each story element in advance in order to create a strong emotional and psychological connection with the viewer and to enhance the unity of the film.

As discussed earlier in the book, you should *"Trust your instincts, but rely on thinking."* I know that there are no rules that will ensure a good film, but there are some principles that provide a means of achieving a well-crafted film when they are properly applied. I encourage you to practice those principles and theoretical approaches to try and rationalize every possible step in advance when you are conceptualizing your film.

This strategy will liberate you artistically and allow you to harness your creativity and communicate your ideas effectively. I don't want to say that there are no other approaches to directing with successful results. Some professionals don't like the idea of analyzing the creative process at all and urge students and novice filmmakers to ignore all books, encouraging them to "Just do it." Some artists make a choice to avoid systematic thinking, rejecting all principles, ideas, schools of thought, theories, patterns, and designs. For them, art is an entirely intuitive process that can never be mastered by rules of thumb and should not be reduced to a formula. And they aren't wrong. *"At the core of every artist is a sacred place where all the rules are set aside or deliberately forgotten, and nothing matters but the instinctive choices of the heart and soul of the artist."* (Vogler, C. *The Writers Journey: Mythic Structure for Writer*, 3rd edition. Michael Wiese Productions, 2007, ISBN-10: 193290736X).

And there is something else you should take into consideration as well, some outrageous thoughts: While flying from the USA to Europe on November 2013, to start pre-production on my feature film *The Lights*, written by Kegan Chandler, I read in *Hemispheres* magazine an interview with Malcolm Gladwell. I did mention him earlier in the book, referring to his magic number for true expertise, where he claims that *"ten thousand hours of practice is required to achieve the level of mastery associated with being a world-class expert – in anything."* The journalist and novelist Dana Vachon, in reference to Gladwell's latest book, *David and Goliath: Underdogs, Misfits and the Art of Battling Giants*, asks the question: *"You are on a course to say that the rules are made by the powerful against the powerless, so the powerless shouldn't play by the rules."* Malcolm Gladwell responds: *"If conventions are stacked against you, challenge the conventions. Don't be passive and lose."* Challenge the conventions! I would bet that now you are going to change the perspective you are using to look at the film.

(*The Lights:* In 1921, two Slovak-American brothers Jerry and Daniel Siakel return to Czechoslovakia to direct the first Slovakian film. The movie is about the classic tale of Jánošík, the famous bandit who died for his people. But when the American censors declare the hero's death in the movie's ending "too violent", Jerry is forced to re-shoot a new "happy" ending behind his brother's back. In doing this, Jerry betrays not only the story, but his brother, and the people that trusted him. The brothers later retire to America and never speak to each other again. But in 1968, a damaged copy of the Jánošík film is re-discovered in Chicago by Daniel's widow. Jerry must decide if he will return to his homeland to restore the film for his brother and risk re-exposing himself to a new generation as "the man who ruined the Jánošík legend". But fear is not the only thing that stands in Jerry's way: the Warsaw Pact has just invaded Czechoslovakia.)

CHAPTER 14:
DIRECTOR'S BOOK

Notebook, Sketchbook Journal, Well-kept Diary

The best way to assemble individual components of a director's vision and stay organized in this task is to build a *Director's Book*. The purpose of the director's book is to communicate as clearly as possible a vision to collaborators. The director's book is a journal in which the director records the conceptualization and preproduction phase of the film in much detail. The book includes everything from visual inspirations to scene breakdowns, which helps a director to see his/her vision with clarity. It captures the visual imagination of the director. The director's book provides the complete record of how the film will be created, along with records, comments from people who read the script and saw the casting and locations, personal notes, inspirational sources, and influences. The director's book addresses every aspect of conceptualization, planning, and visualization involved in the film directing process in the stages of conceptualization and preproduction. It is a complex activity combining research and practice and is designed to reflect on director's individuality, as well as to develop and enhance his/her creative work.

This chapter shows the structure of a director's book, including all breakdowns, along with the inventory sheet.

1. *Artist's Statement*

   Why does this story need to be told? Why is making this film an inevitability? Why is this film important to you? Why does your voice have to be heard? Showcase the level of commitment, dedication, and passion you have for your film.

2. *Script*
   - First draft
   - Script critiques, script analysis
   - Newest version of the script
   - Shooting script

3. *Directorial-dramaturgical Analysis*
   - Vision Statement, Historical Context, Setting of the Story, Theme
   - Genre (stylistic elements and narrative conventions that define a genre), *Genre Compilation* (visual style, tone, shot types, shot sizes, composition, camera movement, blocking and staging, cinematography, color palette, lighting).

When you rip films and put together clips from other films, which stories are set in the territory of the similar genre you want to use for the interpretation of your story, you create a *Genre Compilation*. A *Genre Compilation* is a video representation of your *Genre Breakdown*. A *Genre Compilation* can be used as a base for a mood reel/tone reel (rip-o-matic). Please, refer below to the *Visual References Packet*, and also to the CHAPTER 16: I. STUDIO – APPLICATION OF GENRE CONVENTIONS. That directing exercise – shooting the scene within the restrictions of a particular genre – will teach you the importance of a genre for narrative purposes and for a visual treatment of the film.

- Personal imprint
- Directorial-dramaturgical analysis
  - Story breakdown
  - Scene breakdown
  - Shot breakdown
- Story charts and diagrams: rising action chart/narrative structure chart/plot diagram/story intensity chart

4. *Art Package*

- *Visual references packet*
  - Lookbook/visual lookbook/ mood book/mood boards/moodies/visual references
    Compilation of images that best represent your vision of your film, including location, costume, makeup, lighting, color palette, shot design, and the overall tone and style of your film.
- *Location book*
  - Location list
  - Location breakdown
  - Location survey checklist for each location
  - Photographs from location
  - Overhead sketches or blueprints of location/location diagrams
  - Diagram/floor plan
  - Written notes
  - Walkthrough
  - Technical scouts
  - Location list with addresses and contact information
  - Map/directions
  - Location permits
  - Scouting tape

- *Art direction package*
  - Production design
  - Costume design
  - Makeup
  - Set design/set dressing
  - Props masters
  - Special effects
  - Visual look/visual concept/visual design
  - Concept for credit sequences w/film clips
  - Credit sequences design
  - Main title design

5. **Previsualization**
   - Visual structure and visual structure chart
   - Concept art/conceptual sketches
   - Storyboard
   - Animatic
   - Photo-script
   - Video-storyboard

6. **Casting**
   - Audition packet
     - Audition flyer
     - Project description
     - Logline
     - Synopsis
     - Character list with character sketches for each character you will be auditioning for (one paragraph long)
     - Sides (audition script pages) for each character that you plan the actors to audition for
   - Character breakdowns
   - Casting tape

7. **Preproduction book**
   - Shooting schedule
   - Budget
   - Financial statement
   - Crew list/contacts
   - Cast list/contacts
   - Budget summary
   - Production summary
   - Call Sheets

8. **Miscellaneous**

Art Package

Here is the breakdown of the fourth part of the director's book – the *Art Package* and its three segments:

I.   **Visual References Packet**
II.   **Location Book**
III.   **Art Direction Package**

I. Visual References Packet

The first task you face in designing your film is creating a visual concept of the film. The *Visual References Packet* contains pictures that closely depict your notion about a particular place, its architectural style, photographic potentiality, color palette, texture, and social codes. The visual packet sort of articulates what you are looking for in terms of visual look and style, mood and tone, and it has to be very close to what you have envisioned in your mind while working on the story, characters, plot, setting, style, and tone. You can replicate or recreate existing imagery or invent your own to fit your vision and suit its purpose. In addition, at first glance, there must be a recognizable attempt to create an original, characteristic, identifiable, visual, formal, personal style that will help you design a visual look for your film, unless you are boarding a running train, where a visual template was laid down way before you got in, like is usually the case with TV series. Without any doubt, the visual and cinematic appeal of chosen locations, along with the cast and cinematic style, contributes to the overall appeal of the film.

The lookbook/mood book could reference lighting from one film, shot design from another film, and characters' costume, makeup and props from additional one. The lookbook/mood book can reference lighting style and shooting style; it can render examples of mood and tone from different resources. It can explore possible reference ideas through photographs of people, actors, props, and the character's environment; it can contain images that suggest the feel and sensibility of the film and communicate the atmosphere. Show your aesthetic choices through magazine clips, archival photos, or original photos. Use whatever visual references and whatever inspirational sources which can help you to set a tone and mood for the film. Aesthetic, the sources and influences from which you draw, can include art, films, and photography. Express your vision by any means necessary. This is the work typically developed by an art department and its designers once a project has been developed and is greenlit, but directors have always to be working on it while articulating their vision or pitching their films.

The lookbook/mood book is overly representative in regards to your vision. In addition, it will help you to find a mutual language with other collaborators in refining a visual look that will enhance the expressive potential of your film. Even though your goal is to lock down the aesthetic, feel and tone for your film, the point of working on a visual references packet is not to cement your preconceived ideas but the other way around: to explore your original ideas actively. And you will be even more open to new points of view and to accepting new ideas from other designers from all department heads. This way, you will be prepared to revise or change your original vision if their ideas turn out to better serve the story than yours. Everything you do must serve the story! There is no doubt that your collaborators and designers will enrich the story. Believe me, your cooperation will be mutually inspiring and challenging because you will support, spark, and stimulate each other's creativity.

I didn't use to work this way. I always thought, in accord with the "auteur theory" that a film director chooses to work with collaborators, and he uses them to execute his vision. Consequently, a director as a film's principal creative source has all rights to impose his vision upon all collaborators. I was also terrified that I might lose the control over the film, if I let them exercise a degree of authorship over the entire film rather than simply doing a service for my vision. Things had changed for me in 1992 when I was preparing a TV film *The Bridge*, a historical epic, an action-adventure story about two modern men who find themselves unexpectedly and against their will in the middle of The Thirty Years' War (1618-48). In the world, far away from their own, they face danger. In desperate strait, the fear of the timid aggravates the dangers that imperil the brave. Only thanks to a courageous girl from the past, and true love, they can return back to the present day. *The Bridge* is a story about accepting and giving up on the love, a sacrifice in the name of love, it is a story of sacrifice. The screenwriter (Peter Koza), costume designer (Zdeněk Šánský), music composer (Peter Šibilev), and film editor (Dušan Milko) tried to develop ideas of how they could best serve the theme and tone of the film. Amazing ideas came out of many brainstorming creative sessions we had. Now I attribute the success of any film to the hard work of all people involved in a creative process of filmmaking. The film is very much a labor of love of all people involved in, and not just director's.

You can easily turn the lookbook/mood-book into a mood reel/tone reel (rip-o-matic), or alternatively you can work on a mood reel/tone reel (rip-o-matic). When you work on a mood reel/tone reel (rip-o-matic) you simply rip films and put together clips from other films about a similar subject, visual style, and tone. This compilation can help you to convey and showcase your vision and the mood and tone of your film. If it is done well, it will reflect your vision, tone and mood, and pace as well. It is a very effective way of transforming your ideas into a visual form. The mood reel/tone reel (rip-o-matic) expresses the look and feel of your film to your collaborators, designers and film crew. It is a video representation of your visual imagination. These days video presentations have become essential. A trailer mash-up/video mash-up combines multiple video sources, and it can contain original shots, or/and mockingjay scenes, and even a test footage/proof of concept (a scene from the script shot as a short film). It assesses a film's viability in the stage of conceptualization and development. It can work as a pitch-reel/pitch-video/pitch-trailer to help potential producers to get a sense of how you have envisioned your film, a sense of the look and style of your film. It can help them visualize the final product because the main mantra here is - this is what the film will be like when it's done. In the past few years, the pitch-reel/pitch-video/pitch-trailer has significantly become more demanding.

II. Location Book

Location scouting is the process of looking for the proper places to shoot your film. While scouting different places, document all places and all possibilities. Location books document the actual research of this part of the preproduction process. Don't forget: You need to judge the value of the location through the issue of the script, so take into consideration overall aesthetic value, and lighting. You need to evaluate the artistic, practical, and logistic demands of the location as well: sound; electric power; special areas such as the dressing room, toilets, and catering area; safety and security issues; travel distance; schedule and budget; location fee; remodeling needs; permission; neighbors; local weather conditions; local film office. Take a look at the realities of the location in regards to the space demands of your desired blocking. I encourage you to focus on some seemingly insubstantial things during location scouting such as daylight, the left-right components of the space, etc.

The location book helps you to stay organized during the location scouting and thereafter. In essence, the location book is a collection of photographs and videos of various location alternatives, stating the suitability of all locations and their variants in order to find the ideal location for your production needs (location selected for filming). The location book records your reconnaissance, documentation, and found locations.

Your location book should have the following parts:

    A.   Location survey checklist for each location
        (You can find the location survey checklist in PART V: QUIZZES, TESTS, CHARTS, TEMPLATES of this book, or you can generate your own.)

    B.   Photographs from location
        1.   Panoramic photographs (document location possibilities) – there are many different phone applications for taking panoramic photos, like PanOMG, Panorama Free Photo 360 by Sfera, and Panorama Camera 360

    2.   Photographs mimicking possible camera views and different camera angles.

    3.   Utilitarian photographs (document the space available for camera set-ups, lighting set-ups, video-assist village, places where camera and lights can be placed, dressing room, toilets, wardrobe room, makeup room)

C.   Overhead sketches or blueprints and floor plans of location/location diagrams
You can use the *Magic Plan* app that allows you create floor plans. It measures rooms by marking the corners, and then it aggregates a floorplan.

D.   Diagrams/floor plans.
-   Camera set-ups
All possibilities for camera set-ups with the camera moves and "choreography" required to stage and block the action taking place in a film. *(If you don't like drawing your floor plans by hand, or your drawing skills are really modest, consider the following applications: Shot Designer app lets you quickly and easily figure out camera blockage. Floor plans/overhead diagrams and schematics can be created with Celtx pre-production software, which I am using in this book.)* StoryBoard Quick is an easy-to-use, easy-to-learn software program that allows you to plan and present your film visually. Or you can consider a *ShotPro* by Shot Professional, which is bringing true previsualization to filmmakers, directors, DPs and storyboard artists.

-   Lighting diagram/lighting set-up
You can use a different phone application to plot the position of the sun while you are at the location. It will help you to figure out the general location of the sun. If you plan to work with artificial lighting, you can either sketch your ideas on paper, or you can use applications like the *Online Lighting Diagram Creator* or *Sylights*.

E.   Written Notes
-   Written documentation of location – electricity, time estimates, etc.
-   Direction to the location
-   Time of day vs. the time of day scripted

- Alternation of script (changes that must be made based on a found location or to accommodate a location)
- Review various location's alternatives while assessing its suitability:
  o Overall aesthetic value
  o Sound conditions (background noises that may interfere with audio)
  o Financial cost
  o Parking availability
  o Use of animals on the property if needed
  o Availability of electrical power – circuit breaker box, who can be contacted if a circuit blows, which circuits can be used and how many watts can run on them, need of extension cords (alternation: power generators) availability of light – indoors and/or outdoors (what types of lights will be needed, how the problem of mixing indoor and outdoor lighting can be solved, the sun's position at different times of day and its effect on the shoot)
  o Weather conditions
  o Information if/when a location requires several days of setup and breakdown prior and following the day(s) of filming
  o Set dressing needs

F. Walkthrough
    Documentation of a walkthrough with the cinematographer, production designer, set dresser, and sound designer

G. Technical scouts
    Grips, electric, camera, etc.

H. Location list with addresses and contract information

I. Location permits
    Location owner, neighbors, film commission

J. Scouting Tape (recorded location)
    While a well-organized location book serves you well during location scouting, a scouting tape can speed up the entire process, as well as give you a good grasp of how a particular place will "behave" on screen. Don't be afraid to look for an appropriate camera angle when you sense that the location might be the ap-

propriate one. Your scouting tape can have signs of staging and blocking. If you scout a location with your production designer, scouting manager, or location manager, or with your director of photography, utilize their presence for blocking some shots and use them as stand-ins. From a practical side, a scouting tape is actually a visual record of location possibilities, documentation of locations, and documentation of locations selected for filming.

You should be using a video camera while you are looking for the proper places to shoot your film and looking for alternative possibilities for solving the visual concept of the film. Being directly in the space helps you to verify the set of semantic and aesthetic significant units in the script that might be realized in the film. Using a video camera (and still camera) narrows down the spectrum of possibilities for potential locations as well as helps you to refine the visual concept for the film according to location demands.

The scouting tape (recorded location) should demonstrate your ability to:

- Estimate which place is filmable (photographic opportunities, visual possibilities, visual potential of a location)
- Find out what is most important in the environment for a story and character
- Present connections between the character, story, and space
- Discover the atmosphere and mood of the place
- Present filmmaking ideas
- Present your viewpoint and attitude about the chosen environment
- Showcase how the found location fit your vision.

III. Art Direction Package

Production design

- Statement of intent – initial design ideas (written statement)
- Guiding principle
- Initial discussions
- Visual research (photographs that display a wide range of possible approaches to the production design)
- Conceptual sketches

- Alternative interpretations of the director's vision
- Architectural drawings of production set
- Finished blueprint drawings
- Details of all needed design elements
- Adjustments, layout, modifications

Costume design

- Statement of intent – initial design ideas (written statement)
- Guiding principle
- Initial discussions
- Visual research (photographs that display a wide range of possible approaches to the costume)
- Costume sketches
- Catalogues
- Samples of fabrics
- Different ideas
- Alternative interpretation of the director's vision

Makeup

- Statement of intent – initial design ideas (written statement)
- Guiding principle
- Initial discussions
- Visual research (photographs that display a wide range of possible approaches to the makeup)
- Sketches
- Catalogues
- Different ideas
- Alternative interpretation of the director's vision

Set design/set dressing

- Statement of intent – initial design ideas (written statement)
- Guiding principle
- Initial discussions
- Visual research (photographs that display a wide range of possible approaches to the set dressing)
- Sketches
- Visual art
- Alternative interpretation of the director's vision

Visual effects

- Statement of intent – initial design ideas (written statement)
- Guiding principle
- Initial discussions
- List of optical and mechanical shots which will need conventional optical trickeries, process photography, and computer produced imagery
- List of CGI (Computer Generated Imagery) - green screen, virtual set - digitally constructed scenes, digital set extension, VFX compositing
- Sketches
- Storyboard
- Pre-rendered CGI
- Animatics
- Script rewrites

Visual look

- Visual style of film (art-cinema narration, visual genre conventions, atmosphere and mood of locations, visual potential)
- Visual rules
- Modes of lighting/light design
- Camera treatment
- Shot design
- Picture composition
- Camera movement
- Lenses
- Color palette
- Staging and blocking

Sound design

- Brainstorming phase
- Initial discussions
- Solving on-set audio problems in advance
- Walk through locations before they are locked

Film music

- Statement of intent – initial ideas
- Initial discussions
- Inspirational sources

- Temp music
- Composed music numbers

Design schedule

- Individual meetings with all the designers
- First design meeting with all the designers – design team
- Different ideas
- Brainstorming phase
- Synergy
- Final design phase
- Technical execution

Conclusion:

There's no doubt that a director's book is a hands-on personal creative exploration of the material, a deep probe into the tone and mood, the atmosphere and texture, of the film. It explores the creative choices and technical possibilities that help you as a director locate the soul of the film. The director's book expresses the look and feel of your film to all your collaborators, designers, potential producers, and crew members. It gives a representation of what the film will look and feel like.

All the elements are lined up, all the elements are in place, and you can start to inspire all your collaborators. The director's book renders your director's vision and gives a sense of your imagination and the direction the film is going. The director's book can be instrumental in bringing finance to the table as well.

> *Most of the studios are expecting visual presentations from directors on meetings for the open directing projects the studio is developing so the studio can now get a feel about a director's vision for their project," comments the Gersh Agency's Scott Yoselowin an email."* (Ariston Anderson. "Mood Reels and Lookbooks: In Today's Pitches, the Image Comes First." http://filmmakermagazine.com/66393-the-image-comes-first/#.WGGfQpIazl8. Accessed December 26, 2016)

Somebody may argue that nowadays individual voices mostly in mainstream films are not welcomed mostly because of current franchise, which has become a very robust economic model for the studios. Christopher Nolan *(Memento)*, English-American film director, producer, and screenwriter after releasing his film *Dunkirk* said: "*But I think that will change. I think that the studios have always valued freshness and new voices. Hollywood has always valued unexpected – even if Wall Street doesn't.*" (TIME, July 31, 2017, pg.55)

CHAPTER 15:
PREVISUALIZATION

Intro

In an artistic endeavor, the creative process begins with conceptualization and passes through several phases of development until completion. From the inception of the idea to its maturation, either the concept degenerates or grows. The static ones exasperate and dismantle entire projects. Since the birth of the cinema, filmmakers have striven to tell stories in the most compelling way possible. The use of previsualization in filmmaking is as old as the medium itself. Directors used previs tools to explain their vision of the film or their thought processes.

Previsualization (Previs):

PREVISUALIZATION ("Previz") is a cinematic process used by filmmakers to preview a film well in advance of principal photography. By exploring the visual aspects of a film early on, the production team is given an incredible opportunity to troubleshoot, discuss, share, and refine their cinematic approaches with each other BEFORE arriving on set, so that the entire team is focused on the same goal once production begins. Properly executed, Previz will strengthen your storytelling skills, and help you identify budget concerns, iron out editorial needs, and maximize your film's quality, while saving you time and money. Chris Olsen *(Beneath the White City Lights)* (Chris Olsen. "Previsualization." MicroFilmmaker Magazine. Iss. 61. Reprinted by permission.)

There are several of types of previsualization: 2D conceptual illustrations, 2D hand-drawn storyboard, 3D animated visualization, 3D storyboard. The ASC-ADG-VES Joint Technology Subcommittee on Pre-visualization formulated all types of previsualization. There are a number of types of previs in current practice, including *Pitchvis, Technical Previs, On-Set Previs, Postvis.* A joint subcommittee comprising members of the American Society of Cinematographers, the Art Directors Guild and the Visual Effects Society has agreed upon all definitions. Please, refer to the "Previs Glossary" which you can find on their web page.

Benefits of Previsualization:

No matter how creative you are, you have a limited amount of time, money, and creative juice to work with on any production. With this in mind, tak-

ing time to create the strongest production plan possible before the day of the shoot is just good filmmaking. If you create a strong creative base which allows your filmmaking partners to add their own enhancements, your film will be that much better. If you can iron out any concerns the team might have before you get to set, production will move that much faster. If you can identify cost concerns early, you can put backup plans into place, and make a budget decision ahead of time, not when everything is already allocated and you have nowhere to turn. PREVISUALIZATION allows the entire production team to aim in the same direction, so your Gaffer is prepared with the correct lighting and grip, your Actors fully understand their blocking, your Cinematographer can come to set with fresh framing for your shots, and your Editor can suggest shot coverage that could make for a stronger story in the edit suite. And with the entire team focused on the same goal, their unified contributions will result in a better, stronger film for you. (Chris Olsen. "Previsualization." MicroFilmmaker Magazine. Iss. 61. Reprinted by permission.)

Previsualization Tools for Film Students and Novice Filmmakers:

I am listing here previsualization tools that address the needs of scenic previsualization in students' and novice filmmakers' films.

2D hand-drawn storyboard:

Images hand drawn by a director or storyboard artist, displayed in a sequence. They are frequently inaccurate and are sometimes impossible to film.

2D Storyboarding Program:

Storyboards generated by 2D storyboarding programs, they are frequently inaccurate and are sometimes impossible to film.

Photoscript:

Still, photographs displayed in a sequence. Optically accurate previsualization. It is thoroughly grounded in the realities of locations, camera lenses, shot design and choreographed action. For more information, please refer to CHAPTER 26: PHOTOSCRIPT.

Animatic:

A series of storyboard drawings edited together and presented on screen in a sequence. Often, storyboards are animated with simple zooms and pans to simulate camera movement. These animations can be combined with sound effects, dialog, voiceover, and music to create a presentation of how a film could be shot and cut together. The end result resembles an animated version of the scene that has yet to be filmed. A lot of creative ideas can be tested this way, as well as detailed planning that can save time and money on the day of shooting. 3D animatic applications can produce pretty optically accurate previsualization of the film.

Photomatic:

Similar to an animatic, but it uses a series of still photographs edited together. Photomatics, just like animatics, are research tools to test the concept or the final product.

3D Storyboarding Programs:

Optically accurate previsualization. It uses 3D animation tools and a virtual environment. Since its introduction, *FrameForge 3D Studio* has made it possible for anyone to produce optically accurate previsualization of their film, commercial, TV show, or whatever without requiring a huge budget, intense programming knowledge, or a daunting learning curve. And by "true previsualization" they mean that when you plan your shots, what you see in the program is what you'll be able to shoot on a live set! That's because *FrameForge's* previs images are not based on forced perspective and imagination, as are 2D or clipart storyboards, but are instead thoroughly grounded in the physics of optics, film planes, and the realities of locations and camera packages.

Video-storyboard:

The most efficient and reliable previsualization tool for film students and novice filmmakers.

- Generates preliminary version of a scene or the film.

- Tests a film's idea, including a concept.

- Visually explores creative and technical solutions of the scene or film.

- Directors visualize what the finished product might look like.

- Directors choreograph the action and block performers in a real environment.

- Directors design shots within the framed environment.

- Cuts down the intended camera set-ups.

- Cuts down errors.

- Provides a means for brainstorming and generating constructive ideas.

- Communicates director's vision to a film crew for the efficient production.

- Keeps everyone on the "same page" during the production process.

When you have finished surveying this chapter, return to the beginning and read it again in more detail. Then you can proceed to the next step – starting the script visualization process. Information related to a photo script, and a video-storyboard can be found in PART III: VIDEO ASSIGNMENTS: CHAPTER 26: PHOTOSCRIPT provides instructions on how to execute a photo script, and CHAPTER 27: VIDEO-STORYBOARD provides instructions on how to execute a video-storyboard, with a thorough checklist for identifying problems.

PART II: STUDIOS – DIRECTING EXERCISES

Studios Goals

The combination of knowledge and practical experience is the key to success. These hands-on, crafted, rigorous directing exercises advance student-directors directing skills through practical studio experience. All directing exercises are designed to help student-directors develop blocking skills, discover the strong connection between blocking and the plot, character, and emotional meanings of the situation, and gain awareness of the different styles of blocking and how to tackle them on a professional level. In addition, student-directors can practice all the directorial concepts and techniques they have learned, all the directorial methods, principles, and concepts they've read in this book. Decision-making practice, originating artistic vision, and clearly articulating an artistic vision to collaborators are other benefits of these directing exercises.

Studios Outcomes:

Upon completing all in-studio directing exercises, student-directors will be able to

- Articulate the manner of narrative treatment.
- Establish and maintain the visual look all the way through the film and enhance the expressive potential of the film through visual design.
- Apply film language standards, composition principles and guidelines, visual rules and regulations, genre narrative conventions and codes of visual genre conventions, directing style conventions, stylistic patterns, and psycho-physiological regularities to shot design.
- Analyze the story elements and structural components that can be translated into a visual story.
- Recognize, analyze, and visually articulate the director's units.
- Apply different manners of sophisticated blocking and staging, staging styles, and staging-editing patterns to two-character scenes, three-character scenes, and multiple-character scenes.
- Use sophisticated visual strategies for rendering a scene based on character perspective and use a wide arsenal of different methods for modeling character perspective in the scene.
- Accommodate a visual narration to different alternations in storyteller's perspective.

- Translate inner feelings, motivations, and insights of the character to a filmable situation.
- Control and manipulate the viewers' own emotions and perceptions of fictional reality.
- Direct viewers' attention to the line of plot by screen direction and to direct and redirect the narrative flow by screen direction.
- Apply psycho-physiological regularities in left-right and right-left orientation to a shot design.

Upon completing all in-studio directing exercises, you are ready to move on and start working on the final film, a *SHORT LIVE ACTION NARRATIVE FILM*. All directing exercises aimed to teach you specific directorial skills through specific directing exercises. The final film should reflect all that you have gained from those exercises.

My experience over the years in the classroom has been that challenging students provides better results in the end. You might argue that not all film students are enthusiastic and concerned with directing, but that doesn't prevent any of you from working hard and doing your best because you will benefit from it. I would rather challenge all of you in the pursuit of your progress in directing than cater to the less-advanced or less-interested student-directors while the truly interested students just sit back. Directing exercises are excellent in teaching a single component of directing, but since films do not consist of only a single component of filmmaking, I am completely convinced that the final film will teach you more. There are no doubts that whatever your path may be, whether it is scriptwriting, editing, or producing, you will benefit from it. But first, you have to practice all directorial concepts covered in this book and the following seven directing exercises. If you concentrate on improving your skills, the quality will follow automatically.

CHAPTER 16:
I. STUDIO – APPLICATION OF GENRE CONVENTIONS

The only thing that I try to make very clear when I start a film is the genre that I want to place it in. - Wong Kar Wai, Hong Kong Film Director

In this directing exercise, student-directors will set the interpretation of the scene in a specific "territory" of the genre and practice how specific genre conventions help in enhancing the expressive potential of the scene and how those conventions comment on the narrative. This directing exercise – shooting the scene within the restrictions of a particular genre – teaches student-directors about the importance of a genre for narrative purposes and for a visual treatment of the film.

Before *proceeding* further and starting work on the I. STUDIO, review CHAPTER 2: VISUAL CONCEPT and CHAPTER 3: CONCEPT OF VISUAL UNITS. Retaining and applying the knowledge described in those two chapters will help you with this hands-on directing exercise.

"Conventional definitions of genres tend to be based on the notion that they constitute particular conventions of content (such as themes or settings) and/or form (including structure and style)." (Chandler, D. "An Introduction to Genre Theory." http://visual-memory.co.uk/daniel/Documents/intgenre/intgenre1.html.   Accessed December 28, 2016)

I encourage you to embrace this aspect of film genres and learn how to incorporate it into your own directing style. In this particular studio, you will practice how to shape one scene using a specific set of genre conventions.

I was the director of the complete season of the TV miniseries *The Goblin* (1995), which tells the stories of two children, Peter and Evka, who encounter characters from *The Adventures of Tom Sawyer*, *The Three Musketeers*, *Peter Pan*, *Snow White*, and many others. With the help of the Goblin, a magical creature who lives inside the computer, the kids are sucked into the computer screen. The Goblin guides children into the magical world of fairy tales. The TV miniseries explores themes of children's fantasy and creativity.

There are differences between designing a whole film and designing just one scene. The particular scene you will work on belongs in its entirety to the TV miniseries *The Goblin*. I have chosen the sixth scene from the first episode, which is a three-character scene. (You can find the scene in PART IV: STUDIO SCRIPTS.) The primary goal of this directing exercise is to practice establishing a genre for a separate, isolated, self-contained scene while maintaining genre consistency throughout the scene. The scene in question has nothing to do with the rest of that particular episode or the TV series as a whole, so design it accordingly. Or you can work with a scene of your own choice. The scene should be a three-character scene, two to three-page long, with a page counting as a minute of screen time.

Studio Goal:

The goal of this directing exercise is to help you to develop your narrative skills and benefit from employing some conventional approaches related to genre in designing a film.

Specification:

In this directing exercise, you are going to set the interpretation of the scene in a specific "territory" of the genre and practice how specific genre conventions help you enhance the expressive potential of the scene and how those conventions comment on the narrative.

Goals – Outcomes:

This directing exercise teaches student-directors how a manner of shaping story can be brought about by genre, and how the choices related to a genre function in relation to the narrative aesthetic effect. This directing exercise teaches student-directors about the importance of a genre for narrative purposes.

Objectives:

Student-directors will be able to efficiently use, obey, stretch, or turn a classical genre inside out, or totally deny the norms and limitations of the genre.

Assignment:

Shoot the scene within the restrictions of a particular genre. Locate your interpretation of the scene within a particular genre and design it to form an organic whole. Clearly define a solid set of the genre visual conventions you plan to use.

The class will be divided into groups of four, maximum five. Without spending any money, bring into class the props relevant to the scene. Each group will produce one scene. During the class that follows the studio class, each group will screen their directing exercise. The screening will be followed by a group discussion.

Bill of Rights:

- In groups of four or five, examine the scene that you have already verbally storyboarded and shaped based on a genre. Choose one verbal storyboard (one principal key) and one genre (solid set of genre visual conventions) or combine two or all of them based on a mutual agreement between all four/five members, and create a visual storyboard (2D or 3D storyboard), or/and shot list (whatever helps you to consolidate your intentions for shooting), and afterward, shoot the scene.
- Work jointly and together constructively.
- Participate in all crew positions, even though you are just "acting."
- Handle disagreements constructively.
- Learn how to work cooperatively with peers.

Homework – First task:

Create a *Genre Breakdown*: stylistic elements and narrative conventions that define a particular genre; critical element(s) of the genre; some other of genre's main stylistic aspects or conventions. Locate your interpretation of the scene within a particular genre and specify the characteristics of this genre. Use the chart template "Genre Breakdown" posted in PART V: QUIZZES, TESTS, CHARTS, TEMPLATES of this book.

Here is the workflow you can follow:

First step:

First, start to look at films with similar thematic, stylistic, narrative, and formal elements. Afterward, try to come up with a solid set of conventions typical for the narrative and visual style of the films you have analyzed, or simply watched. In other words, try to sum up what those films have in common (common features) in terms of a narrative style, and visual style. Or you can work backwards by selecting a theoretical category of a genre you would like to set this scene in and afterward study a group of films officially marked by this genre to come up with a solid set of conventions typical for the narrative and visual style of the films in this group.

Second step:

Start to mentally design the scene by applying the set of conventions typical for the visual style of the genre you want to employ.

Third step:

Rationalize each step and visually design the scene with the intention of highlighting the narrative and visual conventions of the particular genre.

Homework Assignment Example – First Task: Genre Breakdown – Akmaral Karbozova, Lauren Longoria:

Genre:
• Thriller
Fundamental elements of this genre: **(theme, dramatic components, narrative conventions, narrative style,** **dramatic action, dramatic structure, and tone of this genre)**
• A life-threatening situation • Common theme: innocent victims dealing with deranged antagonists • Red herrings, cliffhangers, plot twists • Suspense, excitement, surprise, anticipation, anxiety • Violence • Music to emphasize fear and rush • Ransoms, captivities, heists, revenge, kidnappings
Critical elements of this genre: **(conventional settings, conventional events, conventional roles, the** **qualities of the main character, the nature of the antagonist)**
• Ordinary protagonist placed in a dangerous situation or a trap.   His/her life is threatened. • High stakes • Villain-driven plot • Cover up important information, serial killers, stalking, paranoia
Some other main stylistic aspects and conventions of this genre: **(visual techniques, camera techniques, shot design)**
• Close-ups used to build tension and suspense and to increase intensity and uneasiness. • Tail-away shots, where the character is most off guard, such as from behind as a character is being followed or watched. • Dolly-in shots are used to push into a tighter shot when story information has been divulged, to align the audience with the character, or to show that the character is in danger. • Wide shots of the villain taken from a distance in order to conceal his identity. • Low-key lighting, shadows, and silhouettes are employed. • Low-angle shots of a villain emphasize how intimidating a villain is. • POV shots of the main character to make the audience emotionally

attached. • Using mirrors and reflections, the audience can see what the main character cannot.
Notable films:
• *Seven* • *The Silence of the Lambs* • *Enemy of the State*

Homework – Second Task:

Work out a verbal storyboard based on the concept of visual units for the scene from *The Goblin,* or a scene of your own choice. Use the template "Verbal Storyboard" posted in PART V: QUIZZES, TESTS, CHARTS, TEMPLATES. Follow instructions from CHAPTER 3: CONCEPT OF VISUAL UNITS, specifically the section "Guidelines for Creating a Verbal Storyboard in Steps."

What Students Said About the I. STUDIO – APPLICATION OF GENRE CONVENTIONS:

I thoroughly enjoyed seeing how much a genre can change one script into multiple stories that look and feel nothing alike. – Joseph Raines

The I. STUDIO (Goblin Studio) helped me to realize how important it is to establish a genre and keep a cohesive look and feel in your film, in every aspect (lighting, shots, etc.). – M. Colton Comeaux

I loved this project using the futuristic genre, and we also put a cartoon filter with aftereffects to make the greatest visual film so far at SCAD. I really enjoyed this studio. – Renee Schlosser

The written concept showed me that organization is key, and the redundancy of coverage. Every single shot must be planned beforehand, and as such, every single shot must support the genre. This studio exercise helped me understand the importance of filming according to a genre, and the techniques that support certain genres. – Sinead McGill

In writing the concept for the I. STUDIO (Goblin Studio), we were tasked with something very interesting. We chose to shoot the genre of Crime/Thriller. We carefully thought of how to apply the genre conventions. We came up with an excellent idea. – Solomon Petchenik

From this exercise, I developed a better understanding of different genres and what is required and excepted for the genre of a film. – Sean Apuzzo

CHAPTER 17:
II. STUDIO – BLOCKING IN DEPTH

A couple of years ago, when I gave my students a simple dialogue scene and asked them to break it down into individual shots, almost none of them were thinking about how blocking actors can affect the whole process. Almost every student lined a script with vertical lines drawn down the pages, indicating which takes would cover which part of the script. Most dialogue scenes between two characters, if the plan was to shift audience attention from one character to another, were structured in order to shoot multiple-shot coverage. The dialogue and action were broken down shot by shot, line by line, according to the action, character importance, or both, depending on a particular director's needs. No one thought that the same effects or similar ones could be achieved by switching the audience's attention to a specific actor through his/her movement. No one took into consideration that the size of a shot can be changed by an actor's movement toward or away from the camera, and no one took into consideration that the point of interest for the audience could be articulated through blocking.

The approach I saw was the employment of basic cinema grammar and the ABCs of coverage: *"This line of dialogue will be covered in a wide shot, and when the interest builds up, I will cut to a tighter shot."* Cuts and shots, no blocking! Mostly because of that, I came up with the idea to assign my students a dialogue-based scene with one emotional turn and ask them to shoot it in one continuous take while providing different varieties of view for mapping the emotional beats in the scene. I was surprised by the results as well as the passion my students had and still have for this directing exercise. I do believe that II. STUDIO will be an eye-opening experience for some of you in terms of the various ways you can shoot a scene and block actors.

In this directing exercise, student-directors will direct the attention of the audience to characters, plot, and emotions not by cut, but by the movement of actors and by different sizes of a shot achieved by actors' movement. The same principle extends to controlling the pace and rhythm: they are going to control the pace and rhythm by the movement of actors and by changes in sizes of a shot achieved by this movement. This directing exercise – shooting the scene in one shot – teaches student-directors how to eliminate the cut and selectively emphasize dramatic elements within one scene shot.

Before proceeding further and starting work on the II. STUDIO, review CHAPTER 5: CONTROLLING SPACE and CHAPTER 6: STAGING AND BLOCKING STRATEGIES. Retaining and applying the knowledge described in those chapters will help you with this hands-on directing exercise.

The American film theorists and film historians David Bordwell and Kristin Thompson made the interesting argument *"about the development of staging-driven cinema (often, but not only, European), as opposed to the editing-driven cinema (usually, but not invariably, American)* in the Bordwell blog. (Thompson, K. and Bordwell, D. "Observation on film art." http://www.davidbordwell.net/blog/2012/07/22/not-quite-lost-shadows/. Assessed December 28, 2016)

Stephen Prince, a professor of cinema at Virginia Tech and the author of numerous books on cinema:

Many filmmakers treat the shot as an extended unit of expression and composition. Such filmmakers as Orson Welles, Akira Kurosawa, Jean Renoir, and William Wyler favored practice of working within the boundaries of a single, extended shot (called a long take), rather than cutting among many camera set-ups (which is the normative practice in cinema) in creating a scene. At its most extreme form, this practice results in sequence shots, an entire sequence lasting several minutes done as a single, extended shot. The Hungarian filmmaker, Miklós Jancsó (Red Psalm, 1971), composes his films as a series of sequence shots; a ninety-minute film by Jancsó may contain as few as ten shots. This aesthetic practice emphasizes the structural integrity of a shot with overwhelming expressive force because the shot takes precedence over editing. In Welles's case, the sequence shot may be coupled with the deep-focus composition; in Kurosawa's, by a static camera emphasizing the hieratic positioning of the actors; in Renoir's, by a continuously moving camera that fluidly reframes the composition. In each case, the design insists upon the real time that exists within the shot and disengages it from the structured cinematic time of the rest of the film as created through editing. Admittedly, by the standards of contemporary commercial cinema, filming in long takes is a very deviant practice. Films constructed from the montage, from very quick cutting, have become the norm today in commercial cinema. Montage, however, devours the structural integrity of the shot as a unit of meaning that can stand-alone. In a montage, no shot stands alone; instead, the total gestalt produced by the montage is what counts. The expressive possibilities, which the shot enables - extension. (Prince, S. "Aesthetics of the Shot." http://www.filmreference.com/encyclopedia/Romantic-Comedy-Yugoslavia/Shots-AESTHETICS-OF-THE-SHOT.html. Accessed December 28, 2016. Reprinted by permission of the author Mr. Stephen Prince.)

Studio Goals:

- The goal of this directing exercise is to help you develop blocking skills and gain awareness and practical, creative experience with different methods and styles of blocking actors, mostly by staging in depth along the camera's Z-axis.

- Eliminating the cut and selectively emphasizing dramatic and emotional elements in one shot by the movement of the actors.

Specification:

In this directing exercise, you are going to direct the attention of the audience to characters, plot, and emotions not by cut, but by the movement of actors and by different sizes of a shot achieved by actors' movement. The same principle extends to controlling the pace and rhythm: you are going to control the pace and rhythm by the movement of actors and by changes in sizes of a shot achieved by this movement. Utilize this great tool – eliminate the cut and selectively emphasize dramatic elements within one scene shot. Try to provide a variety of visually interesting views – different shot sizes within one scene shot (a shot based on inner montage).

Goals – Outcomes:

- Main goal: figuring out how to communicate the ideas of a scene through staging and blocking in one shot.
- Articulation of scene ideas and emotions through blocking actors in depth along the camera's Z-axis.
- This directing exercise teaches student-directors how to:
  - Control the space by moving actors around.
  - Change the size of a shot by moving actors along the Z-axis.
  - Engage the audience with the events and emotions of the scene through changes of sizes of a shot achieved by moving actors along the Z-axis.
  - Align and distance the audience from a character by his/her movement toward or away from the camera.
  - Increase or decrease the emotional and dramatic intensity of the scene through physical action.
  - Control levels of emotional intensity.
  - Raise or lower the audience's emotional arousal.
  - Exaggerate the emotional impact on the audience.
  - Amplify or diminish emotions.
  - Foster intimacy and emotional attachment with a character.
  - Prevent intimacy and create emotional distance between the character and the viewer.
  - Motivate and control the movement by deeper emotions.
  - Change emotions by movement.

Objectives:

- Develop blocking and staging skills.
- Eliminate cuts and selectively emphasizing dramatic and emotional elements within one scene shot.
- Direct the audience's attention to substantial in-the-scene events and control the pace and rhythm of a scene by movement of actors.
- Articulate the audience's focus at a particular moment.
- Control the audience's perception of events and emotions in the scene.
- Engage the audience emotionally with characters and story events.
- Hold and shift the audience's attention.
- Map a character's responses to dramatic and emotional events.
- Shift the audience's perspective from a spectator to a participant.
- Consider the role that pictorial rhythm has in regard to the articulation of the audience's point of interest and comprehension of a character's emotional state.

Assignment:

Communicate the ideas and emotions of a scene through blocking actors in depth along the Z-axis.

The class will be divided into groups of three. Each group will produce one scene. During the class that follows the studio class, each group will screen their directing exercises. The screening will be followed by a group discussion.

Description of the Directing Exercise:

Blocking and staging for one static shot – scene shot, sequence shot, integral shot. The movement of actors achieves changes of shot size and different varieties of view. Usually, you figure out your camera placement based on actors' movement. This case is reversed. You have a fixed camera position, so move the actors from the background to the foreground and around. That means the position of the actors is determined entirely by the way the scene is going to be shot (one static shot), and the actors are blocked accordingly. You are not allowed to use any movement of the camera – the camera remains fixed and on a tripod, and only lens manipulation is permitted – a rack focus and/or pull focus is permissible using a constant-fixed focal length of the lens, but no zooming.

Technical Requirements for the Directing Exercise:

- Change the size of a shot by moving actors along the Z-axis
- Change the screen direction by switching a screen position of actors within a shot.
- Cover the lens by the movement of an actor.
- Uncover the lens by the movement of an actor.
- Allow an actor to pass the shot in the foreground (exit and enter) while you are keeping another actor in the background in focus.
- Allow an actor to pass the shot in the foreground in focus (exit and enter) while you are keeping another actor in the background out of focus.
- The actor can exit the shot in FS and again enter the shot in CU.
- Cover the bigger part of shot with a prop or an actor in the foreground.
- Change the camera angle by the movement of an actor.
- Clear the shot and use OS dialogue (off-screen dialogue - dialogue spoken by someone not currently seen on the screen).
- Focus on the external action. (You are going to shoot the external movement.)
- Even though you are going to shoot external movement, keep in mind the relation of external and internal action. (They interplay, they reflect each other, they feed one another – physical behavior reflects the emotional state.)
- Consider using a distinct character's rhythm.
- Try showing the action that is motivated by the conflict and by emotions.
- Try to translate inner feelings, motivations, and insights into the filmable situation – seek external events and action. (Contemplate using action or/and "film visual language" – render an inner state of mind through the visual means of film.)
- Try to visualize the inner motivation of a character – concentrate on outside events. (Don't forget that film renders the inner state of mind through outer manifestations of action.)
- Try to reveal a character's thoughts and emotions through actions.
- Motivate (justify) each change in the shot and each movement inside the shot based on character emotions and attitude.
- Justify the external action. (On the screen, you can show only what you can shoot. Look for a playable action. Try to find the inner needs of a character. The inner needs drive the action. Motivations for character movement include: spontaneity, curiosity, small job, controlling territory, discomfort, intimacy, privacy.)

- Define the character objective. (The action springs naturally from character objective and everything the actor does, as the character, must be justified by growing directly out of his/her needs.)

Instruction:

- Determine whom you want to associate the audience with, and accordingly block the scene.
- Determine the basic blocking and staging principle within one shot:
  - In depth
  - On line
- Determine how you can employ and benefit from "shot-reverse-shot pattern" within one shot.
- Determine the staging pattern within one shot:
  - Approaching and receding pattern
  - Accompanying the emotion pattern
- Determine the camera set-up based on the line of action.
- Focus on "lining up a shot" and "framing": camera placement, framing, camera angle, lens selection, and composition.
- Contemplate using different shot sizes inside one "integral shot" for a two-character scene:
  - FS – single shot
  - 2FS – two shot: OTS, fifty-fifty, front-face/selective focus, direct two shot to camera
  - 2MFS – two shot: OTS, fifty-fifty, front-face/selective focus, direct two shot to camera
  - MFS – single shot
  - 2MS – two shot: OTS, fifty-fifty, front-face/selective focus, direct two shot to camera
  - MS – single shot
  - 2CU – two shot: OTS, fifty-fifty, front-face/selective focus, direct two shot to camera
  - CU – single shot
  - ECU – single shot

    Single shot:
    - Front-face/Head-on shot
    - Profile (L, R)
    - Semi-profile (L, R, Front)
    - Semi-profile (L, R, Rear)
    - Tail-away shot

Bill of Rights:

- In groups of three, maximum four, examine the scene that you have already analyzed and verbally storyboarded. Choose one verbal storyboard or combine two or all of them based on a mutual agreement between all members and create a concept for the scene – simply how you are going to accomplish your goal. You are going to translate your concept for the scene based on the concept of visual units, mostly by staging and blocking. Since your visual means are limited (you have to design the scene for one shot), try to envision staging and blocking like you have a small box in which you have to squeeze your concept in. The box is smaller than your concept, but your concept won't be delivered to your viewers without the box. So do your best in order to communicate your idea. In other words, adjust your concept to the main "obstruction" imposed on this directing exercise, which is shooting a scene in one continuous shot, and try to achieve the same or similar result as you have originally conceived with multiple-shot coverage.
- Work jointly and constructively.
- Participate in all crew positions, even though you are just "acting."
- Handle disagreements constructively.
- Learn how to work cooperatively with peers.

Homework:

Create a verbal storyboard based on the concept of visual units for the scene you have decided to work with for the II. STUDIO. You will be able to access the scene in PART IV: STUDIO SCRIPTS.

- *Kramer vs. Kramer*
- *Closer*
- *The Bridges of Madison County*

No doubt, there are differences between designing a whole film and designing just one scene. Particular scenes you will work on belong to the entirety of the film – *Kramer vs. Kramer, Closer,* or *The Bridges of Madison County* – but for our purposes, you can take it as a separate, isolated scene, a self-contained scene. You can also work with a scene of your own choice. Choose a scene with the following list of characteristics: character-driven, dialogue-based, one emotional turn, two characters, two to three pages, with a page counting as a minute of screen time.

Do not get bogged down in too many details. Just state whom/what you want to have in the shot. Shots in your verbal storyboard do not have to inevitably indicate the size of a shot, composition, camera angle, and camera movement. You will work this out during the II. STUDIO.

Here is a workflow you can follow:

1. Determine the following:
    - Emotional state of characters
    - Emotional dynamism and intensity of the scene
    - Tension
    - Focal point
    - Fulcrum point
    - Emotional turn
    - Point of view

2. Work out a verbal storyboard based on the concept of visual units for the scene. Use the verbal template storyboard posted in PART V: QUIZZES, TESTS, CHARTS, TEMPLATES. Follow instructions from CHAPTER 3: CONCEPT OF VISUAL UNITS, specifically the section "Guidelines for Creating a Verbal Storyboard in Steps." Divide the scene into directorial units, title each directorial unit with a distinct dramatic function, and determine a pivotal beat within it. (A pivotal beat is an important beat in which the action of the scene takes a significant turn or something really important to the outcome of the scene happens. In a pivotal scene, the character makes a decision that alters the direction of the story.)

3. Try to apply and incorporate into your concept, and thereafter execute, visual strategies and techniques for creating a flat space and deep space listed in CHAPTER 5: CONTROLLING SPACE.

4. Try to apply and incorporate into your concept, and thereafter execute, visual strategies and techniques for blocking on line, blocking in depth, shot/reverse-shot pattern, approaching-and receding-pattern, accompanying-the-emotions pattern, and integral shot listed in CHAPTER 6: STAGING AND BLOCKING STRATEGIES

What Students Said About II. STUDIO – BLOCKING IN DEPTH:

Amateur filmmakers have a peculiar tendency to block and stage action on the line, in a very theatrical style. For some films, this is perfectly acceptable and works well; for most, however, it is an inappropriate style. Staging and blocking in depth is one of the magic elements of the film, which no other medium can really contend with. Try moving your actors parallel to the camera's field of vision instead of horizontally. Pull your actors away from the wall and give them space to move. You may be surprised at the wonderful things you can accomplish. – William P. Hammargren

This was our first journey as a class into the numerous studio exercises. This studio was one of the more difficult studios due to the fact that the camera could not be moved. All movement, pace, staging, blocking, and rhythm had to be achieved by the use of actor movement. We also used in-camera editing, which made things a little more difficult as well. This studio began teaching me some of the many techniques for staging and blocking. It was like a foundation of a house. This studio laid the groundwork, allowing the following studios to build our knowledge and experience from the ground up." – Jeremiah Frazier

I have learned a great deal from the studio exercises. Having to complete a number of these throughout the quarter and under strict time limitations helped me to see my progress over time and under pressure. II. STUDIO showed me my faults right away, how I was staging on line and not in depth. The fact that we could not move the camera helped too because it focused my attention on blocking. Using the blocking and movement in the frame for depth and dynamism is a tool that will stay with me forever. – Richard Webb

I couldn't understand why you wanted us to do this assignment when you knew we had so much else to worry about. In the end, however, these exercises proved to be very useful, and very applicable to every aspect of any film project I may undergo in the future. The II. STUDIO was probably the most challenging, and I think the most beneficial. That's probably why you had us do it twice. As I recall, the first attempt we made in class did not impress you. And I'm glad you made us do it again. Doing a scene in one static shot is difficult because you want to create a sense of movement and dramatic energy, but at the same time, you are not allowed to move the camera or cut to another angle at all. – Michael Lippert

Unfortunately, as we found out, we couldn't all direct, and I was happy to let someone else direct while I acted. This did not mean I did not participate in the direction of the piece, but I was not looking in the camera, and what seemed to me like depth in our shots was in fact on line on the screen. I think, all in all, the results of the studio benefited the class in a lot of ways because we had to learn from our mistakes, of which there were many. – Angela Gunn

The STUDIO II was an eye-opening experience for me. First off, I was shocked that no one lived up to the teacher's expectations. Second off, my own illustrious ego was wrong: I had failed an assignment. And last but not least, I learned a new technique for directing actors. It was a failure that taught me the most in the class. – Chris Osman

CHAPTER 18:
III. STUDIO – BLOCKING IN 360-DEGREE SPACE

Film studios are now seeking films that take artistic risks and break all the rules of conventional cinematographic practice set by traditional Hollywood filmmaking. We all have a certain perception of how comfortable we are taking risks. Think about how you deal with and handle risk, such as creative risk, intellectual risk, career and financial risk, and social and relationship risk, and try to learn about your risk profile and your risk tolerance. There are globally recognized risk profiling systems that have been widely used to help determine your personal risk tolerance. So if you lean more toward an "aggressive" risk profile, this directing exercise will definitely help you because it challenges the basic 180-degree rule. If you are risk averse and worship the invisible film technique, this exercise is exactly right for you, because it will teach you how to break the 180-degree rule legally. This is a very important studio for all of you, but all studios tend to be. When you want to learn more about the invisible film technique, please take the quiz "Invisible Technique," which can be easily located in PART V: QUIZZES, TESTS, CHARTS, TEMPLATES. This directing studio will be very useful to you all as you prepare the shot design as directors for your final film and perhaps in all future projects as well.

In this directing exercise, student-directors will practice a subjective treatment: treating the audience as participants of the dramatic situation and not as observers (shifting the audience's perspective from being a spectator to being a participant). Student-directors have to break the "stage fourth wall" and stage and block the scene with the closed proscenium, with the fourth wall of the "box set."

Before proceeding further and starting work on the III. STUDIO, review the following chapters: CHAPTER 6: STAGING AND BLOCKING STRATEGIES, CHAPTER 7: MULTIPLE-CHARACTER SCENE, and CHAPTER 8: DEMYSTIFYING THE 180-DEGREE RULE – CROSSING THE LINE. Retaining and applying the knowledge described in those three chapters will help you with this hands-on directing exercise.

Good composition is the best arrangement of the subject matter in sympathy with the function of the shot. It should have simplicity and intensity and achieve its objective with clarity, precision and economy. (Ward, P. *Picture Composition for Film and Television*, 2nd edition. Focal Press, 2003, ISBN: 0240516818)

Studio Goal:

The goal of this studio is to help you develop blocking skills, discover the strong connection between blocking and the plot, character, and emotional meanings of the situation, and gain awareness of the different styles of blocking, by staging and blocking in a 360-degree space.

Specification:

Aspiring and novice film directors will learn the most effective blocking in this particular studio and build a huge inventory of different techniques of blocking, and more experienced directors will lift their blocking skills to the higher level. This studio also helps to build skills when dealing with multi-character scenes.

Goals – Outcomes:

- This directing exercise teaches student-directors how to stage, block, and shoot multi-character scenes in a 360-degree space, and how to get rid of the fear of breaking the 180-degree rule.

Objectives:

- Develop of blocking and staging skills.
- Master different strategies of blocking and staging multi-character scenes in a 360-degree space so that student-directors learn how to
    - Learn proper 180-degree rule handling.
    - Benefit from breaking the fourth stage wall - staging and blocking a situation with a closed proscenium, with the fourth wall of the "box set."
    - Benefit from crossing the line (adding physical, psychological, and emotional dynamism and energy to the scene).
    - Establish and favor the subjective manner of treatment over the objective treatment
    - Follow the formal paradigm of the classical invisible style and conceal the breaking the 180-rule.
    - Break a set of guidelines that the films tend to follow and still employ the classical invisible style.
    - Benefit from compositional stereotypes.
    - Reject conventional visual and narrative codes.

Assignment:

Staging, blocking, and shooting a multiple-character scene in a 360-degree space.

The class will be divided into groups of four (five max). Each group will produce one scene. During the class that follows the studio class, each team will analyze the directing exercise of another team. You will be asked to identify the technique that was used for crossing the line, so make sure that your own work is carefully conceptualized and accordingly executed.

Description of the Directing Exercise:

This scene must be very well established. You are not allowed to "fish" for a shot here (casting simultaneously with a few fishing rods and hoping that something will get caught). In this exercise, you are not allowed to shoot "coverage." "Dump-truck directing" and "shotgun moviemaking" is forbidden! You have to design each shot individually and uniquely in context of the entire scene. Don't use "all-purpose coverage!" Don't fish! Each shot should have a clear and relevant intention behind it. Pay attention to sightlines. Create a very clear plan when you want to have a new shot. Do not shoot the scene in one continuous take – use multi-shots. Move the character through space – from the background to the foreground and around (like you did in the II. STUDIO). Move the camera around your character and keep the audience oriented.

Note: Each time you cause a disorienting effect, your grade for this directing exercise will be lowered by an entire letter grade.

Technical Requirements for the Directing Exercise:

- Break the "stage fourth wall." (Block and stage in 360-degree space: staging and blocking with the closed proscenium, with the fourth wall of the "box set.")
- Cross the line. (Use all techniques that can be used for crossing the line; refer to CHAPTER 8: DEMYSTIFYING THE 180-DEGREE RULE – CROSSING THE LINE.)
- Adjust the eye line of actors in a single shot.
- You are allowed to use any movement of the camera. Lens manipulation – a rack focus and/or pull focus – is also permissible, as well as zooming.
- Break a consistent screen direction of all characters throughout the scene. Do you recall the rule of thumb noted earlier: the "closed box" results in a more subjective treatment (the viewers are treated as par-

ticipants of the situation), the alternation of screen direction brings dynamism to the scene?

- Try to cross the line as many times as you can, at least six times, each time using a different strategy.
- You can rewrite the lines, and you don't have to follow the scene description, scene action, and parenthetical directions.
- It is not about lighting or technical execution of the shot, not even about actor's performance. (You don't need a full-out performance; you are going to shoot the blocking.)
- Determine everything stated below in the instruction section.

Instruction:

- Determine the basic blocking and staging principle.
- Determine the staging style.
- Determine the staging-editing pattern.
- Determine the camera set-up based on the line of action.
- Determine an emotional meaning of the situation.
- Keep continuity of action.
- Keep spatial orientation. (Three-dimensional continuity/spatial continuity and demand for solid spatial orientation must be satisfied.)
    - Spatial relation between shots (convergence of the eye lines from shot to shot)
    - Screen direction (Do not maintain consistent screen direction of all performers throughout the scene and keep viewers oriented where the performers are in relation to one another. Do not treat the space by staying only on one side of the line of action and try to avoid a disorienting effect.)
    - Eye lines have to match (leveling the eye line – a) adjusting the camera angle, tilt and height; b) adjusting an actor eye line looking at camera height or above or below; c) cheating the eye line – adjusting the eye line of an on-screen actor in a single shot to an off-screen actor. The eye-line in a single shot is slightly closer to the lens than in an OTS shot.
- Use various shot sizes.

Homework:

Carefully review all instruction in CHAPTER 8: DEMYSTIFYING THE 180-DEGREE RULE – CROSSING THE LINE before you attempt to break down the scene into individual shots.

Create a floor plan, a visual storyboard (2D or 3D storyboard), and a shot list that will help you to consolidate your intentions for blocking and shooting the scene you have decided to work with for the III. STUDIO. You will be able to access the scenes in PART IV: STUDIO SCRIPTS. You can also work with a scene of your own choice. Choose a scene with the following list of characteristics: character-driven, dialogue-based, one emotional turn, two or three characters, two to three pages, with a page counting as a minute of screen time.

- *Sex, Lies, and Videotape*
- *Closer*
- *The Notebook*

Your in-studio directing exercise has to fulfill the requirements stated above in the section "Technical Requirements for the Directing Exercise." Also, pay attention to the section "Instruction" above.

Note: Without spending any money, bring into class the props relevant to the scene you will work on.

Here is the workflow you can follow:

The written homework is the individual homework assignment; shooting a directing exercise is a group project.

First step: floor plan

Draw the floor plan. In it, depict each character's position and indicate the camera set-up for each shot by drawing a camera symbol (outline or solid, depending on whether you plan to have a static shot or shot with camera movement.) The floor plan has to show the camera path and the choreography required to stage the action and block the camera movement in the scene.

Second step: visual storyboard (2D hand-drawn storyboard or generated by 2D storyboarding program or 3D Storyboarding Programs)

Assign a particular shot to each camera set-up as an output from the camera. Draw a sketch for each shot. Sketches must show the size of the shot and content of the shots. If you have envisioned a shot in movement, you are supposed to draw two sketches for that particular shot – the opening composition of the shot and the closing composition of the shot. For a static shot, draw just one sketch.

Third step: shot list

Create a shot list and then point out the technique you are using for crossing the line and state the justification for crossing the line. Also, state what you intend to employ from the II. STUDIO – STAGING AND BLOCKING IN DEPTH. The shot list chart is posted in PART V: QUIZZES, TESTS, CHARTS, TEMPLATES. The shot list will help you to consolidate your ideas, stay organized, and stay focused on your goals.

Before you work on a shot list, try to determine:

- Emotional state of characters
- Emotional dynamism and intensity of the scene
- Focal point (associative point, point of interest, alignment)
- Fulcrum point (The critical moment – the most important moment in a scene, sometimes in the whole story. It can be character's realization.)
- Pivotal moment
- Emotional turn
- Point of view
- Divide the scene into directorial units, title each directorial unit with a distinct dramatic function, and determine a pivotal beat within it

What Students Said About the III. STUDIO – BLOCKING IN 360-DEGREE SPACE:

Planning out why we were breaking the 180 line and for what reasons (beats) was really quite interesting. It made me really think outside the box as far as shot design goes. It's usually very easy for me to design my shots in OTSs and medium shots and close-ups, but thinking of how I was going to cross the line now makes me think about how different kinds of shots could be more interesting. – Joseph C. Bauer

This was the most complicated planning session yet, and I was grateful to have collaborators. We broke down the scene to find the important beats again and decided that each of our six "line crossings" would happen on one of those beats. Then we determined what type of line cross would be most appropriate given the beat, and sketched a rough floor plan. – Nick Livanos

Highlighted the utmost importance of previsualization in terms of crossing the line – and the visual nature of the written concept really helped my understanding. Actually, doing it seemed to bring me right back to square one of insecurity with the concept, but by the end of the exercise, I understood it pretty concretely, particularly how imperative it is to motivate a move or jump across the line. – Sinead McGill

When shooting the Studio III exercise, the value of shot listing and story-boarding became very apparent. I was immediately able to see the design of the shot. I was able to execute it very well. I will forever apply this to my work. I successfully created the scene. – Solomon Petchenik

I also learned a great deal from watching other students' work. I began to see how the other students are blocking and understand similar strengths and weaknesses amongst the class. This helped me a lot because I get to judge my blocking methods by looking at other work in the same conditions. – Richard Webb

In the STUDIO III, I learned about the economy of camera manipulation within a script. It had never occurred to me that during the first part of the film, the shots, set-ups, and the story have yet to be fully revealed. This relates to another lesson I have pulled from the narrative as well as all of my other film classes: keep it simple. – Chris Osman

My group's first attempt at this studio was a failure, so we attempted a second time and failed again. In the end, the failure of this studio turned out not to be a failure at all, but a great learning experience. I learned a tremendous deal from failing, and I was perfectly fine with that. Victory even in defeat. – Jeremiah Frazier

CHAPTER 19:
IV. STUDIO – MODELING CHARACTER PERSPECTIVE

In CHAPTER 9: CONCEPT OF CHARACTER PERSPECTIVE, I said:

> *A director makes critical choices in designing each scene, and the decision about character perspective is one of the most important that a director makes. The character's attitude, feelings, emotions, thoughts, perspectives, or unique view of the situation or world lead the scene. The narrative, emotional, and psychological importance of a character can be achieved by emphasizing his/her visual dominance within the shot, within the scene, within the film.*

In this directing exercise, student-directors will develop the scene out of the character perspective. They have to come up with a clear plan, how they are going to articulate the character perspective visually, how they are going to interpret the concept visually, how they are going to use a change in a visual pattern when they want to execute a switch in character perspective, how they are going to use a change in visual pattern, when they want to map emotional beats.

This directing exercise teaches student-directors:

- how to manipulate the audience's perception
- how to stimulate the audience's emotions
- how to modify, control, and regulate the audience's own emotions
- how to control the audience's perception of story events
- how to control and regulate the level of response to characters and story events how to engage the audience with the story events and with characters' emotions
- how to make the audience emotionally invested
- how to keep the audience emotionally invested
- how to form a bond between a viewer and character
- how to physicalize characters' emotions, thoughts, feelings, dilemmas, and attitudes
- how to show how a character views the situation or world around him/her
- how to signal transitions to memories and reminiscences of a character
- how to articulate the emotional focus of the scene
- how to map emotional beats
- how to favor one character over another
- how to visualize emotional transitions, dramatic twists, turning points, fulcrum points, and pivotal moments

Before proceeding further and starting the IV. STUDIO, review CHAPTER 9: CONCEPT OF CHARACTER PERSPECTIVE. Retaining and applying the knowledge described in that chapter will help you with this hands-on directing exercise.

Studio Goal:

- Visual articulation and execution of the character's perspective within a self-contained scene.
- Practicing different methodology and visual strategy for rendering a scene based on character perspective.
- Practicing different effective ways of communicating the narrative, emotional, and psychological importance of a character to the audience.
- In this directing exercise, you will utilize diverse varieties of visual factors for emphasizing a character's narrative dominance, externalizing a character's emotional state, physicalizing character's interiority, manifesting a character's thought process, drawing the audience's attention to a character's unique view of the world, or simply showing how a character views the situation around him/her.
- The goal of this studio is to make the transition from the scripted word to conceptualizing an entirely visual story, a story where the film's narrative and themes are supported by all aspects of filmmaking. You will begin to formulate your own visual schematic for scenes you will be directing in future.

Specification:

Since directors can control and regulate viewers' perceptions of a scene through visual narrative, student-directors have to master the *concept of character perspective* and its execution. *Strategies and Methodologies for Modeling Character Perspective* in the scene will help student-directors better articulate and communicate a scene's ideas and better direct viewers' attention where they want.

Goals – Outcomes:

- Articulation of character perspective and communication of it through staging, blocking, shot design, and camera treatment.

Objectives:

- Student-directors will be able to more closely align the audience with characters' attitudes, feelings, emotions, thoughts, perspectives, and points of view.
- Student-directors will be able to render the subjective state of a character (inner state of mind) through visual means.
- Student-directors will be able to transport the audience to the inner life of the character through visual means.
- By mastering the *concept of character perspective* and practicing it in this particular directing exercise, student-directors will be able to:
  - Articulate a point of interest for the audience (associative point)
  - Align the audience with a character
  - Distance the audience from a character
  - Favor one character over another one
  - Visualize a character's emotional attachment or distance to another character
  - Articulate an emotional focus of a scene
  - Physicalize and externalize emotions, thoughts, feelings, and attitudes of characters
  - Signal a transition to memories and reminiscences of a character
  - Visualize a narrator's attitudinal point of view (judgments)
  - Accommodate the audience's ability to understand a story and characters
  - Establish a subjective manner of treatment
  - Visualize emotional transitions
  - Visualize emotional and dramatic twists, turning points, and fulcrum points
  - Visualize a character's transformation
  - Map emotional beats in a scene
  - Emphasize the dramatic and emotional intensity of a story
  - Evoke empathy, sympathy or interest for character

Assignment:

Modeling character perspective in a scene through shot design.

The class will be divided into groups of three. Each group will produce three scenes. During the class that follows the studio class, each student will screen his/her directing exercise. The screening will be followed by a group discussion.

Description of the Directing Exercise:

You must control the audience's perception of events and emotions in the scene. The decision of how to engage the audience with the events and emotions of a scene is your first and most important decision in visual storytelling. This decision will help you to break down a scene into individual shots or help you decide where to put the camera.

Instruction:

Even though the primary goal in this directing exercise is the articulation of a character perspective, take into consideration everything stated below:

- Determine the basic blocking and staging principle
  - In depth
  - On line
- Determine the staging style.
  - Shot-reverse-shot pattern
  - Shots based on the inner montage
  - Integral shot, scene shot, sequence shot
- Determine the staging-editing pattern
  - Approaching and receding pattern
  - Accompanying the emotion pattern
- Determine the camera set-up based on the line of action.
- Focus on "lining up a shot" and "framing": camera placement, framing, camera angle, lens selection, and composition.
- Determine if using static and moving shots will result in all of the above. Also, determine the type and needs of the action in other types of shots used in the scene and the rhythm of the action of the whole scene.

Homework:

Write a one-page concept for character perspective for the scene you have decided to work with for the IV. STUDIO. You will be able to access the scenes in PART IV: STUDIO SCRIPTS. You can also work with a scene of your own choice. Choose a scene with the following list of characteristics: character-driven, dialogue-based, one emotional turn, two characters, two to three pages, with a page counting as a minute of screen time.

- *Kramer vs. Kramer* (consistent character perspective)
- *Closer* (fluid character perspective)

- *Still Life* (fluid character perspective) written by Noël Peirce Coward
- *The Bridges of Madison County* (neutral stance)

Like with all studios, going from paper to screen will help you tremendously in your understanding of the goals of the directing exercise.

Develop the scene based on the concept of character perspective and state how you plan to interpret it visually. Elaborate accordingly on all six components below and number them.

Here is the workflow you can follow:

1. Clearly articulate either a consistent character perspective based on Ted's character or Joanna's character (*Kramer vs. Kramer,* or two-character scene of your own choice), or the fluid character perspective in the scene with one legible switch from one focal character to another focal character (*Closer, Still Life,* or two-character scene of your own choice), or a neutral stance *(The Bridges of Madison County,* or two-character scene of your own choice).

2. Justify the character perspective, and in case of applying the fluid character perspective, justify a switch in character perspective.

3. Clearly state what you want to achieve in terms of emotions, which feelings you want to evoke, which feelings the audience has to understand, and how you plan to modify, control, and regulate viewers' emotions.

   - *How do you want your audience to feel?*
   - *What it is that your audience should feel?*
   - *Which feelings do you want to evoke within viewers?*
   - *What feeling do you want to engender and/or grow in the audience?*
   - *Which feelings does the audience have to understand?*
   - *What emotion do you want to elicit, and ultimately, what do you want to communicate to the audience?*
   - *With whom does the audience share feelings?*
   - *Which emotional response do you expect from the audience?*
   - *What is the emotional dynamic of the scene?*

4. Explain how you intend to communicate the concept through shot design and camera treatment. Clearly specify all visual factors you will use for emphasizing a character's narrative dominance, externalizing a character's emotional state, manifesting a character's thought process, drawing attention to a character's unique view of the world, or simply showing how a character views the situation around

him/her. There are some factors and some visual elements that you must consider in designing your scene, like visual weight, depth of field, lines, frame within the frame, color coding, and distorted image. Try to employ as many factors and visual elements as you can. Which method you employ depends upon what you will try to accomplish with your scene in terms of character perspective, as well as how you want the audience to feel about the character.

5. Determine the camera set-ups.
   (Go over the "Instruction" section and try to apply everything to the scene. Also, state what you intend to employ from II. STUDIO – STAGING AND BLOCKING IN DEPTH, and III. STUDIO – BREAKING THE STAGE FOURTH WALL.) It can be done in narrative. Floor plans are optional.

6. Incorporate into your written concept and execute the change in a visual pattern. A "turning point," an "emotional turn," or a "fulcrum point" has to be accompanied by the change in visual pattern. See the segment *"Shift in Character Perspective"* in CHAPTER 9: concept of character perspective. Utilize the change in a visual pattern for visualizing a switch in character perspective.

Recommendation:

Consolidate all possible solutions down. If you think that working on a verbal storyboard, floor plan, shot list, and 2D or 3D storyboard can help you better consolidate your ideas and help you stay organized and focused on your goal, work on it as well. Choose what best suits your needs.

I want to make sure that everyone understands the given homework, so let me sum it up:

- Create a concept for the character perspective for the particular scene. Develop the scene out of the character perspective and state how you plan to interpret it visually, how you plan to articulate the character perspective visually, how you plan to use a change in visual pattern, when you want to map emotional beats, and when you want to execute a switch in character perspective, map a fulcrum point, or map an emotional turn. Simply write down how you plan to achieve your goals.

- During studio class, each student will direct his/her concept and portray one of two characters in a directing exercise of his/her teammates' work.

- IV. STUDIO directing exercise is NOT a group project. Each one of you will shoot your own project with the help of your group members, so each one of you should have separate homework to hand in.
- Have a clear plan for each shot you plan to shoot and be prepared because you only have 1/3 of the class time to get your footage before you have to hand the camera over to your teammate.

Note: Without spending any money, bring to studio class the props relevant to the scene you will work on.

Sample of Student's Written Homework for the Scene from *Kramer vs. Kramer* – Franz Gatzke

1. *Articulate Character Perspective Based on One Character or Another for the Scene from* Kramer vs. Kramer*:*
   I intend to use a consistent character perspective. I've chosen for this to be Ted's scene.

2. *Justify Character Perspective:*
   Aligning the audience with Ted will allow them to experience his range of emotions during this surprising break up. He has significant emotional shifts in the scene, while Joanna seems to remain emotionally consistent.

3. *Emotions and Feelings That the Audience Must Understand and How I'm Going to Create Them:*
   I want the audience to feel sympathy for Ted and identify with him. I want them to share his feelings of disbelief, desperation, and frustration. He expects to come home and celebrate, but that is instantly disrupted by Joanna's declaration that she's leaving him. The audience has to understand that Ted is initially more irritated that he has to deal with a moody wife than he is worried that she's going actually to leave. When her serious demeanor brings him to realize that she's not just making threats, the audience must also feel this change in emotion. This is the pivotal moment when Ted becomes apologetic and concerned that this isn't just a quick-fix situation. She continues what she set out to do, and Ted becomes increasingly desperate. He tries warning her, and when that gets him nothing, he panics.

4. *Intended Communication of Concept Through Shot Design and Camera Treatment:*
   To highlight these emotional beats in Ted's character, I chose to limit Joanne's screen appearances to profiles, long shots, soft focus, or not even cutting to her at all. After Ted enters the scene first, she passes

quickly across the screen, telling him that she's leaving, but we stay on Ted for his delayed reaction. Handheld camera movement and blocking will bring Ted into a CU as he realizes what she just said. As Joanna moves behind us off screen, Ted's eyes follow, crossing the camera and establishing a new line. When he walks towards her, we can stay close to him by panning around 180 degrees, revealing Joanne in the kitchen in soft focus. From there, we cut to a CU of Ted weakly apologizing for being late. Ted's eye line crosses the camera again while she continues completing her checklist. We pan over into a 2S as she enters the right of frame in profile. She says she took $2000 out of their account and again walks off into the background into soft focus. Ted stays in the CU for a moment, frozen. From there, we cut to the reverse shot. Joanne exits the frame past us, and Ted walks from the background into a CU during his genuine apology. This gets us close to him during an emotional shift, as he completely changes his tone. She doesn't buy it and heads for the door, causing him to leave the frame. He chases her into a 2S, closing the door and begging for an explanation. She gives an answer and exits, leaving him alone in CU and distorted image through the door.

5. *Camera Set-ups*
   From II. STUDIO – BLOCKING AND STAGING IN DEPTH, I will be using changes in shot size as characters travel along the Z-axis. Ted's importance will dominate because he'll be traveling towards camera into tighter shots, while Joanna will be traveling away from the camera into wider shots. Lessons from II. III. STUDIO – BREAKING THE FOURTH WALL will be employed as well. I will be using character movement, camera movement, eye lines, and shot-reverse-shot pattern to use the entire 360-degree space and cross the line. Character movement will allow them to alternate position in the frame, with the goal of putting Ted on our left to aid us in aligning the audience with him.

6. *Change in Visual Pattern*
   The fulcrum point, where Ted realizes that Joanna really is going to leave, will be marked by the shift in visual pattern from nearly static shots to moving shots. Also, we will go from wider shots to tighter shots either with cutting or blocking in depth.

Sample of Student's Written Homework for the Scene from *Closer* – Francesca Crichton

1. *Articulate Character Perspective Based on One Character or Another*
   Throughout the scene in Closer, I want to portray a consistent character perspective in order to experience the scene through the heightened

emotions and dialogue that Larry and Anna are experiencing. In this scene, the truth and reality of their marriage is revealed: Larry has cheated on Anna, and Anna has also had an affair. Even though they are both in the wrong, I choose to make Larry's perspective privileged because I want the audience to feel the shock, betrayal, and distance he has experienced with his wife. In doing so, the audience will be able to go further into his head and understand his side of the situation and why this moment is a crucial point for him as a character.

2. *Justify Character Perspective:*
    This scene is not only a crucial turning point in Larry and Anna's relationship but also for Larry as a character. By maintaining a consistent perspective, I will allow the audience to ally with Larry in order to create tension not only between the couple but also between the viewers and Anna.

3. *Emotions and Feelings That the Audience Must Understand and How I'm Going to Create Them:*
    It is important for the audience to feel exactly what Larry is experiencing in this scene: betrayal from his wife. I want them to be able to relate to the situation even if they haven't actually experienced something like this before. I will aim to show them what it's like to free yourself from what you once thought you loved. I am going to create this "mood" that consists of feelings/emotions by making Anna linger further and further away from Larry all throughout the scene to go with the mindset of finally taking that one step and saying goodbye. I want to give her the spotlight sometimes, while also making all her lines look ridiculous. I want to use OTS/POV like we were taught in class, but I also want close-ups for reactions to fill the studio with tension.

4. *Intended Communication of Concept Through Shot Design and Camera Treatment:*
    I intend to start the scene in medium close-ups and a couple of wide shots. I'll do this to show the distance between the characters, not only physically but also to symbolize the distance in their relationship. But as the scene intensifies, I want to transition into close-ups of Larry to demonstrate his aggression and emotions while also bringing the audience closer to him. In contrast to this, I will keep Anna in medium/medium close-ups to show her distance from what is happening and disinterest in her current relationship.

5. *Camera Set-ups*
    I want to utilize the staging and blocking that we learned in Studio I in this particular scene. The beginning of the scene will be static (like their emotions), and then, as the mood and emotions intensify, so will the blocking within the scene. I want to close the fourth wall to create tension between these two lonely characters. I want Anna looking off into the distance, out of frame, because she can't look at Larry (when she isn't staring at Larry, she is staring at her future). Considering the previous idea, I want also to frame Larry in a certain way, either taking up the negative space or in the BG of shots.

6. *Change in Visual Pattern*
    As I've stated before, I intend on beginning the scene with medium close-ups, progress to close-ups, and the end in a wide shot. This will be accompanied by static blocking that progressively becomes more dynamic to emphasize Larry's emotional progression from feeling guilty to angry and betrayed. I will signal the turning point of the scene when Larry's tone changes, as his framing begins to consist of low-angle shots and close-ups.

What Students Said About IV. STUDIO – MODELING CHARACTER PERSPECTIVE

The STUDIO IV was interesting in that it required a certain amount of homework revolving around something I rarely considered before: character perspective. The assignment forced me to consider whom the audience should associate with. This aided in freeing me from my objective habits and started me en route to subjectivity. Immediately after writing the assignment out, I changed a series of shots in both my final project and my senior project and, in my opinion, pushed the quality of the project higher.
– Chris Osman

By STUDIO IV, I felt I had a basic and fundamental grasp on blocking. I felt comfortable working with the line of action and knew what to do if I wanted to cross it. This may have been where I saw some real improvement, and I saw a more confident approach to my blocking techniques. – Richard Webb

STUDIO IV was the studio I think we were most prepared for and able to do out of all the studios up to this point. We were able to utilize the skills and theory we had learned in STUDIO II and III to create the best piece of work that we did in the studios this semester. We didn't have spent as much time blocking the scene before shooting because we had more of an idea of where to place the camera around the actors in order to create the depth and size of shots we wanted. – Angel Gunn

The shifting of character perspective is a subtle and tricky thing. STUDIO IV forced me to rethink a scene I had conceived before. Going back over allowed me to distill the scene to its essence, creating a minimalistic but more effective film. – Manuel Valdivia

CHAPTER 20:
V. STUDIO - ALTERNATION IN STORYTELLER'S PERSPECTIVE

I like a good story well told. That is the reason I am sometimes forced to tell them myself. - Mark Twain, American writer *(The Adventures of Tom Sawyer)*

In this directing exercise, students-directors try to master different narrative techniques for articulating the classical paradigms: attached/detached narrator, biased/unbiased narrator, the reliable/unreliable narrator, judgmental or effaced narrator. This directing exercise teaches student-directors how to use diverse visual strategies and make the implied narrator either virtually invisible or how to make the overtly manipulative narrator visible. This directing exercise teaches student-directors how to affect the audience's responses to characters and the story through *Storyteller's Perspective*. In this directing exercise, student-directors translate and/or modify Storyteller's Perspective, which is imprinted in a screenplay to the screen, and accordingly decide on the manner of narrative treatment.

Before *proceeding* further and starting working on the V. STUDIO, review the CHAPTER 10: CONCEPT OF STORYTELLER'S PERSPECTIVE. Retaining and applying the knowledge described in that chapter will help you with this hands-on directing exercise.

You will try to figure out your own way around filmmaking without realizing that some of your "discoveries" have already been discovered. The *Concept of storyteller's perspective* is one of them. Do not lose your precious time by digging for something that is already at your disposal. Just reach for it and use it!

Studio Goal:

- To accommodate the visual narrative to different alternations in a storyteller's perspective.
- To use different narrative strategies and narrative techniques in visual narrative related to storyteller's perspective.
- To align a manner of visual treatment with the subjectivity in storyteller's perspective.
- To use diverse visual strategies and make the implied narrator (low profile narrator) virtually invisible.
- To use diverse visual strategies and make the overtly manipulative narrator (high profile narrator) visible.

- To master different narrative techniques for articulating the classical paradigms: attached/detached narrator, biased/unbiased narrator, the reliable/unreliable narrator, judgmental or effaced narrator.
- To manipulate the audience's perception through a storyteller's perspective.

Specification:

The audience's responses to characters and story events are influenced by storyteller's perspective. In this directing exercise, you are going to affect the audience's reaction to characters and story events through storyteller's perspective.

In this directing exercise, you are going to modify and alter storyteller's perspective. This directing exercise will also teach you that the modification and/or alternation of the scripted storyteller's perspective can:

- heighten the emotional impact of the story on the audience
- enhance the audience's emotional experience
- produce additional responses from the audience to characters and story events
- strengthen a weak story
- accommodate the psychological immersion – the audience's ability of being transported into the story

Goals - Outcomes:

- Visualizing the alternation of storyteller's perspective through staging, blocking, shot design, and camera treatment.
- This directing exercise teaches student-directors how to affect the audience's responses to characters and the story through storyteller's perspective.

Objectives:

- Student-directors will be able to translate scripted storyteller's perspective to the screen.
- Student-directors will be able to control the film narration through storyteller's perspective.
- Student-directors will be able to choose the appropriate storyteller's perspective or modify or change scripted/existing storyteller's perspective to accommodate the emotional and dramatic needs of the story.

- Student-directors will be able to control the audience's responses to characters through storyteller's perspective.
- Student-directors will be able to help the audience to interpret the events and emotions through storyteller's perspective.
- Student-directors will be able to fix discontinuous or broken narrative in post-production by modifying or changing the storyteller's perspective.

Assignment:

Practicing different narrative and visual treatments in transforming five different *Storyteller's perspectives* to the screen. You will alter storyteller's perspective five times in this directing exercise.

The class will be divided into groups of three, maximum four and that depends on if you plan to work on a two or three-character scene. V. STUDIO directing exercise is NOT a group project. Each one of you will shoot your own project with the help of your group members, so each one of you should have separate homework to hand in. Each student will screen his/her directing exercise. The screening will be followed by a group discussion.

Description of the Directing Exercise:

You have to write a scene employing five different storyteller's perspectives, and then decide on narrative treatment and visual treatment, which will help you to transform a specific storyteller's perspective to the screen, and then you will shoot it.

Technical Requirements for the Directing Exercise:

Even some of the storyteller's perspectives might look similar to you, but there are certain noticeable differences. Construct each section of your V. STUDIO by applying the narrative concept of storyteller's perspective. Each section has to be distinctively separated with the information for the credits about storyteller's perspective displayed on a card.

1st section: First person perspective - limited
2nd section: First person perspective - extended
3rd section: Third person perspective - covert narrator (anonymous narrator)
4th section: Third person perspective - the overt narrator - Off-screen (Inisible)
5th section: Third person perspective - the overt narrator - On-screen (Visible)

Homework:

Write a one paragraph long Concept for each storyteller's perspective you will employ in the V. STUDIO. You are supposed to have 5 short sections in this STUDIO, each section based on a different storyteller's perspective. (See the Requirements below)

1. You can take any Studio (II. STUDIO, III. STUDIO or IV. STUDIO) in its entirety and use it to demonstrate a particular storyteller's perspective.

2. You can use a portion(s) from each STUDIO and use it (them) to demonstrate a particular storyteller's perspective.

3. You can take any studio in its entirety and use it to show a particular storyteller's perspective. If something must be added (voice-over, interior monologue, commentary) for making the storyteller's perspective more distinguishable, utilize the studio time of the V. STUDIO for it.

4. You can pick one STUDIO (the work which came from the STUDIO) from the past and cut it up into segments illustrating one of the storyteller's perspective. You can utilize the studio time for taking pick-ups or reshooting some parts or just recording the voice over, or interior monologue or commentary, in order to show a particular *Storyteller's perspective*.

5. You can make up a new scene(s), and link it (them) to the rest of your material.

6. You can utilize your footage (shots) from previous STUDIOS and utilize the Studio time just for shooting needed pickups or reshoots.

7. You can use the script(s) from the past studios and shoot a completely new scene applying the concept of the storyteller's perspective. For that purpose, you have to break the scene up into five segments.

8. You can write a new scene.

9. You can combine all of the above-listed practices.

Here is the workflow you can follow:

Let's say you want to follow the idea described in point five above: "*You can make up a new scene(s), and link it (them) to the rest of your material.*" Suppose you have worked with the scene *Kramer vs. Kramer* for IV. STUDIO – MODELING CHARACTER PERSPECTIVE. You have extremely good material to use in this scene for demonstrating the *First Person Perspective – Extended* by just adding the voice over of Joanna or Ted. It depends on from whose perspective you have narrated this scene. Let's assume you "gave" this scene to Joanna. Then, you can make up a new scene when Joanna is alone at home waiting for Ted and cut in this new scene in front of the scene you worked on and apply to it the *First Person Perspective – Limited*. Thereafter, you can make up another new scene when Joanna leaves the apartment and Ted stays alone, and cut in this new scene after the two scenes you have already connected and apply it to the *Third Person Perspective - Covert Narrator.* Now, when your two characters are apart, one of them could meet you - by you I mean you the Director as a next lover - and all of a sudden you can turn toward the camera and address the audience. By executing this, you have a *Third Person Perspective - Overt Narrator - On-screen.* All four of these scenes can be framed (bookended) as a whole by the *Third Person Perspective - Overt Narrator - Off-screen (Commentator).* By doing this, you have met all requirements for this STUDIO, since you have 5 different storyteller's perspectives there.

Note:

You don't have to care about the consistency of storyteller's perspective in the V. STUDIO. Actually, there cannot be a consistency! This Directing exercise is designed to help you visually articulate different variants of storyteller's perspective and practice a visual translation of those perspectives to the screen. So, feel free to model the scene in any way that you want. Do not forget that there is a direct link between the way the events are presented and the way they are visually narrated. It is not sufficient to just add voice-over narration to the material, which has been treated objectively, and believe that you have a very subjective first-person perspective narration. The scene should be shot subjectively.

Recommendation:

Review the CHAPTER 9: CONCEPT OF CHARACTER PERSPECTIVE, particularly the section *"Methodology and visual strategy for rendering a scene based on character perspective"* You can apply some visual solutions for rendering a character's perspective in a scene for articulating a *Storyteller's perspective.*

Sample of Student's Written Homework - Tyler J. Kupferer

For V. STUDIO, I choose to demonstrate the various storyteller perspectives throughout a single narrative, switching perspectives as the story progresses. This particular story is one I wrote to satisfy the needed story changes in V. STUDIO, simply about a young man's attempt to acquire a bottle from an evil wizard.

Because three out of the five storyteller perspectives are based on my character, Tyler, the shots are designed to favor Tyler the majority of the time subjectively. The scene begins with a close up of old Tyler's face as he enters the room and pulls back to establish the area in which he is reminiscing. Then, another close-up shot of Tyler's face is shown to increase empathy with the character, as the narrative enters a flashback. Shot A is repeated at the beginning of the flashback, only now with young Tyler. Shot B is also repeated, to show that this flashback is taking place in the same location with the younger character.

At this point, we switch from First Person Perspective Extended to First Person Perspective Limited to show Tyler's direct point of view as he is experiencing the scene. Once Tyler is on the floor, the perspective switches to Third Person Perspective Covert External Narrator. Again, despite the covert storyteller, the camera still focuses on direct CU's of Tyler and features on a shot from his POV (although not directly related to the first-person perspective limited shot). Stuart also enters this sequence from the left side of the frame, strengthening his identity as the antagonist.

In the climax is the one time the scene belongs to Stuart, as he reveals he is not an evil wizard but just an old guy trying to tease Tyler. Here the scene switches to Third Person Perspective On-Screen Overt External Narrator as Stuart reveals his true identity directly to the audience, breaking the fourth wall. The shot is in 50/50 profile, so when Stuart does turn, he is directly facing the camera.

Finally, we switch to Third Person Perspective Off-Screen Overt External Narrator as the scene comes to an end, Tyler gets the soda bottle and trots away victoriously. The camera maintains the same side of the line of action until Tyler exits the room, in which case the line is broken using a modified tail-away to head-on shot.

PERSPECTIVE	SHOT	VISUAL IMAGE	DESCRIPTION
First Person Perspective - Extended	**A**	*Tyler*	*CU on old Tyler's face as he walks through the door with V.O.*
	B	*Tyler*	*Wide shot of old Tyler approaching the table nostalgically*
	C	*Tyler*	*CU on Tyler's face as the remembers the days of yore*
	D	*Tyler*	*Flashback: CU on young Tyler's face as he enters the same room, notices something on table*

First Person Perspective - Limited	E	Soda Bottle, Stuart	*Continuous medium shot of Soda bottle and Stuart, as seen from Tyler's POV. Stuart then blows the viewer over with his wind breath.*
Third Person Perspective - Covert External Narrator	F	Tyler, Stuart's feet	*Full CU of Tyler on ground. Stuart's feet enter frame from screen direction left as he announces the second challenge*
	G	Soda bottle	*CU on soda bottle as Stuart tips it over*
	H	Tyler	*Full CU on Tyler as the soda is poured over his face.*
Third Person Perspective - On-Screen Overt External Narrator	I	Tyler, Stuart	*Full shot of Tyler and Stuart in 50/50 profile sitting at table and Stuart explains the third challenge to Tyler, then turns from Tyler and addresses audience*
Third Person Perspective - Off-Screen Overt External Narrator	J	Tyler, Stuart	*Medium shot of Stuart presenting bottle to Tyler*
	K	Tyler	*Full CU on Tyler's face as he celebrates his acquisition of the bottle, off-screen overt narration begins*
	L	Tyler	*Full shot of Tyler skipping over chairs with the bottle, then exiting room*
	M	Tyler	*Full shot from hallway of Tyler emerging from inside the room, victorious*

Sample of Student's Written Homework - Emma Branch

I analyzed the scene from "Closer" according to five different storyteller perspectives. The overarching perspective (in that it runs consistently throughout the scene) is the overt third-person perspective. I have inserted title cards throughout the piece, commenting on the characters' various psychological subtext, such as, "Denial", "Self-condemnation as a ploy for clemency", "Self-deception" and "Manipulation through intimidation."

I added a scene at the beginning to include a 1ˢᵗ person extended perspective from Larry, in which he tries on different outfits for the impending breakup and a V.O. informs of his state of mind prior to the confrontation.

Next, I open the scene from Larry's 1ˢᵗ person limited perspective, which I shot handheld, to convey a sense of unbalance and nervousness. I pull out at the end of the first beat to a two-shot, to show the characters' shared space *and then Anna conspires with the audience in a 2nd person perspective that the reason "it's fine" is because of Dan.*

I continue with a series of panned CUs back and forth between the characters during the beat in which Larry's and Anna's perceptions are most highly contrasted: when he says "he's our joke" and she says" I love him." Anna exits the frame and establishes a distance between the two, which I cover in on-the-line Wide Shots.

I go back into CUs for two lines, just after Larry's biggest moment of self-deception, "But...we're happy, aren't we?"

When Larry loses his temper, the camera takes on highly subjective, yet 3rd person perspective as it follows him in a CU dolly back as he charges toward Anna.

Next, I designed a 2-shot with Anna in the foreground and Larry behind her, both facing in the direction of the camera. She says, "I was scared" and Larry whips her around. The last shot catches Anna in a CU, Larry's aggressive hands gripping her, as he accuses her of being "a spoiled bitch."

CHAPTER 21:
VI. STUDIO - EXTERNALIZING/PHYSICALIZING INNER STATE OF MIND OF THE CHARACTER

Of course, I'm playing with emotions, what else should I play on? What else is there other than emotions? What is important? Only that. - Krysztof Kieslowski, Polish film director *(The Double Life of Veronique)*

In this directing exercise, students-directors develop their skills in visualizing emotions and the inner state of mind of characters by purely visual means. This directing exercise teaches student-directors how to connect the audience with the character by externalizing the psychological state of the character, how to make the audience aware of the inner state of mind of the character. This directing exercise teaches student-directors how to associate the audience with a character's feelings, emotions, thoughts, goals, views, and memories.

Before proceeding further and starting working on the VI. STUDIO, review the CHAPTER 11: EMOTIONAL MANIPULATION/EMOTIONAL DESIGN. Retaining and applying the knowledge described in that chapter will help you with this hands-on directing exercise.

Studio Goal:

The goal of this studio is to help you to develop your skills in visualizing emotions and the inner state of mind of characters by purely visual means.

Specification:

The toughest task each director faces in the visual narrative is externalizing the inner world of the character by visual means of film. It is the biggest challenge for every director.

Goals - Outcomes:

- Transporting the audience into the inner life of the character.
- This directing exercise teaches student-directors how to: connect the audience with the character by externalizing the psychological state of the character, make the audience aware of the inner state of mind of the character, make the audience understand the inner state of mind of the character by visual means of film.

- This directing exercise teaches student-directors how to enhance the audience's' emotional experience.

Objectives:

- Student-directors will be able to associate the audience with a character's feelings, emotions, thoughts, goals, views, and memories.

- Student-directors will be able to control and regulate the audience's own emotions.

- Student-directors will be able to manipulate the audience's perception of characters and story events.

- Student-directors will be able to affect the audience's perceptual immersion

Assignment:

In this directing exercise, student-directors practice making critical choices for narrative and aesthetic purposes. Students choose every element within the frame and utilize all possible elements of visual-storytelling in order to immerse the audience in the inner world of the character. Student-directors will communicate and render the meaning, ideas, cognition, emotions, and unspoken thoughts of characters to the audience entirely by visual expressive means. The student-directors in this directing exercise control the design of the shot and fashion each visual element to create a strong emotional and psychological connection with the viewer.

The class will be divided into groups of three. Each group will produce one directing exercise. As for homework, please work out the concept for a directing exercise linked to the particular script that has been assigned to you, or you have chosen, along with the particular "Subjective State of a Character." Write a one-page long concept for the scene. You can work individually on the concept, and at the beginning of the Studio Class, you can pitch your concept to your teammates and afterward you will choose one concept based on a mutual agreement between all three members, and thereafter you will shoot that concept. You can also work together on the concept for a directing exercise, or you can appoint one student from your team to work out the concept for this particular directing exercise. Whatever solution you choose, all of you bear a mutual responsibility for the result. Handle disagreements constructively. During the class that follows the studio class, each group will screen their directing exercise. Screenings will be followed by a group discussion.

Description of the Directing Exercises No. 1 - INTENTION:

Each character must have a goal. A goal is something the character wants, something the character is trying to achieve in a scene. The goal is actually a scene objective, which carries the character through a particular scene. The actions are what the character does to reach the goal. The character's efforts to achieve the overall story goal result in success or failure. The outcome tells if the character reached the goal. There is a complicated relationship between a need and a goal. They can parallel each other, they can contradict each other, they can conflict each other, and they can support each other. In this exercise, you have to articulate a character's goal - what he/she wants - and be able to visualize it. If you clearly articulate a character's goal, which is supposed to reflect his/her needs, you shouldn't have any problem translating it into visuals.

Technical Requirements for the Directing Exercise No. 1 - INTENTION:

Keep in mind, your task is to visualize what your character intends to do or/and intends to say.

- Clearly articulate/identify the INTENTION you want to portray in your Directing Exercise. (Clearly, state what your character wants to accomplish in the scene and how you want the audience to feel about it.)
- In this directing exercise, you are not allowed to use dialogue.
- Do not use non-diegetic means of the film in this directing exercise.
- Do not rely only on the actor's performance.
- Carefully consider how the shot design and camera treatment carries and expresses emotions.
- Direct the viewer's attention by emphasizing what is essential in the shot.
- Determine the camera set-ups.

Homework Exercise No. 1 - INTENTION:

Write a one-page long concept for the scene you have decided to work with. Develop the scene out of the character objective and state how you plan to interpret it visually.

Here is the workflow you can follow:

If you choose to work with the scene *Kramer vs. Kramer:* suppose that Joanna, after arguing with Ted, spends her time in a café and reflects on their entire married life, recalling everything good and bad. Based on her consideration, she has changed her mind and has decided to give him one last chance. She heads home with the intention of telling him the news. Your scene begins with her entering the apartment while Ted is preparing dinner.

Description of the Directing Exercises No. 2 - FEELING:

From CHAPTER 11: EMOTIONAL MANIPULATION/EMOTIONAL DESIGN you know that you as a director have to control the audience's perception of events and emotions in the scene for the sake of engaging the audience emotionally with characters and story events. You also know about the need to use emotional triggers for eliciting an emotional response. In this exercise, you have to articulate the character's feeling. In this exercise, you will control the design of the shot and fashion each visual element to create a strong emotional and psychological connection with the viewer.

Technical Requirements for the Directing Exercise No. 2 - FEELING:

- In this directing exercise, you are allowed to use dialogue but do not rely on a power of dialogue in this directing exercise.
- Do not rely only on the actor's performance.
- Do not use non-diegetic means of the film in this directing exercise.
- Carefully consider how the shot design and camera treatment carries and expresses emotions.
- Direct the viewer's attention by emphasizing what is essential in the shot.
- Determine the camera set-ups.

Homework Exercise No. 2 - FEELING:

Write a one-page long concept for the scene you have decided to work with. Develop the scene out of the mood of the scene, and characters' feelings, and state how you will visually execute the concept. Create a clear plan and specify, what the audience should be feeling, and which tools you plan to use to make them feel it.

1. Clearly articulate/identify the MOOD and EMOTION you want to portray in your Directing Exercise. (Clearly state what you want to achieve in terms of Emotions, which feelings you want to evoke, which feelings the audience has to understand, state how you want to make them feel.)
2. Explain what stimuli (emotional triggers) you plan to use, in order to create emotions. (Review the section *"Guidelines for controlling viewers' emotions/feelings in the scene"* in CHAPTER 11.)

3. Decide how you will create the feeling you want the audience to have.

4. Explain, how you plan to accentuate/intensify stimuli in order to enhance emotions.

5. Explain how you intend to communicate your concept through shot design, camera treatment, production design, and costume design. It will be very beneficial for you to review the CHAPTER 9: concept of character perspective, particularly the segment *Methodology and visual strategy for rendering a scene based on a character perspective.* Try to consider using some of the elements listed in the aforementioned segment, like screen time, frame composition, physical size, depth of field, camera movement, psychological weight, and time. Definitely, employ in this directing exercise the Natural Distortion factor for externalizing the inner world of the character. As for different ways of achieving the time expanding effect, please refer to the chart EXPANDED TIME in CHAPTER 4: MANIPULATING FILM TIME.

6. Use the CONCEPTUAL MAP TEMPLATE FOR EMOTIONS, which can be located in PART V: QUIZZES, TESTS, CHARTS, TEMPLATES of this book.

Here is the workflow you can follow:

1. Determine the feeling of the scene. (What the audience shod be feeling.) MOOD

2. Determine what can trigger the feeling(s) you want your audience to have.

3. Clearly, state what you plan to portray for triggering the feeling you want your audience to have.

4. Determine what else can intensify/accentuate the audience's feeling. (Engage as many of "senses" as you can.)

5. Determine how you intend to communicate your concept through production design and shot design.

Description of the Directing Exercises No. 3 – MEMORIES:

In this directing exercise, you have to visualize the character memories and bring them on the screen from the character perspective, not from the omniscient narrator, not from a storyteller's perspective.

Technical Requirements for the Directing Exercise No. 3 - MEMORIES:

- In this directing exercise, you are allowed to use dialogue but do not rely on a power of dialogue in this directing exercise.

- Do not rely only on the actor's performance.
- From non-diegetic means of a film, you can use music in this directing exercise.
- You can utilize your footage from previous STUDIOS and utilize the STUDIO time just for shooting needed pickups or reshoots for this directing exercise.

Homework Exercise No. 3 - MEMORIES:

Write a one-page long concept for the scene you have decided to work with. Create a clear plan and specify the visual representation of memories

1. Clearly articulate/identify the MEMORIES you want to portray in this Directing Exercise. (Clearly state why the character contemplates the past, how memories affect the character and how you want the audience to feel about it.)
2. Explain how you plan to communicate your concept through shot design and camera treatment. Review the CHAPTER 9: concept of character perspective, particularly the segment *Methodology and visual strategy for rendering a scene based on a character perspective.* Try to consider using some of the elements listed in the aforementioned segment, like screen time, frame composition, physical size, depth of field, camera movement, psychological weight and time. Definitely employ in this directing exercise a Natural Distortion factor for externalizing the inner world of the character. As for different ways of achieving the time expending effect, please refer to the chart EXPANDED TIME in CHAPTER 4: MANIPULATING FILM TIME.
3. Utilize "screen directions" as a factor that can help you to redirect a narrative flow from present to past, and prepare a smooth transition to memories or flashbacks if you plan to use them. (Deliberately think how to direct and redirect "narrative flow" by screen direction. Review CHAPTER 12: PSYCHO-PHYSIOLOGICAL REGULARITIES IN LEFT-RIGHT/RIGHT-LEFT ORIENTATION.)
4. Determine the camera set-ups.

Here is the workflow you can follow:

If you choose to work with the scene *Kramer vs. Kramer:* Suppose that Joana is alone at home waiting for Ted contemplating her past; or Ted is alone at home, after Joanna left, contemplating his past. You can also consider to intercut memories from both characters, when they reflect on same issues. You can show the conflicting physical representation of memories from two different perspectives, how both characters differently interpret the events in their memories.

Sample of Student's Written homework (INTENTION) - Kim Travis, Ben Barbour, Abosede Copeland

For VI. STUDIO we have chosen to do INTENTION. We have chosen to convey the scene similar to that in Abosede' s final film "Rammed". This scene consists of a woman walking up to her car and then being attacked by a man.

We want the audience to fear for the victim, and also sew what the attacker has to do to win power over her (struggling dragging away from the car). We can show this in two separate ways. First, we can show it from the victims POV of being attacked and trying to do everything she can to get away. The second way we can show it is from the attackers POV, and the waiting and anticipation of striking on his victim. We also might want to show the different ways of him approaching the situation and what he intends to do.

Since there is no dialogue or music allowed we will enhance the studio assignment with many different camera angles (above, below, head-on, Dutch, etc.) and different shots (WS, MS, CU, etc.) to enhance what is going on in the scene. The actors will perform, however, the real feeling and emotion behind the scene will be made better by the camera angles. In other words, the actors will only enhance the scene. We feel to make it more lifelike we will go hand-held and do long takes. We believe by focusing on an object as well as the talent we can achieve the intention behind the action. I think the most powerful shot we could have is seeing the reflection of the victim and the attacker in the car window while the attack is happening.

Sample of Student's Written Homework (INTENTION) - Austin Saya, Britt and Kyle

For my VI. STUDIO, I am working with Britt and Kyle. We have decided to think a little bit outside the box and shoot a whole new idea. We wanted to stray away from the scripts we always use to bring a more creative look into this studio. Our topic is the intention.

We plan on clearly stating the needs of our main character, Sue, as she waits in an endless line for food. The food will be a clear objective for her because we will visually show how hungry she really is. The drama will be added to this situation because the closer Sue gets to the food, the faster the food is disappearing into the mouths of the people that are in front of her in this endless line.

*We will be employing all the techniques from studios I.-V. Sue will be seen in
multiple perspectives and be shown crossing the line multiple times as well.
Preliminary shots include but are not limited to:
CU of Sue looking off into the distance.
CU of food in the distance.
MED of people in front of Sue.
WIDE of the entire line.
CU of a clock ticking
MED of Sue as she gets very nervous"*

Sample of Student's Written Homework (MEMORIES) - Cecyl Cabán

*The scene I have chosen for this exercise is from "The Bridges of Madison
County". This scene takes place right after Robert leaves. The scene will focus
on Francesca's emotional response to the events that have just transpired,
the dinner and the conversation that followed. Francesca watches through
the screen door as his car drives off. She turns and looks down at her hands,
which Robert held just minutes ago. Then she goes back to the living room
and sits down in her original spot. She sees Robert's half-empty glass of
brandy on the table next to hers.
The overall mood that wishes to convey is a contemplative mood, in which
Francesca reflects on the events of the night and her feelings for Robert. His
question about leaving her husband really shocked her, as were his final
words. The audience needs to be aware of Francesca's growing attraction,
which foreshadows the impending internal conflict within her: being attracted to a man who is not her husband.*

*The emotional triggers for this scene are the door closing, Francesca's hands,
and Robert's glass of brandy. These three triggers mark the main emotional
beats of the scene. The door closing symbolizes the ending of her evening
with Robert, and she can now begin to process what has happened. Her
hands, which Robert just held, are a trigger for her growing attraction to
Robert, a sensory reminded of his touch. Finally, the brandy represents their
conversation- when he asked her if she wanted to leave her husband.*

*I intend to show these emotional responses by portraying the sources (door,
hands, brandy) and how Francesca reacts to them. Her facial expressions are
a doorway to the emotions of the scene, so close-up and even extreme close-
ups will be employed. The camera frames the screen-door as it swings
closed, and Francesca is staring out as Robert leaves. Close-up shots of her
hands as she looks at them. Here the depth of field is shallow, the light soft.
She remembers what his hands felt like. Then, the action moves to the living*

room, where Francesca notices Robert's glass of brandy, next to her own. Again, an extreme close-up of this shot, with a shallow depth of field will emphasize its importance. The brandy evokes the response she felt to his question. Also, I want to empathize with Francesca and how she feels.

CONCEPT MAP FOR EMOTIONS

STIMULUS (Emotional triggers)	ACCENTUATING/ INTENSIFYING STIMULUS (Engage as many of "senses" as you can)	EMOTION (Response or reaction triggered by stimulus)	ENHANCING EMOTIONS (Multiplying emotions)	EMOTIONS DESIGN (Physical and mental components of emotion; visual design; shot design)	MOOD
The door closes.	Sound of the door. Sounds of the night (cicadas etc.), music Car driving away	Finality	Framing Francesca looking out the screen door. Close up shots of her face as she watches him drive away. Camera stays focused on her. She is processing Robert's words to her about not being a simple woman.	Lighting: very soft, focus on Francesca's face. She looks as if illuminated by moonlight.	Contemplative
Hands	Looks down at her hands. Takes a deep, shuddering breath. Touches them, rubs them together.	Attraction	Francesca turns away from the door. She comes into a wider shot, and looks down at her hands. Everything else is quiet.	Francesca remembers the touch of Robert's hands in her own.	Contemplative
Glass of brandy	Shot of Robert's half-empty glass.	Attraction	Francesca sits down and looks at Robert's drink.	Close-up shots of the brandy glasses. Shot of Robert's empty seat	Contemplative

Sample of Student's Written Homework (FEELING) - Grey Gowder

I was drawn to the scene THE BRIDGES OF MADISON COUNTY due to the strong potential for exploring the feelings of the characters in the moments that precede and follow this particular scene. While the soul-searching moments for both characters after the scene could be particularly riveting, I believe that the moments leading up to this scene could yield hilariously tense moments. The moment I am interested in the time, Robert must have spent at the dinner table waiting as Francesca finished preparing their meal in the kitchen. He is alone with his thoughts, his desires, with time to run through all sorts of personal pep talks and moments of doubt before having an unofficial dinner date with a married woman for whom he pines. The sexual tension must be excruciating. He is left sitting alone at a table set for two, listening to the woman that he cares for but could never have right in the next room. He can barely see her, only catching glimpses of her bustling about, preparing everything for them. He could call to her, but a physical wall would still divide them. He could get up and talk to her, or he could even take her in his arms and profess his love and maybe even make love to her there on the kitchen counter, but he cannot bring himself to act on such rash and youthful thoughts. No, he must sit there, alone, silent, waiting for her.

Emotions: Anxiety, longing, yearning

Mood: tense, uncomfortable

In order to achieve these feelings, I will play with the stimuli of empathy and sound to influence the audience. His emotions and sense will be running high from adrenaline so quick and tight shots of things like his fingers tapping, feet shuffling, throat clearing, fingers scratching, and body shifting will create a layer of tension in which the audience recognizes this nervousness and will grow in anxiety with the character, hoping for a positive resolution. His insecurities become our insecurities as we become more on axis with him and are framed closer to him. His eyes, his mouth, his hands, and his feet will be the keys to unlocking his mind.

By shifting the camera to tighter shots with shallow focus, the intensity of the scene increases as we become more uncomfortable with being in such close proximity to this person and will be unable to avoid picking up on even the subtlest insecurities of this person. It is almost as if we were becoming Robert as we adopt his fears and his apprehension.

MOOD (Audience's feeling; the general feeling or atmosphere of the scene created within the viewer.)	EMOTIONS DESIGN (Physical and mental components of emotion; visual design; shot design)	ENHANCING EMOTIONS (Multiplying emotions)	EMOTION (Response or reaction triggered by stimulus)	ACCENTUATING/ INTENSIFYING STIMULUS (Engage as many of "senses" as you can)	STIMULUS (Emotional triggers)
Sexual Tension	- Tight shots of Robert - Family photos without Robert - Shallow focus, Robert tries to see Francesca around the door frame	- Single, fixed point of view of Robert - Setting: dimly lit dining room in another family's home - Sound: Francesca hums in the next room as she cooks, his fingers tap, his feet shuffle, he clears his throat and groans	Anxiety	Family portraits Table set for two Ticking clock	Waiting for Francesca

Sample of Student's Written Homework (FEELING) - CONCEPT MAP FOR EMOTIONS – L.K.

Scene:
A couple came to the restaurant to celebrate their wedding anniversary. It is the most romantic place you can imagine. Interesting food, dim lighting, warm and pleasant atmosphere. We know that their son is the first time away from home because he is in US Navy serving in the war. The father is proud of a son that the can serve and help protect their country. In the restaurant is a flat-panel LCD on the wall. Suddenly, a breaking news report appears on the TV screen and brings a news spot from the battlefield.

STIMULUS (Emotional triggers)	ACCENTUATING/ INTENSIFYING STIMULUS (Engage as many of "senses" as you can)	EMOTION (Response or reaction triggered by stimulus)	ENHANCING EMOTIONS (Multiplying emotions)	EMOTIONS DESIGN (Physical and mental components of emotion; visual design; shot design)	MOOD
Breaking News	Pictures of wounded soldiers from the battlefield. Anchor's commentary. Sound of explosions.	Sadness	- Applying different point of views: Father: guilt Mother: anger). - Setting (Restaurant) Characters' emotions and the atmosphere of the setting play off each other in discord. - An empathetic sound: restaurant radio continues to play a happy tune.	War footage Mother leaves the restaurant Father is crying American Flag Dutch angle shots	Depression

Sample of Student's Written Homework (FEELING) - Scene: Game of Thrones - Dining Scene; - Miles Nera

Sam returns home after a long absence, but he brings along a woman named Gilly as well her son Little Sam and they eat dinner together with Sam's Family. The dining hall is a luxurious location with an interior dimly lit by candlelight. The atmosphere is pleasant due to the welcoming nature of Sam's family. Although, all is not well with the master of the house, Sam's Father, Randyll, as he discovers that Gilly is actually a wildling, an enemy of his family. After some brief small talk, Randyll begins to engage and accost Sam for bringing home a wildling. This incident upsets everyone, eventually leading Sam's mother to walk out with Gilly.

STIMULUS	ACCENTUATING/ INTENSIFYING STIMULUS	EMOTION	ENHANCING EMOTIONS	EMOTIONS DESIGN	MOOD
Randyll suddenly insults Sam and points at him with an accusing finger	*- Gilly stands up raises her voice.* *- Randyll slams the table.* *- Flashback: Sam killing a Then and Whitewalker. -* *Flashback: Images of the wildling invasion.*	*Apprehension*	*- An Epiphany: From static shots to a dolly in for Randyll as he confirms his suspicion as to who Gilly really is.* *- Sharp Sounds Break the Ice: Glass break and cups fall to the floor as Randyll slams the table.* *- Uneasiness: Long drawn out takes to accentuate unease.* *Uncomfortable framing. - Setting: Musicians stop playing.*	*- Glass breaking* *- Cups falling* *- Children are crying* *- Sam is timid and helpless* *- Sam's mother leaves with Gilly*	*Unease*

What Students Said About the VI. STUDIO - EXTERNALIZING/PHYSICALIZING INNER STATE OF MIND OF THE CHARACTER

STUDIO VI was a lot of fun. Not having to worry about the dialogue kept me focused on the blocking and the mood we were trying to get across. I now focused on blocking along with the camera movement. This added a new element, movement of the camera that I could use along with what I had learned about blocking. I feel this was my most dynamic exercise of all the Studios and showed me all that I have learned so far. Without these Studios, my work would suffer, my final would lack in a confidence in blocking and my thesis film that I will shoot next year would not be as successful I am sure. - Richard Webb

As we got deeper into the workshops, we were allowed more freedom with the camera, and that's where things started to get fun, but there wasn't one workshop that I didn't learn from. More than anything, each one forced me to work in a group under pressure, and I believe that's where I learned most. Having only an hour and a half at the most to the plane, organize, and execute many of these assignments, made it a very difficult but educational experience. - Michal Lippert

*The ways of using blocking and staging to create more dynamic composi-
tions along with an emotional meaning of a scene became more clear, allowing me to think of filming in a new way, giving me new ideas of how to
use that aspect of filmmaking. Overall, I would have to say that workshops
opened up my thinking to shooting a scene, giving me a new understanding
of what can be done, while making me do this quicker and more precise at
the same time.* – Jeff Sears

*I think these studios are very beneficial to have. I am glad I was able to learn
all of this theory and put it into practice.* - Angela Gunn.
*I think that's the most important thing I learned from the entire experience;
to be proud of your work. The act of creation itself is enough reason to feel
joy over your accomplishment. Even if the end result isn't what you intended
it is still miraculous that you put it down in the first place. I learned to accept even the harshest criticism without backlash, though it took me a serious mistake to realize that. I feel like a new, better, artist after this whole or-
deal; and that's something I wouldn't trade for anything.* - Chris Osman

*I think the biggest thing I learned out of this whole experience is that as a
director you have to know what you want and be aggressive about it, but at
the same time put your crew at ease and make sure they're happy. It is a difficult job but fruitful one, at time is self-consuming but your discovery, your
passion for life and for looking at life in a different way. I think that my perception is forever changed and I see people in a certain angle or light I will
think that's a perfect shot or that's a great story. I think that I will go onto to
make a documentary film or even a feature film with the passion that I have
discovered.* - L.M.

CHAPTER 22:
VII. STUDIO - HARMONIOUS PORTRAIT AND DISCORDANT PORTRAIT

If you want a happy ending, that depends, of course, on where you stop your story. - Orson Welles, American film director *(Citizen Kane)*

I am here to show you something that has been of practical use to me. The concepts that the film schools mandate and include in classroom instructions do not contain this one. This is a skill-centric concept with a universal application. The quality of your work will really shine through when you adopt it and use it in your films. You will connect the improved results to the implementation of this concept right away.

The unity and wholeness is an essential quality for each film. This directing exercise will give student-directors tools for creating a style-consistency film; tools for accomplishing the outer and inner cohesion of the film, which will support the unity of the film and heighten the emotional impact on the audience. All directorial components - directing actors, cinematography, shot design, art direction with all its aspects - all have to come together in a unified and seamless way. In this directing exercise, the student-directors have to arrange all elements of a scene in a harmonious or discordant manner and have to combine them in a larger structure of the scene, to make that scene a unified whole with a heightened emotional impact on the audience. This directing exercise also teaches student-directors that the change of the scripted location can: heighten the emotional impact on the audience; enhance the audience's emotional experience; produce an additional response from the audience; strengthen a weak scene. Student-directors in this directing exercise are acquiring a "real-world experience" that the scene can be well-balanced, and its compositional elements can be either harmonious or discordant. The key knowledge and learning experience from this exercise can be transformed into capital that can be used in the future.

Before proceeding further and starting working on the VII. STUDIO, review the CHAPTER 11: EMOTIONAL MANIPULATION/EMOTIONAL DESIGN. Retaining and applying the knowledge described in that chapter will help you with this hands-on directing exercise.

Studio Goal:

The student-directors have to demonstrate in this directing exercise the ability to choose and control all components of the scene for the complete composition of the scene. The student-directors in this directing exercise have to confirm the ability and professional skills to control the design of the shot within a self-contained scene, and prove the ability to fashion each element to create a strong emotional and psychological connection with the viewer, to strengthen the unity of the scene, or to strengthen a weak scene.

Specification:

- Composition is the arranging and organizing of the component parts of a work into a unified whole. Unity is the relationship among all the elements of a scene that helps all the elements function together. Unity gives a sense of oneness to a portrait of the scene. The elements of a scene have to work together as a total portrait of a scene. In this directing exercise, the student-directors have to arrange all the elements of a scene in a harmonious or discordant manner and have to combine them in a larger structure of the scene to make that scene a unified whole with a heightened emotional impact on the audience.

- The student-directors design a pivotal film scene from an original screenplay integrating and implementing the newly acquired theoretical knowledge and directing skills related to the aesthetics of the shot.

Goals - Outcomes:

- This directing exercise teaches student-directors that aesthetically pleasing arrangement of a scene components can be guided by a principle of harmony or by a principal of discord.

- This directing exercise teaches student-directors how to create a well-balanced scene, where its structural and compositional elements can be either harmonious or discordant.

- This directing exercise teaches student-directors that the discordant portrait of a situation (informal balance) is much more interesting, and more dynamic than a harmonious portrait of a situation (formal balance), and keeps the audience's attention focused on the message, emotions, or drama.

- This directing exercise also teaches student-directors that the change of the scripted location can:
  - heighten the emotional impact on the audience
  - enhance the audience's emotional experience
  - produce an additional response from the audience
  - strengthen a weak scene

Objectives:

- Student-directors will be able to create a well-balanced scene, where its structural and compositional elements relate to each other and complement each other (a harmonious blend of all the elements within a scene); and student-directors will be able to create a well-balanced scene, where its structural and compositional elements contradict each other, but the resulting scene is still balanced (balance is established by equalizing the element forces in spite of their differences.)

- Student-directors will be able to intensify and heighten the emotional experience of the audience by creating a more convincing mood for the scene through the atmosphere of a different place than was a scripted location.

- Student-directors in this directing exercise are acquiring a "real-world experience" that the scene can be well-balanced, and its compositional elements can be either harmonious or discordant.

Assignment:

To possess the knowledge is one thing, and applying this knowledge is another one. Confucius, a Chinese philosopher of the Spring and Autumn period of the history of China, said, *"The essence of knowledge is, having it, to apply it; not having it, to confess your ignorance."* Student-directors design one scene applying the theoretical knowledge and practical experience acquired from all directing exercises they worked on so far. In this exercise, student-directors have to demonstrate that they can use the class experience and personal and artistic experience, their professionalism, and strengths in designing one film scene. This directing exercise should be the culmination of their experience acquired by reading this book, and working on all directing exercises, and must demonstrate how they can employ their current skills along with the artistry in designing a film scene.

The class will be divided into groups of five max. Each group will produce one scene. During the class that follows the studio class, each group will screen their directing exercise. Screenings will be followed by a group discussion.

Description of the Directing Exercise:

Creating a HARMONIOUS PORTRAIT of the scripted scene, and creating a DISCORDANT PORTRAIT of the same scene.

Instruction:

- Instruction for creating a HARMONIOUS PORTRAIT of the scripted scene: Use all of the possible techniques and strategies to create a HARMONIOUS PORTRAIT of the scripted scene, and try to resolve any dissonance in the scene.
- Instruction for creating a DISCORDANT PORTRAIT of the scripted scene: Use all of the possible techniques and strategies to create a DISCORDANT PORTRAIT of the scripted scene, and try to heighten dissonance in the scene.

Homework:

Create a HARMONIOUS PORTRAIT of the scene you have decided to work with for the VII. STUDIO, and then create a DISCORDANT PORTRAIT of the same scene. *You will be able to access the scene in* PART IV: STUDIO SCRIPTS in this book. You can also work with a scene of your own choice. Choose a scene with the following list of characteristics: character-driven, dialogue-based, one emotional turn, two characters, two to three pages, with a page counting as a minute of screen time.

- *Kramer vs. Kramer*
- *Closer*
- *The Bridges of Madison County*

Here is the workflow you can follow for creating a HARMONIOUS PORTRAIT of the scene when all the elements that comprise the scene's mood and tone work together in unison:

1. Choose the PLACE with the atmosphere, which will produce a pleasing or distasteful mood. It depends on the original mood of the scene. Create consonance.
2. Choose all the visual components (LINES and SHAPES, TONE, MOVEMENT and RHYTHM) and try to create affinity or contrast. Create consonance.
3. Select the COLORS, which will produce a pleasing or distasteful visual experience. Create consonance.
4. Select mood-setting SOUND, which will establish and maintain positive or negative attitude. Create consonance.
5. Evaluate all employed elements and reexamine if all components are appropriately combined together and create a harmonious portrait of the scene.

Here is the workflow you can follow for creating a DISCORDANT PORTRAIT of the scene when the filmmaking elements contrast or work against each other in order to intensify interest or emotion:

1. Choose the PLACE with the atmosphere, which will produce an unpleasant-conflicting mood or pleasing mood. It depends on the original mood of the scene. Create dissonance.
2. Choose all the visual components (LINES and SHAPES, TONE, MOVEMENT and RHYTHM) and try to create contrast or affinity. Create dissonance.
3. Use the COLORS in a discordant fashion, colors that clash with each other; or use COLORS in a harmonious fashion, colors which work with each other. Create dissonance.
4. Select the SOUND, which will establish and maintain dissonance.
5. Design each shot individually and organize all individual elements of the shot into a unified whole.
6. Evaluate all employed elements and reexamine if all components are appropriately combined together and create a discordant portrait of the scene.

Use a chart template *"HARMONIOUS PORTRAIT AND DISCORDANT PORTRAIT"* posted in PART V: QUIZZES, TESTS, CHARTS, TEMPLATES of this book.

Sample of Student's Written Homework for the scene *Closer* - Ernesto Fuentes, Jana Acevedo, Masha Jones, Tian Lan:

The scene from the *Closer* is a breakup scene, where Larry, after admitting to having cheated on Anna with a prostitute, he's flipping out when Anna admits to her affair with Dan.

DISCORDANT PORTRAIT

1. *Choose the PLACE with the atmosphere, which will produce a conflicting mood, contrasting the original mood: The place is a hotel resort. A bright sunny place with vivid colors like the blue sky, blue sea, and green vegetation.*
2. *Choose all the visual components (LINES and SHAPES, TONE, MOVEMENT and RHYTHM) and create contrast, which will oppose the original mood: All shapes in this place are organic. The hotel's architecture is Moroccan and not jagged at all. This atmosphere should completely contrast.*
3. *Select COLORS in a harmonious fashion, colors which work with each other, contrasting the original mood. Create dissonance, the disharmony: All colors are very bright and vivid.*

4. Select the SOUND, which will establish and maintain dissonance, disharmony: All sounds are calm ambient nature sounds. For example, the winds caressing the leaves and the ocean.

5. Design each shot individually and organize all individual elements of the shot into a harmonious and unified whole: The shot begins with the woman outside wearing a nightgown. The man goes outside, and she notices he is already dressed. This starts the argument.

HARMONIOUS PORTRAIT

1. Choose the PLACE with the atmosphere, which will produce a distasteful mood, going hand in with the original mood: This takes place on a hot, humid, summer night on the side of a highway inside a broken-down car. There are semi-trucks rushing by, and each one leaves the small car rocking.

2. Choose all the visual components (LINES and SHAPES, TONE, MOVEMENT and RHYTHM) and try to create affinity, which will go hand in with the original mood; Create consonance, the harmony: In terms of Lines - There are the lines made by the small car and the high way on the wide shots and the lines made by the small boxy car in the two shot and close-ups. These two shots contrast with each other and create a rhythm that accentuates the anxiety both characters are feeling not just because they are in physical danger but because their relationship is ending. In terms of tone, the audience should feel anxiety and an awkward discomfort.

3. We have decided to use the COLORS in a discordant fashion, colors that clash with the original tone of the scene, and not the colors which will highlight the original mood, what actually the harmonious portrait is calling for. So, we have departed here from the harmony, believing that the discord would better serve the tone of the scene here: Both characters will be wearing 90's style clothes. The woman specifically is wearing a flower-patterned dress that is unbuttoned. The man is wearing a button-up shirt and a sports coat with it –making him very sweaty. The car is a boxy thing from the 90's

4. Select the SOUND, which will establish and maintain negative attitude: As the scene plays out the audience will constantly hear the semi-trucks flying by. But we have also decided to add elements of dissonance, disharmony here: They will also hear a song on the radio from the 90's called "Can you feel the love tonight." This will amp up the anxiety.

5. Design each shot individually and organize all individual elements of the shot into a unified whole: There are basically two shots for this scene using the consonance scenario. The first involves a wide shot of the small car on the side of the freeway in clear danger. And the second

is a two shot of both characters cramped and uncomfortable inside the car.

6. *Evaluate all employed elements and reexamine if all components are appropriately combined together and create a harmonious portrait of the scene: When we considered all elements in both portraits (Harmonious and Discordant) we decided as a team that the best one was harmony because it has elements that lend themselves quite well to the underlining mood of the scene (Contempt, Anxiety and discomfort)*

Sample of Student's Written Homework for the scene *Closer* - Leanna Kemp, Jon Kelly Shelburne, Alexandria Ducksworth, Allison Hirsh:

DISCORDANT PORTRAIT

1. *Choose the PLACE with the atmosphere, which will produce a conflicting mood, contrasting the original mood: In the den of the characters' house.*

2. *Choose all the visual components (LINES and SHAPES, TONE, MOVEMENT and RHYTHM) and try to create contrast, which will oppose the original mood: Long shots with both characters sitting close together. Use of deep, layered space. Many layered textiles soften the shot. Rounded forms of the couch and pillows. Characters are closely focused on each other.*

3. *Select the COLORS in a discordant fashion, contrasting the original mood:*
    Warm colors and soft daylight lighting. There is a balanced range of colors, but all are muted slightly and warmed by the lighting.

4. *Select mood-setting SOUND, which will establish and maintain establish and maintain dissonance: Natural outdoor noises come in through an open window, including the breeze through the trees, wind chime, and small birds.*

5. *Design each shot individually and organize all individual elements of the shot into a discordant and unified whole: The first shot is medium-long, establishing the room and showing the closeness of characters to each other while the camera ever so slightly tracks in toward the characters. When Anna says, she loves Dan the camera switches to close-ups alternating at a semi-slow pace.*

HARMONIOUS PORTRAIT

1. Choose the PLACE with the atmosphere, which will produce a dis-
    tasteful mood, going hand in with the original mood: *Waiting in line
    for a dilapidated small town fair.*

2. Choose all the visual components (LINES and SHAPES, TONE,
    MOVEMENT and RHYTHM) and try to create contrast, which will go
    hand in with the original mood: *Harsh lines, sharp textures, spinning
    of ride, camera moves quickly, shots are tight, and the characters never
    move. The tone is dusky, harsh, dim and sickening, very disorienting.*

3. Use the COLORS which will create a distasteful visual experience,
    highlighting the original mood: *Rotten, dark with green and orange,
    clashing and not cheerful with a sense of nighttime falling quickly.*

4. Select the SOUND, which will establish and maintain negative atti-
    tude: *Crazy game noises, carnies yelling, various annoying and ca-
    cophonous carnival sounds.*

5. Design each shot individually and organize all individual elements of
    the shot into a unified whole.
    *Starts with a medium OTS shot that cuts back and forth from the faces
    of the characters. When Anna says she loves Dan the camera leaves the
    OTS position and moves slightly outside of the characters, circling
    around them. For the last line, the camera switches to a low angle shot
    where faces of both characters are framed with harsh lighting and a lot
    of anger.*

MOOD - Contempt

EMOTION DESIGN *(Physical/mental components of emotion; visual & shot
design)*

- Extreme close-ups showing the anger in each character's mouth
  and eyes as they deliver each line.
- Quick cuts between the characters feel disjointed and angry.
- Flat space where characters are confronted "against the wall" in
  this situation that has inevitably come forth and cannot be avoid-
  ed.
- Rarely showing the characters together in the same frame, giving
  them the maximum emotional separation.
- Strongly contrasting and harsh lighting with sort of a sickly glow.
- Outdated apartment that does not feel at all homey or loving.
- Colors are sickly orange and green. Appliances are outdated.
- Daylight darkens until Anna turns her back to flip on the fluores-
  cent light.

ENHANCING EMOTIONS (Multiplying emotions)
-   *Even though characters are angry, their skin doesn't appear red or flushed.*
-   *They each feel very cold and harsh rather than heated.*
-   *Everything (setting, dialogue, color, sound) has a crisp and biting quality. The hatred has an evil and calculated quality rather than a passionate feeling. They feel as though they actually have hated each other for a long time and this is the culmination of a complete absence of love.*

EMOTION (Response or reaction triggered by stimulus)
-   *Discomfort*

ACCENTUATING/INTENSIFYING STIMULUS (Engage senses)
-   *Crisp, cut sound and lines, almost spitting the words.*
-   *Between the lines, there is a harsh, repetitive noise of a dryer shaking clothes.*
-   *The texture is sharp and disconnected. Nothing feels soft or layered.*
-   *Fluorescent light washes characters of color or feeling. The scene becomes more cold and calculated.*

STIMULUS (Emotional triggers)
-   *The revelation of infidelity by each character.*

Sample of Student's Written Homework for the scene *Closer* - Gregory Roberts-Gassler, Jing Ge, Robert Faris, Amie Flanagan:

DISCORDANT PORTRAIT

1. *Choose the PLACE with the atmosphere, which will produce a conflicting mood, contrasting the original mood: Restaurant in an aquarium.*
2. *Choose all the visual components (LINES and SHAPES, TONE, MOVEMENT and RHYTHM) and try to create contrast, which will oppose the original mood: Bubbles, circles, horizontal lines, fluid movement, calming atmosphere.*
3. *Use the COLORS in a discordant fashion, contrasting the original mood: Blue, white orange, chartreuse*
4. *Select mood-setting SOUND, which will establish and maintain an attitude contrasting the original tone of the scene: Sounds of water, ambient restaurant sounds, harp music.*
5. *Design each shot individually and organize all individual elements of the shot into a and unified whole.*

Isolated but balanced characters in the frame, rule of thirds, characters facing each other. Shades of blue and green. Aligned with Anna, Larry in the Right.

HARMONIOUS PORTRAIT

1. Choose the PLACE with the atmosphere, which will produce the tone, which will go hand in with the original tone. We have decided against it, believing that the discord would better serve the tone of the scene here: Candyland, by a pink waterfall.
2. Choose all the visual components (LINES and SHAPES, TONE, MOVEMENT and RHYTHM) and try to create contrast, which will go hand in with the original mood: Both are in black and white structured outfits, vertical, triangular, organic buildings. No horizon, organic squares. Staccato rhythm, jump editing.
3. We have decided to use the COLORS in a discordant fashion, colors that clash with the original tone of the scene, and not the colors which will highlight the original mood: Chartreuse, puce, mauve, fuchsia, orange, pink, conflicting with the characters' monochromatic black and white clothing.
4. Select the SOUND, which will establish and maintain a negative attitude. Also, here we have decided to go against it, and use the sound which will create dissonance with original tone, and by doing this, it will highlight the conflict: Playful children singing, repetitive.
5. Design each shot individually and organize all individual elements of the shot into a unified whole: Long shots, long Depth of Field, unbalanced frames, jump cuts, crossing the line illegally, characters framed with little breathing room and dwarfed by the environment in the frame.

Samples of Students' Written Homework for the scene *Kramer vs. Kramer*

MOOD	EMOTIONS DESIGN (Physical and mental components of emotion; visual design; shot design)	ENHANCING EMOTIONS (Multiplying emotions)	EMOTION (Response or reaction triggered by stimulus)	ACCENTUATING/ INTENSIFYING STIMULUS (Engage as many of "senses" as you can)	STIMULUS (Emotional triggers)
Anxiety	Include a baby's birth to create empathy	Build defensiveness upon anger and discontent	Exhaustion	Annoying	Clock
Hopeful			Happy	Hospital Noise	Wheelchair
Anxiety	Enters next to a sickly man	Heightening urgency by compressing time, maybe give her some reason to leave.	Hopeful Confused Regretful	Smells of flowers	Gift
Sympathy	Establish her in a baby room, she must exit to hallway with him			Sterility	Baby
				Cold and smoothen	Form/List
					Family mourning

HARMONIOUS PORTRAIT	**PLACE** Choose the PLACE with the atmosphere, which will produce a distasteful mood, going hand in with the original mood.
	Hospital
	VISUAL COMPONENTS *Choose all the visual components (LINES and SHAPES, TONE, MOVEMENT and RHYTHM) and try to create a mood which will go hand in with the original mood.*
	Hallways, jump cut, focus, characters pacing
	COLORS *Use the COLORS* which will produce a distasteful visual experience, highlighting the original mood.
	Cool, blue + green, harsh, falloff
	SOUND *Select the SOUND, which will establish and maintain dissonance.*
	Sickness, mechanical, P.A. system, crying or very quiet still.
	SHOT DESIGN *Design each shot individually and organize all individual elements of the shot into a unified whole.*
	Deep, 2 point, wide, ECU, MS
	FINAL TOUCH *Evaluate all employed elements and reexamine if all components are appropriately combined together and create a discordant portrait of the scene.*

What Students Said About the VII. STUDIO - HARMONIOUS PORTRAIT AND-DISCORDANT PORTRAIT

In 7 short studios, I learned more about filmmaking than reading books, practicing or going to school. With the correct guidance and influence, a lot of necessary time is not wasted in learning. The principles are simple and powerful, and the practice and execution are what we need to learn. Each workshop, whether it is Staging and Blocking for the single camera system, modeling character perspective, or visualization of the inner state of mind was beneficial and necessary to my growth as a filmmaker. Each technique we learned will be used in my later work, hopefully by that time, unconsciously and as a good habit. We learned how to break the fourth wall, cross the line, adjust eye lines, make a line of action, develop character perspective, pull emotional meaning from the situation, model a certain perspective, or show a visualization of the inner state of mind. This list is long, but it is necessary to learn and practice these techniques in order to make your-self a great filmmaker. - Amardeep Kaleka

In conclusion, each student in the Directing the Narrative course has his or her own perspective on their studio experience. Mine was genuinely positive, and I appreciate all that I have done and understood along the way. Even the mistakes that I made, I love them and want to understand why they detract from what I am trying to achieve, that is, what we are all trying to achieve... a good film. - Amardeep Kaleka

PART III: VIDEO ASSIGNMENTS

All Video Assignments help readers to reinforce concepts they have been studying by reading this book, and by working on STUDIOS - DIRECTING EXERCISES. The main benefit of these video-assignment is that student-directors will tap into their creative wells to produce the content, which will help them to introduce themselves in a cinematic way (Self-Portrait), and help them with shooting a Short Live Action Narrative Film (Video-Study of Character, Video-Study of Place, Ptotoscript, and Video-Storyboard.)

CHAPTER 23:
SELF-PORTRAIT

Assignment:

Student-directors may choose to work on the SELF-PORTRAIT applying the manner, which suits them best. They can rely on their physical features, exploring physicality and outer appearance to portray themselves, or they can reveal themselves through "abstract" shapes, exploring different aspects of their personality and psychological makeup. They might build up a portrait on the facts and events linked to their personal history or family history. Or they may portray objects, which make their identity. Whether it will be an in-depth exploration of their own psyche or simply just a "model" of their Self-Portrait, the work has to offer cinematic insight into personal and professional life. Student-directors are encouraged to take this assignment as a mean of self-exploration and self-expression through visual media. Take it as an extended expression of the self.

Description:

- You can present yourself in a video assignment through picture and word.
- You can present yourself through the personification of a certain type of temperament (Choleric, Phlegmatic, Melancholic, Sanguine), through the emotional reaction (pleasure, fear, anger, depression, frustration). Don't be afraid to over exaggerate; don't be afraid to overdraw your type.
- You can use any genre, any type of film, any style, even a reality television show style like a documentary-style of "Celebreality," or "Docudrama" or "Candidcamera" or any hybrid of it.

- You can apply a documentary approach, or you can stage situation(s) or combine both approaches.
- You can use the parts/citations from your video-portfolio.
- Your Self-Portrait shouldn't run over 5 min including opening and closing credits.

Goal and Purpose:

- The goal of this assignment is to introduce you as a person as well as a filmmaker and to present your filmmaking skills, visual storytelling abilities, visual thinking and visual literacy.
- To evolve and utilize means of visual media for self-expression.

Instruction:

Show

- how you perceive and reflect the world around you
- how you interpret your perception
- how you re-create, manipulate and modify aspects of your perceptions through a visual media
- your attitude, your perspective, your viewpoints
- your style, your individuality, your uniqueness, inimitability, imagination
- how you visually think
- how you use the filmmaking means
- your efficiency with using visual film language
- how you construct an event
- how you create the feel you want the audience to have
- how you visually translate feelings
- what you consider as a filmable situation
- how you render an inner state of mind, psychological state, feelings, and thoughts by visual means of film
- how you articulate and visualize an idea
- where your passion lies
- what you are committed to as a human being
- inspirations, influences, role models

Paramount Advice:

Feel comfortable to talk about yourself. From now on everything will reflect you and your feelings. No one knows you better than yourself. Show us that!

What Students Said About the SELF-PORTRAIT:

I learned a lot about who I am and who I strive to be as a filmmaker in this project – I really enjoyed having the opportunity to portray myself visually and through my work for the self-portrait! - Rachel Horstmann

In filming my self-portrait, I felt that I completed a self-contained short film. The mood, theme, and director's critical choice were all successfully established. I wanted the audience to feel that I cannot be silenced without extreme consequences. This went to lengths to communicate my filmmaking style and personality. - Solomon Petchenik

I learned to talk about myself comfortably, and use creative methods to express myself. - Kristen Hall

I was really excited to do the self-portrait. It made me think of what I wanted to convey about myself. Since there were no constraints on how we could film, I was able to do what I wanted and not worry about having to conform to a certain style. This helped my future work about anything having to do with the character. With the lack of constraints, I realized that in film there are many different ways to learn about and introduce a character, not necessarily the most overdone ways. - Stacie Gliniak

CHAPTER 24:
VIDEO-STUDY OF CHARACTER

For an actor to be effective on the screen it is not enough for him to be understandable. He has to be truthful. What is truthful is seldom easy to understand, and always gives a particular sense of fullness, of completeness - it's always a unique experience that can be neither taken apart nor finally explained. - Andrey Tarkovsky, Soviet director *(Ivan's Childhood)* (Excerpt from SCULPTING IN TIME by Andrey Tarkovsky, translated by Kitty Hunter-Blair, translation copyright © 1986, 1987 by Kitty Hunter-Blair. Used by permission of Alfred A. Knopf, an imprint of the Knopf Doubleday Publishing Group, a division of Penguin Random House LLC. All rights reserved.)

Student-directors start to explore the world of scripted characters in a real setting. This is the most effective methodology that can help them to create believable characters through research. This video assignment will help them to convert abstract ideas (concept) about characters into a more concrete (material, figurative) form, to make those scripted characters more palpable, more tangible and eventually more believable.

When you are working on a character as a director, you try to create the basis of a truly believable and plausible character. In order to achieve this goal, you have to sketch an outline of the character's personality, age, family background, relationships, professional definition, social status, birth, friends, hobbies, political views, hopes, dreams, ambitions, talents, education, physical appearance, etc. You also try to work out a backstory of a character (the events preceding the script's story; biographical details that substantiate the backstory; character's biography): like family, childhood experience, personal taste – music, books, movies, hobbies, political affiliations, religious affiliations, hates, loves, fears, dreams, goals, needs, wants, education, career, economic status, personality. This is the way of shaping a character and creating an abstract notion of the character. When you have full knowledge of a character, a full abstract notion about a character based on a character breakdown (described above), you can start your video exploration (VIDEO-STUDY OF CHARACTER) and find out if your abstract notion (concept) of the character has roots in the real world or if you need to change or incorporate something else into it. After the VIDEO-STUDY OF CHARACTER, you can incorporate traits from the study to the character or even completely change your notions about a scripted character. You might discover idiosyncrasies you have never thought about and some habits or traits that enhance the character that you may have overlooked.

Assignment:

The assembly cut of raw documentary footage from the shoot of a VIDEO STUDY OF CHARACTER.

Assignment Goal:

There are a couple of different ways you can do research about a scripted character. But how can you possibly portray a believable character, you have never met before? How can you portray a believable character, in a situation that you have never been in? To get into the mindsets of your character, you have to do practical research. One of them is the VIDEO STUDY OF CHARACTER. You go out and start to explore the world of your character in a real setting. The characters come to life based on your research. This is the most effective methodology that can help you to create believable characters through research.

Principal Goal:

To carve out a scripted character based upon a real model(s) found in the real world.

Outcomes:

This video assignment will help you to convert/translate abstract ideas (concept) about the character(s) into a more concrete form, to make the character more palpable, more tangible and eventually believable. This is the place, where your characters will be developed.

Description of the Assignment:

VIDEO STUDY OF CHARACTER is a real-world study of scripted character(s) from your script for the *Final Film*. You will utilize the VIDEO STUDY OF CHARACTER for the study of a concrete person or group (in a concrete space), that resembles or is similar to the dramatic character(s) in the script of your *Final Film*. Try to catch the trivial (ordinary, every-day) situation(s) of a particular person or group in a concrete space.

Practical Requirements:

You have two options to choose from:

1st option:
Study three different individuals to represent one character in your script. The small size of study makes it difficult to say anything conclusive about its finding. However, I recommend choosing this option, because it will give you a more generalized idea about the type of the character than just studying one individual. The results of a video-study can be generalized to a scripted character, based on "external validity." The external validity of the video-study is high because it is taking place in the real world, with real people, who are more diverse than just one scripted character, or just one person you will base the character on, even it was you. The findings from a video-study of one person cannot be generalized to a scripted character. That being said, a video-study is carried out on more samples from a population, but still, it is not easy to draw the rigid lines.

2nd option:
Study one individual for each of the three different characters from your script.

The Goal of the Exercise

- To create a real authentic character rather than a fabricated one.
- To learn about the internal and external factors that shape the character.
- To find some connections between the character, story and space.
- To verify the set of semantic and aesthetically significant units of the script that might be realized in the film.
- To align your imagination with the practical requirements of the real world, even a Sci-Fi world.
- To adjust the script and incorporate the elements learned in this part of conceptualization to the script (to incorporate what you have learned from the study into your character and characterizations of the character)
- To determine what dialogue can be omitted by using visuals to get the point across.
- To create a solid foundation for the actor's performance (preparation for his/her role). It will help you in directing actors to become the characters that they represent truly.

- To provide actors with information which will help them to deliver a believable performance.

This exercise along with a VIDEO STUDY OF PLACE launches the process of putting the abstract ideas (concepts) of a story, character and place into a more concrete form. In addition, a thorough character sketch helps you to create the basis of a believable actor performance.

Video Study should demonstrate your ability to:

- Employ your sense of authenticity, and sense of place.
- Provide the doorway into a scripted character.
- Find material in the real word for more character's depth.
- Present your viewpoint of what you consider as motivation, needs, and traits of the character.
- Observe movement, gesture and facial expressions of people.
- Discover unconscious movement.
- Explore what causes each person to speak and act in a particular way.
- Find the dominant trait of the person.

Technical Requirements for the Assignment:

There are plenty of different ways to do the VIDEO-STUDY OF CHARACTER:

- Record the model for your character.
- Record people who remind you of character(s) from your script.
- Observe people with a "candid camera." (Ask people for permission and record people in a trivial situation.) See how much you can discover about them.
- Create a situation that has a similar "psychological profile" as a situation from your script and observe (record) your friends in this situation.
- Record an interview with a person who reminds you of a character from the script.
- Observe people and make "video-notes" with your comments about their appearance and what it tells you.
- Record a person who does not have any similarities with your notion of your character, and try to find out the most important thing about that particular person - the main character trait. (What is his/her dominant trait? Can you show this trait with just him/her walking? Analyze what you have learned from it. Can you use something from this for the sake of your scripted character?)

- Record a personal interview. Personal ticks can be applied to your characters' mannerism.
- Record the environment, your characters are in.

Concentrate on unconscious movement: the ways the person moves his/her body, the way he/she walks, his/her gestures and mannerisms, his/her facial expressions. Gestures are largely unconscious movements and therefore good indications of character. What character traits might these gestures indicate? Observe the gestures of people you know or of strangers with whom you come in contact. How the facial expressions of people talking relate to their emotional state. How do these mannerisms fit what you know or surmise of their traits? Observe people – what makes them interesting? Develop your own technique that allows you to recognize, what is most important from a particular person. Train your eye to discover one element that reveals the person's personality, attitude, or unique mannerisms or one feature or trait that forms the individual nature of the person. Observe people and discover the *pars pro toto*, which will tell everything or at least something important about the person.

What is not acceptable as a VIDEO STUDY OF CHARACTER:

- Recorded audition
- Recorded actor's rehearsal
- Portrait of the person
- Staged situation(s)
- Fabricated character
- Edited video-compilation using stock footage or clips from films

The VIDEO STUDY OF CHARACTER is supposed to result in a final sketch of your character. It is expected after the video-study of your character that you will be able to incorporate some elements learned in this process to the script.

Guidelines for Opening Credits

1st single credit card:

VIDEO-STUDY OF CHARACTER

2nd single credit card:
NAME OF CHARACTER (S) A character sketch. One paragraph long description for each character you have been video-studying.

Sample:

> **LIZA**
>
> Early to mid-twenties. Classically beautiful, has the aura of a 40's Hollywood actress or singer. She is a master of manipulation and carries a dark past with her. Her ultimate goal is to be a singer in the style of Ella Fitzgerald or Billie Holiday and the Aces fit her taste, although they are suspicious of a hidden agenda involved.

3rd single credit card:

Applied approach. One paragraph long description you have applied for studying the character, something similar to the *Assessment Report*. Describe here your original concept for the assignment, projected goals and real outcomes. Be as specific as you can. State what you have learned about the scripted character and what you can use from it in shaping your character. You might even have learned a new skill.

Some hints:

- From the VIDEO STUDY OF CHARACTER, I can incorporate to my character...
- On the basis of the VIDEO STUDY OF CHARACTER, I can add to my character...
- My notion of the scripted character has been affected by...
- I learned that I could communicate emotions to the audience by...
- I learned that physicalization could be magnified by...
- Since acting is supposed to mirror true-life behavior, I learned from working on the VIDEO STUDY OF CHARACTER...
- I learned that real stimuli...

Sample:

> Originally, I was thinking that I would utilize the VIDEO STUDY OF CHARACTER for studying the minor behavioral patterns unique to stage singers. I have even prepared a list of questions for an interview. I got the permission to shoot during the show and to be in her dressing room before and after the show, during the intermission. I was surprised by what I got to observe. The documentary approach enabled me to see the depth of a character I could have never scripted myself. The real person blew my mind. Some footage is not even usable for in-class screening purposes for its obscenity. Even though I had a clear vision of what I wanted my character to be, based on video-studying the real model

> for my fictional character I am going to rewrite that particular character from scratch and will take Carla as the model for LIZA in my final.

The assignment is presented and discussed in class. You can present the assembly cut of raw documentary footage from the shoot up to 10 minutes.

What Students Said about the VIDEO STUDY OF CHARACTER:

This tool gave me an extraordinary insight into the mind of a character that I thought I knew...only to discover that I didn't really know him at all. It allowed me to develop my character further, making him a more meaningful part of the film. - M. Colton Comeaux

Very interesting, it was really essential as I decided to change certain parts of the script to make it more real. - Clemy Clarke

I've always liked just to study people. This project helped me really focus on the way people act. Since acting is supposed to mirror real life, one thing I learned is that you can't tell someone to act certain things. Something I really liked about this project was that I could tell my "actors" just to ignore me and that should pretend that the camera wasn't there. I was lucky because the people I chose already knew me, so they had no problem just acting like I was hanging out with them like I do all the time. I wouldn't tell them I was filming, in fact, there were a couple of times that they didn't even know that I was filming them because I would just set the camera down and let it record while I talked to them and left the camera alone. I've learned that sometimes, words are not what's important, it's the way a person behaves without speaking that's important when a person is being his normal self, and things just happen naturally. - Jori Karoll

My goal was to learn how to present a convincing, strong-willed Southern woman by interviewing my ex-girlfriend. Indeed, our interview was entertaining. Professor Kocka enjoyed the fact that I interviewed her while she was performing tasks she already needed to do. That way, she was more comfortable and didn't think so much about being on camera. That's a good point for actors in general, who, in most cases, should be doing something on screen besides just sitting and talking. In real life, people usually are trying to get stuff done - whether it's cooking, paying bills, etc. In interviewing Alexandra, I found some very specific things I used for my final project, including the location itself and one of Alex's quirks - She likes to wear funny hats and tiaras while she is typing away at her computer. - Eric Williamson

What I learned from doing this character study was that the personality traits we see a person exhibit on a day-to-day basis are a small piece of who they actually are as a person. While in much of the footage I used, she is playing to the camera somewhat (which is unavoidable), the few moments where she seemed to forget that I was filming her were – to me – the most compelling. It was only then that I saw through the public face that she puts on (that we all put on), and was able to understand the complexity that is our humanness. - Jeff Taylor

CHAPTER 25:
VIDEO-STUDY OF PLACE

Above all, the place tells something about the life of the people who live there.

A particular place/environment/location/setting has a special atmosphere, atmosphere creates mood, and mood generates a feeling. Can this be exaggerated, or modified by a camera treatment and shot design? Student-directors video-study a particular place, where they plan to situate a story of their Short Live Action Narrative Film. The goal of this video assignment is to translate the dominant tone of the place to the mood, which will generate the desired feeling; or to change the dominant tone of the place by a camera treatment and shot design, to accommodate the desired feeling. Student-directors will be able to intensify and heighten the emotional experience of the audience by creating a more convincing mood for the scene through the atmosphere of a different place, if a scripted place does not enhance the expressive potential of the scene, and if the way how the place is filmed cannot change the feel of the place to the desired feel. Lessons from VIDEO-STUDY OF PLACE assignment will show, how to determine a visual potential of the place, how to determine main characteristics of the place, how to determine the dominant tone of the place, and how to determine a graphic aspect of the place.

Assignment:

The assembly cut of raw documentary footage from the shoot of a VIDEO-STUDY OF PLACE.

Description of the Assignment:

VIDEO-STUDY OF PLACE is a study of a particular place, where you might situate a story for the *Final Film*. VIDEO-STUDY OF PLACE could go hand in hand with the Final Film, or it can be a freely chosen space without any relationship to your story space. Also, it could be an EXT. or INT. place; exercise your free will.

Assignment Goal:

- A location influences a mood of a scene. The goal of the assignment is to capture the mood and atmosphere of the place, and characteristic elements of a particular space without actor's action, just by camera treatment.

- A director's choice in regard to a shot design influences the way space is perceived by the audience. The goal of the assignment is to express or change the feel of a place by camera treatment and shot design.

Outcomes:

- To decide whether the scene set (INT. or EXT.) or the specific location or the time of day serves the dramatic and emotional needs of the scene in the best possible way.
- To recreate the aspects of own visual experiences.
- To improve your spatial reasoning skills.
- To develop and evolve visual-spatial skills.
- To make some changes in the script on the basis of information and experiences gained during this process. (Alter the script.)
- To adjust the script and to incorporate the elements learned in this part of pre-production to the script. (Accommodate the script.)
- To find some connection between the character, story and place.
- To evolve and develop your graphic sense.
- To evolve and develop your sense of graphic aspect of visual storytelling.
- To evolve your narrative, visual filmmaking skills.
- To evolve and develop your sense of authenticity, and sense of place.
- To train your eye for location.

Video study should demonstrate:

- your ability to accurately perceive the visual world and to re-create, manipulate and modify aspects of your perceptions through a visual media
- your ability to interpret the spatial world through a visual media
- your visual-spatial ability
- your attention to visual details
- your good visual imagination.
- your visual-spatial intelligence
- your ability to estimate, which place is filmable
- your ability to find a place with a visual potential (photographic opportunities, visual possibility)
- understanding of three-dimensional design
- understanding of a Visual vocabulary of 3D design (Mass, Relative scale, Proportion, Volume, Texture, Color, Line, Positive and Negative space, Symmetrical and Asymmetrical balance)
- your ability to find out what is most important about the place

- your ability to discover the *"pars pro toto"* from a place
- your ability to discover the main trait of the place, which leads to its own mood
- your ability to find out the "character of the place"
- your ability to express or change the atmosphere and mood of the place by filmmaking means (camera, framing, angles)
- your ability to present your observation skills
- your ability to present filmmaking thinking
- your ability to present your viewpoint and attitude about the chosen environment
- your ability to reveal a character through space

Guidelines:

- How do I want the audience to experience the mood of location?
- How will a setting contribute to the mood I want to convey?
- How can I create the feeling I want the audience to have?
- Can I emphasize, accentuate some existing characteristic of the place?
- Am I able to express the truth?
- Can I make a familiar place unfamiliar?
- Can I make the place which is not visually dramatic by itself, visually dramatic by filmmaking means?
- Am I more focused on story and character, and therefore want to suppress graphic aspects of place?
- Am I able to communicate the character traits, am I able to introduce a character through the place?
- Am I able to lay down the foundations for the overall mood in a scene by choosing an appropriate place?
- Am I able to establish a "look" of location, which can involve the audience emotionally?

Practical Requirements:

- Determine the mood of location and setting by itself.
- Determine a visual potential of the place.
- Determine characteristics of place.
- Determine a graphic aspect of the place.
- Focus on: camera placement, framing, camera angle, lens selection, composition, movement.
- Take into consideration: influence of color, lines, light, texture, design.

What is not acceptable as a VIDEO STUDY OF PLACE:

Even though a VIDEO STUDY OF PLACE is not a Location Scouting, you still need to judge the value of the location through the issue of the script (artistic demands of location), but you don't have to evaluate the practical demands of location, like a power source or sound conditions. You don't need to take a look at the location through - what is needed to be done in order to adjust the space to the script and accommodate the story needs.

The assignment is presented and discussed in class. You can present the assembly cut of raw documentary footage from the shoot up to 10 minutes.

What Students Said About the VIDEO STUDY OF PLACE:

From the video study of place, I learned that you could completely change the mood of a location just based on the way you film it. You can also learn about the person associated with that location by what is in the place or even if there are only certain things that you film, you can leave something out of filming and change the character. You can change the rhythm of a place by the way you film too. If you change your shot sizes or your camera movement (or lack of camera movement) you can change the feel of a place. I learned a lot from this video study. I have a better understanding of how to film a place to achieve the look I want. - Jori Karoll

From this assignment of documenting a space, I learned that there are other ways to view space than just the way it appears at first glance. It is possible to make space feel uncomfortable and foreign to you, even if it is somewhere that you go all of the time. Space or place can tell a story by itself without any words or characters to go along with it. A place can have completely different feels in daytime vs. the night time. Extreme close-ups of the space give us details and images that we normally wouldn't associate with the place. This assignment made me start to evaluate the place I go more. I find myself thinking about what I could film, and what is interesting about the place, what type of scene could be filmed there, if I could film anything there, etc. The assignment made me re-think the locations for my project. I think it helped me to take the location of where I am shooting more seriously because I realize that the location is a character in itself. It can really add a whole new dimension to your film. If you can set up interesting and meaningful shots of your location, then you can begin to convey a mood to your audience without using any words or characters. It's less work for the characters and story then. You won't need as many shots or dialogue. - Brian Millard

CHAPTER 26:
PHOTOSCRIPT

A *photo script* represents your vision in a real setting and provides an accurate design for a scene with some production components included. A *photo strip* is a photographic representation of your vision.

As student-directors continue with the script visualization process, they will create a photo script (*"photographic scenario"*, *"photo-boards"*, *"photo-sketch"*, *"photo-storyboard"*) of one scene for the final project.

Even though the photo script is the director's second stage in the visualization process (a 2D or 3D storyboard is the first one), it has some similarities with a *Storyboard* in that the basic plan for visualization comes from the dramatic necessities and emotional necessities of the story. That means you can begin to work on a photo script without being absolutely sure about the locations. Unlike the *Storyboard*, you work with an actor; you work in a real environment, not in abstract or virtual one; and with a still camera. Unlike the *Storyboard*, which sometimes represents shots unable to be created, the photo script is taken with a real still camera, giving you precise ideas about real shots. Limitation of the medium, lens field of view, the real size of the shot, actor's features, needs of character movement, real setting, and space limitations may force you to design the shot quite differently than you might have originally intended. A *Storyboard* is more or less an abstract representation of your vision, the photo script is a more accurate representation of your vision because it is something you'll be able to physically shoot on a film set, even if you are shooting your photo script with substitute actors at a substitute location.

The list of benefits:

- Photoscripting mental image (pictorial representation of visual mental imagery) of the scene by means of still photography.
- Rendering a mental image of the scene - turning an abstraction into reality.
- Converting/translating abstract ideas into images.
- The application of abstract ideas to a real setting (the process of putting the abstract ideas of a story, character and place in a concrete form).
- Communicating meaning through images.
- Physical proof of a visual notion.
- It can help crew members to get a sense of how you have envisioned a scene.

Main Goal:

The goal is to bring your idea of the film down to earth, and see how a dramatic development is unfolded pictorially, and how an emotional and dramatic architecture of a scene can be rendered visually.

> *Your choice of the shots is all you have. It's what the movie is going to be* *made up of. The main questions a director must answer are: "where do I put* *the camera?" and "what do I tell the actors?"; and a subsequent question,* *"what's the scene about?* (Mamet, D. (1991) On Directing Film; Viking Adult; ISBN-10: 067083033X)

Format:

1st variant: (simple)

> Each still picture represents a shot you will later shoot. Each photo should represent the characteristic moment of each shot (the key moment frame) and altogether must represent one scene for your project. Each shot should be united in editing continuity with the other shots, and each pho-to must subsequently link up with the other. It's not enough to link the photos together only by the inner idea of the scene. You need to choose the required size of the shot, the appropriate position for the performer within the image area, including the direction of the performers' action, eye-line and anticipated movement.

2.variant: (advanced)

> A row of three or four photos represents one shot you will later shoot. The 1st photo represents the beginning of the shot, the 2nd photo represents the middle of the shot, the 3rd photo represents the end of the shot, and the 4th photo depicts a characteristic moment of one particular film shot - key moment frame (optional). Each row of photos has to be united in editing continuity with the others rows of photos. Photos must show how the last frame of the shot matches with the first frame of the following shot, but it doesn't have to adhere to any certain technical standards. Also, lighting, costumes and set design don't matter, and scenes can be blocked using substitute actors. (Note: If you can sum up the scene in a single photo/one keyframe, use only one photo for the entire film shot. Use the three-image format [beginning, middle, and end] only for moving shots, capturing ei-ther camera movement or a performer's movement within the shot.)

Technical Layout of the Photoscript:

1. Folder:
    Photos can be presented in the optional format (Academy movie format): photos are attached side by side onto cardboard sheets of paper. The bottom space of the paper must contain the explanatory information of the individual takes like the shot number, size of the shot, angle, anticipated camera movement, the *focal length* of the lens, dialogue and description of the scene. The whole set of photos is arranged in the form of a folder so that the photos touch each other with their shorter sides.

2. Album:
    The standard album view features three picture thumbnails in each row, representing one film shot. Printed photos can be on an 8 ½" by11" paper. Multiple sheets create a photo-script.

Instructions:

Prior to taking photos:
  - Create a *Shot List* for the scene based on the *Storyboard.*
  - Design each shot in the context of the entire scene.
  - Take photos in the actual location or substitute location with the real actors or substitute actors.
  - When you set up the shot, take into consideration: camera placement, camera angle, lens selection, composition, framing, selective focus and time.
  - For one shot, take a lot of variants of shots – change camera set-up, change the camera angle, recompose the shot, change the lens, even block actors differently.

After taking photos:
Print all variants of shots and choose one that suits your story best and analyze the chosen shot:
  - What am I trying to say with this shot? What is the main storytelling reason for this shot? What is the shot's purpose within the overall story? (If a shot does not support the story, it works against the story!)
  - Does the shot communicate the intended information?
  - Does the shot conform to the visual look of the film?
  - What is the visual advantage of this shot?
  - Why this way and not another way?
  - How does it fit into the whole?

- How will it cut with the previous and next shot?
- Is the shot totally concrete, or so abstract that the audience can miss the intended message?
- Assess dramatic tension, imaginative involvement, aesthetic value, informative value and emotional impact.
- Asses Dramatic Elements, Theatrical Element, Technical Elements, Visual Conventions
- Time limitations - take into consideration a realistic shooting schedule: number of camera set-ups in the scene, technical difficulties, complicated staging and blocking, emotional weight.
- Study and analyze the results and change (correct) your shooting script.
- Carefully review and analyze the photo script. Be prepared to revise your original concept (not just a visual concept) or even change the concept completely.

Photoscript components:

Your photo script has to communicate your vision and meaning through images clearly. Please write one paragraph on each section from the list below. Whatever your artistic approach will be, whatever format you choose for your photo script, stick to the following guidelines:

A. Scene description: State what the scene you have chosen to photo script is about.
    This is the climax of "Happily Never After." In this scene, Michael, who has refused to believe that Stephanie is a controlling and psychotic person, realizes that he cannot spend his life with her. In the midst of the proposal, he bails out and attempts to run away from her. On the other hand, Stephanie rushes after him and roughs him up, forcing him to propose to her. - Sagar Desai

B. Purpose/reason (statement of necessity): State why you have selected a particular scene for photoscripting.
    I chose to do this scene because though there is not much description about the climax in the scene, it is a difficult scene to stage. I knew that I needed to run through the scene and visualize with a camera – not with words on a script – because there is strong movement and in-depth staging. In addition, I needed to understand how to create a fight scene. - Sagar Desai

C. Self-assessment: State what you have accomplished, realized, plan to exaggerate, change or omit.

I was very surprised to see the helpfulness of this assignment. It really helped me figure out the faults of my storyboard. They were not visible to me until I had a chance to review my photos. I compiled a list of changes to my storyboard after reviewing my photo-script. Overall, I was very happy with the results of this assignment. - Amanda Kulkovski

D. Actual photo script:
Whatever format you have chosen, whatever layout you have applied, each shot has to have explanatory information of the individual takes like: shot number, size of the shot, angle, anticipated camera movement, the focal length of a lens, DOF, description, staging, blocking and dialogue.

Note:

The content and structure, blocking and a shot design of the photo script is your primary focus. The technical needs, like exposure, sharpness and depth of field do not have to be completely satisfied. You are required to take all pictures on your own, no matter what your skill level may be. Work with a still camera. Use a tripod, careful setups, and of course use only horizontal formats! The concept of vertical photos is polluting your mind, and in order to become a good filmmaker, you must rid yourself of this habit. Access your Photos App on your phone and go into your albums. Review your last 10 photos. Count the number of photos taken on vertical. You will be amazed! The point of this "test" isn't to shame yourself for using so many vertical photographs. It's to become more mindful about when and how you use them - so you can avoid them in the future. Actually, I should have been more adamant: No more vertical photographs! That means no more vertical holiday pictures! Film format is still horizontal!

Never use computer generated figures, life-imitating digital models, puppets, inflated figures or toys to stand in as substitutes for actors for your photo script. Work with flesh and blood actors. Don't use single images (still frames) from a video clip, compose each shot individually. It will teach you the discipline and practice that can push you towards greatness in composition. Feel free to use the trial and error method of taking still photos.

Advice:

- Be creative, be sensitive, be emotional and be unique!
- Try to find original viewpoints.
- Experiment and risk failure.

What Students Said About the *Photoscript:*

Utilizing the photo script provides a director with the opportunity to refine her vision by economically reading and revising each sequence of shots. Every successful effort to nurture a film during preproduction inevitably contributes to a coherent, clear and succinct piece of work. - Jason Tatum

Doing a photo-script can be very useful. Visualizing a scene mentally and visualizing with actual equipment is very different. This process allows the creator to see how his planning and visualization appears in the sequence. This process forces you to decide between camera placement, lens size etc. It's the first time you can get an idea if your shots are working or not. When I had to do the photo script, I didn't think very highly of it. I just figured it could all be covered with the video storyboard, but after completing the photo script, I realized how useful it could actually be. The earlier you can fix the mistakes in your shots the better. - Jeremiah Frazier

I found this assignment extremely valuable, and much more challenging than I had anticipated. At first, I thought that doing both this and the video storyboard might be redundant, but the photo script really helped prepare me for doing the video storyboard. I found out that some of the storyboards I had drawn could not actually be created: I had come up with impossible compositions that couldn't fit into the frame. - James Krokee

The photo script process was a bit more tolerable than the storyboard. Actually, after doing the photo script, I realized that the photo script was more helpful than the storyboard. Taking a picture with the camera allowed me to get the angles I wanted without my lack of drawing inhibiting me. Also, I got a great sense of how the actor's faces filled a shot so that when I film, I feel more confident in experimenting and deviating from the photo script. - Frank Bologna

The photo-script was helpful since it let me know which shots were unrealistic from the storyboard. Besides finding unrealistic shots, the photo-script was a preview of what my final project would look like. I didn't like what I saw. I wound up coming up with a new concept of shots for my final project. It was good I did the photo script, because it let me find out what my shots would really look like and made me change it so I could try something new. - Stacie Gliniak

CHAPTER 27:
VIDEO-STORYBOARD
ONE SCENE - TWO WAYS OF APPROACHING

A *Video-Storyboard* represents your vision in a real setting and provides an accurate design for a scene with all production components included. Since a video-storyboard is thoroughly grounded in the physical limitations of the medium, setting, space limitations, lens, field of view, camera possibilities, size of the shot, actor's features and choreographed action, it gives you an accurate picture of what the finished scene might look like. A video-storyboard is one of the most powerful pre-visualization tools because it will help you to see your vision, test your ideas and find original and unique ways of communicating your ideas.

As student-directors continue the script visualization process, they will create a video-storyboard of one scene for the Final Project. He/she will shoot one scene in two different ways.

A script is never the final product. It's a work in progress until the end of post-production. Although a student creates a video-storyboard, he/she has to be aware that the entire concept of the film is a subject to a constant verification and validation. The final shooting script, which is the eventual result of the video-storyboard, is not the goal of pre-production of the film, but its starting point.

The list of benefits:

- Launches the process of putting the abstract ideas of the story, characters and place, in a more concrete form (converting abstract ideas into visuals).
- Generates preliminary version of a scene or the film.
- Visually explores creative and technical solutions to the scene or film.
- Verifies the *Visual Concept* of the film.
- Verifies the *Visual Structure* of the film.
- Verifies the *Dramatic Architecture* of the scene (how emotions are structured within a scene).
- Verifies the *Passing.*
- Test and verify one or more aspects of the narrative.
- Tests and verifies the alternative possibilities of designing a *Visual Look* of the film.
- Tests and verifies the semantic and aesthetic elements of the script.

- Tests if the manner of staging and blocking the scene supports the scene in terms of drama and emotions or diminishes the conflict.
- Tests if the audience's attention is oriented/directed toward the substantial in a scene, and to the line of the plot.
- Tests if the intended shots are what the scene actually requires.
- Tests how many shots the scene really needs.
- Tests the director's critical choices related to a character perspective.
- Tests if the shot design is mapping turning points.
- Tests the economy of the entire shoot.
- Tests the logistics related to the shoot.
- Help potential producers to get a sense of how you have envisioned a scene or entire film, a sense of the look and style of your film.

Main Goal:

Student-directors practice conceptual approaches and rationalize every possible step in advance when designing the scene for video-storyboarding. For this project, student-directors practice making critical choices for narrative and aesthetic purposes. Students interpret the scene, choose every element within the frame, design the actor's performance within the shot and utilize all elements of visual-storytelling in order to create a scene that will communicate meaning and emotionality. Student-directors have to make critical choices, which include determining the mood, tone and the feel of the scene.

Instructions:

Prior to taking photos:

- Create the shot list for the scene based on the results from the *Photoscript*. (1st Approach)
- Pick one from the criteria stated in the chart below and apply it for rendering the same scene in a different way (2nd Approach). Or create your own criteria for what you want to test, verify or prove in your video-storyboard.
- Review the Instruction section – "Prior to taking photos" from the *Photoscript* and create a shot list for the 2nd Approach
- Shoot the *Video-Storyboard* in the intended shooting location (or appropriate substitute location) with the real actors (or substitute actors) and with a DP.
  a.   You don't have to utilize all elements of sound unless you need to test it as well.

b. You don't have to care about costumes and set design unless it is something you want to test in your *Video-Storyboard*.

After shooting:

-   Compare two scenes (Two-Ways of Approaching) and decide which one better serves the story and expresses the meaning, atmosphere, mood of the scene, emotional impact, and try to objectively assess, if your video-storyboard meets the scene objectives you have determined in advance, and if your director's choices serve those objectives in the best possible way.

-   Analyze each shot in the scene and apply the same checklist as you did while you were analyzing the *Photoscript*:

    ▪ What am I trying to say with this shot? What is the main storytelling reason for this shot? What is the shot's purpose within the overall story? If a shot does not support the story, it works against the story!

    ▪ Does the shot communicate the intended information?

    ▪ Does the shot conform to the visual look and feel of the film?

    ▪ What is the visual advantage of this shot?

    ▪ Why this way and not another way?

    ▪ How does it fit into the whole?

    ▪ How will it cut with the previous and next shot?

    ▪ Is the shot totally concrete or so abstract that the audience can miss the intended message?

    ▪ Assess the dramatic tension, informative value, imaginative involvement, aesthetic value, and emotional impact.

    ▪ Asses Dramatic Elements, Theatrical Element, Technical Elements, Visual Conventions

    ▪ Time limitations (take into consideration a realistic shooting schedule: number of camera set-ups in the scene, technical difficulties, complicated staging and blocking, emotional weight.)

- Carefully analyze the video-storyboard. Involve the crew members and discuss any changes that need to be made. Be prepared to revise or even change the original concept completely.
- Analyze the results and change/correct your shooting script. (Make a final decision about how many shots you need, make a new shooting script and a shot list for this scene. Thereafter, apply the result to your entire script if possible.)

One thought about a shot: Concrete vs. Abstract

A shot in a narrative film should lead viewers toward the intended meaning without being totally concrete. Give your audience a bit of room to think and interpret the shot for themselves. Do not attempt to say it all. Don't be too on the nose. Is your shot totally concrete or so abstract that the audience could miss the intended message?

> *Cinema consists of drawing the audience's attention to the significant elements and eliminating the superfluous. (...) All of this corresponds to our own way of perceiving the world, for we eliminate from our field of vision everything that does not hold or attract our attention.* (Wajda, A. WAJDA ON FILM: A MASTER'S NOTES, 3rd edition; ACROBAT BOOKS; 2015, ISBN-10: 0918226295)

Pick one from the following criteria and use it for rendering one scene in two different ways, or create your own criteria for what you want to test, verify or prove in your video-storyboard. The point of working on two different approaches is simple. It is a process of determining if the original concept accurately represents your vision, and serves the story and emotional needs of the scene in the best possible way. The second approach can provide you with a deeper understanding of the dramatic mechanism and emotional mechanism of the scene; it can give you a chance to recognize of new or yet undiscovered phenomena of the scene; it may reveal information that would not be identified through the first approach. Or the other way around, the second approach will reassure you that the original concept rendered in the first approach is the best one for the scene.

VIDEO-STORYBOARD TWO WAYS OF APPROACHING		
CRITERIA	**1ST APPROACH**	**2ND APPROACH**
Character Perspective	Consistent, Fluid, Neutral (The execution of a standard visual approach.)	Consistent, Fluid, Neutral (The execution of an unconventional visual approach.)
Storyteller's perspective	3rd Person Perspective	1st Person Perspective
Location (Emotional impact)	Atmosphere and Mood (Setting for creating the mood you want to convey.)	Different Atmosphere and Mood (Different setting for creating the mood you want to convey.) (Consider: changing the location, color, texture, design, lighting, camera framing, movement,..)
DAY or NIGHT (Foundation for mood)	DAY	NIGHT
Time of day (Tremendous impact on the interpretation of the scene)	Morning	Dusk
Setting – Atmosphere of the place (Foundation for mood)	INT.	EXT.
Emotional impact (Relation of each shot to an emotional meaning of the situation)	Emotional value of the situation (What feeling you want to engender and grow in the audience)	Different emotional value of the situation, or a different approach to rendering the same emotional value.
Assess the rhythm and pace and decide, how many shots you really need	Break down the scene into several shots and cover situation using a multiple shot coverage.	Cover situation in one scene shot (sequence shot, integral shot), which is based on inner montage and keep the same blocking.
Blocking	In-depth	On-line
Blocking style	Shot-reverse shot pattern	Shots based on the "inner montage"
Blocking pattern	Approaching and receding pattern	Accompanying the emotion pattern
Rhythm	Pattern of Repetition	Pattern of Alternation
General narrative principle	Subjective treatment	Objective treatment
Cinematic realism	Very well framed shots, conceived compositions	Shaky, jittery camera
Acting style	Classical	Natural

Casting	Actor	Different actor
Casting	Typecasting	Cast against type
Organization of storytelling	Chronological time	Non-linear time
Movement	Static shots	Moving shots
Cinematic realism	Appearance of realism	Drawing attention to its own aesthetic
Montage	Invisible editing	Editing dominates the narrative
DOF	A shallow depth of field	Deep focus
Composition	Opened composition	Closed composition
Editing pattern	Editing pace	Different editing pace
Visual look	Mode of lighting	Different mode of lighting
Psychological time	Compressed time	Expended time
Narrative ambiguity	Clear (transparent) message	Clouded (hidden) message
Genre conventions	Genre code	Against or different genre code, genre deviations
Artistic ambition	Visual clichés	Non-conventional visual approach
Viewer's treatment	The viewer is treated as a participant	The viewer is treated as an observer
Film stock	Color	Black and white
Consonance and dissonance	Harmonious portrait of the scripted situation	Discordant portrait of the scripted situation
Emotional engagement	Passive engagement	Active engagement
Create the feel you want the audience to have	Portraying the source that triggers the emotional reaction	Portraying the emotional reaction of the character to the source

Video-Storyboard – Checklist:

The film tells a story not only through the content of the story and the actor's performance but also through the director's control of the shots. Visual narrative, and directing the viewer's attention by emphasizing what is essential in the shot, is one of the most important parts of film directing. Carefully consider how the shot design and camera treatment carries the story forward and expresses key emotions. As a director, it is your job to practice making critical choices for narrative and aesthetic purposes.

Carefully review and analyze the video-storyboard with all crewmembers, and identify the problems. Discuss any changes that need to be made. Reexamine the scene focusing on its fundamental structure from every possible perspective. Try to troubleshoot and refine your chosen cinematic approaches.

1. The video-storyboard should demonstrate a:
   - Successful application of abstract ideas to the real setting.
   - Successful confirmation of the visual concept for the film.
   - Sense for the graphic aspects of visual storytelling.

2. The video-storyboard should demonstrate a skillful manner of controlling the space by:
   - Camera position (flat, deep, limited, ambiguous)
   - Lenses
   - Staging and blocking

3. The video-storyboard should clearly articulate:
   - Storyteller's perspective
   - Character perspective within the scene
   - Visualization, which is in accord with the meaning of the scene
   - Principal rule (Subjectivity, Objectivity)
   - Shifts in the pattern of shots if something important is advancing the plot
   - The visual style (Does the style carry the content and emotions? Is the style presented as a substitute for a week narration? Does the style simulate the thematic extremes of the narrative? Does the style overwhelm the content?)

4. Does the staging support emotions, story, drama, and rhythm? What is a dramatic advantage of this staging?
   - Does a physical action externalize the character's emotional state?
   - Is the blocking dynamic and supportive?
   - Does the staging make the character objective easily readable for the audience?
   - Does the staging support the characters' relationship?
   - Are there better staging and blocking possibilities?

5. Does the sequence of shots support emotions, story, drama, and rhythm? (Don't forget, you stage and block the scene for the camera not for a theater stage, other filmmaking means are at your disposal as well.) Think about following:

- Emotional dynamic of the scene (relation of shot to the emotional meaning of the situation).
- Physical dynamic of the scene.

6. Do the staging and blocking guide the viewer's attention to the substantial in the story by withholding and revealing information?

7. Do the staging and blocking carry the story and express emotions?

8. Where does the scene take place?
   - How does this place support the story, emotions and drama?
   - What is the dominant mood of the place and how does it contribute to evoking emotions? Does it work for the scene, is it ambivalent, or must it be fixed because it works against the scene?
   - Does the atmosphere of your location create the mood you want?
   - Does the mood generate the feeling you want?
   - What would happen if you changed the location? Would it benefit the story?
   - Should you consider changing the atmosphere of your location from one of harmony to one of discord in order to heighten the emotional impact of the scene?

9. Does the scene communicate with the audience? Did you get across the message?

Video-Storyboard components and credits:

Whatever your artistic approach will be, stick to the following guidelines and use them to create the first five title cards in your opening credits sequence and two title cards for the closing credits sequence.

Opening credit sequence:

Scene description
    state what the scene you have chosen to video storyboard is about.
Purpose/reason (statement of necessity)
    state why you selected this particular scene for video storyboarding.
First approach
    state what you have tried to accomplish or test with your first attempt.
Second approach
    state, what you have tried to accomplish or test with your second attempt.
Director's name

Closing credit sequence:

Identification of problems
Changes that need to be made

Conclusion:

A video-storyboard is a research tool to test and verify the concept or the final product or to test and verify one or more aspects of the narrative. It falls into qualitative research. Qualitative research here is an in-depth exploration of what the audience will possibly feel by watching your film. Verification is the product of checking the whole concept of the film, or one or more aspects of the research process to ensure that a video-storyboard is a true representation of what you have originally envisioned. From a business marketing perspective, a video-storyboard can help you to convey and showcase your vision and the mood and tone of your intended film to potential producers. It is a video representation of your visual imagination, and as a "proof of concept," it can be incorporated into a pitch-reel/pitch-video/pitch-trailer, to help potential producers to get a sense of how you have envisioned your film, a sense of the look, style and feel of your intended film. It will showcase your talent, craftsmanship, industry, artistry, professional voice, expertise, creative potential, the capacity of your creative control, and your ability to perform director's duties.

What Students Said About the Video-Storyboard:

On first consideration, the idea of shooting your film, before actually shooting your film, may seem redundant. However, having done it, it is difficult to imagine undertaking a serious production without first completing a Video-Storyboard. It is amazing the number of errors even a simple video storyboard can correct, as well as the incredible amount of constructive ideas it can generate. And if that's not enough to convince you of the power of video storyboarding, ask a few professionals and you will learn that it is a standardized practice. - William P. Hammargren

From the video storyboard assignment, I learned a great deal about character's placement and location. I realized the location that I originally was planning to shot my scene in was not appropriate for the situation. It was not laid out how I had envisioned. Therefore, I found a new location to shot the final project. By assigning us to direct and edit in two different styles, it forced me to look at different ways to direct the scene. I was forced to figure out whose scene it was. I found this assignment and the photo script as-

signment very useful. It gave me a chance to practice directing the scene and figure out its strengths and weaknesses. - Amanda Kulkoski

Video-Storyboard enhances and reiterates the rarefaction of her vision by analyzing the following: 1) the duration and mobility [camera moves] of shots, 2) choreography of her players and their composition within the framed environment. Every successful effort to nurture a film during pre-production inevitably contributes to a coherent, clear and succinct piece of work. - Jason Tatum

Video Storyboards can be a very useful tool. It is almost like pre-filming your project. It very clearly lets you see if your shots and sequences are working or not. It is something that before this class I had never done. Now that I have done one, I can see how useful it actually is. It can save you lots of time and money, but most importantly it allows you another chance to perfect your work. After this assignment, I will definitely create a video storyboard for any big project I take on. - Jeremiah Frazier

Video-Storyboards will show you what storyboards alone cannot. They will reveal certain impossibilities and limitations in relation to the physical space around you, not to mention, blocking and staging, and composition. So, find the time and effort, because these videos can save your butt. They will show you the error of your ways, and reveal new ideas, before you start shooting costly film. - Rhyan Taylor

My video storyboard was helpful because I was able to walk through the shots I was needing for the final with my DP and camera person. It really helped as a practice for the real thing. I learned that I would have to have a dolly instead of hand-held and I learned that I would have to find rolling chairs to move the actors off screen the way I needed them to move. I also enjoyed getting feedback from my professor about what I was planning. It was helpful to see if it was all working. - Susan Flores

CHAPTER 28:
SHORT LIVE ACTION NARRATIVE FILM

If I wanted a long, boring story with no point to it, I have my life. - Jerry Seinfeld, American stand-up comedian

A student-director works on a *SHORT LIVE ACTION NARRATIVE FILM* from conception to completion. For some of you, this will be most likely the biggest project you have directed so far. This challenge should not scare you. You have to think of it as an opportunity to utilize all that you already learned. All directing exercises aimed to teach you specific directorial skills through specific directing exercises. The short film should reflect all that you have gained from those exercises. Directing exercises are excellent in teaching a single component of directing, but since a film does not consist of only a single component of filmmaking, I am completely convinced that the bigger project will teach you more.

Specification of the SHORT LIVE ACTION NARRATIVE FILM:

This film is a combinative Interior and Exterior short live-action narrative film with or without dialogue, based upon an original screenplay, or adaptation, with a limited number of characters, filmed on location, in length up to 10 minutes, including opening and closing credits. Cooperation with actors is required. Although student-directors are allowed to use dialogue, only filmable topics are taken into consideration and emphasis is put on communicating meaning through visual means of film. Visual aspect should be dominant.

By working on this project – Final Film, student-directors will be able to expand filmmaking abilities, while learning how to do it. Their own project will help them practice and use the new knowledge and skills. A short live-action narrative film is project-based learning, where student-directors will demonstrate mastery of directing by creating a short film, which is driven by their own interest and passion, industry and artistry. The first and foremost beneficiary of this project is a student-director. While the short film can assess student-director's knowledge about directing, it also allows a student-director to showcase his/her talent, imagination, sensitivity and workmanship, and also his/her temperament, emotionality and mannerisms. It is expected that this project will reflect student-directors' style, storyteller's voice, knowledge, the range of talent, experience, creative potential, ability to perform director's duties, and his/her ability to hit the ground because at this point he/she is eminently qualified and capable.

When short films are at their best, they are the exact opposite of "a long, boring story with no point to it." I love brief narratives that are rich in texture, saturated with meaning and tell their stories without wasting a moment on filler of any kind. It is widely known that the short film is the poetry of filmmaking, and the other quote I'd like to share is the most relevant definition of poetry I have ever seen. A Chinese master said: 'The writer's message is like rice. When you write prose, you cook the rice. When you write poetry, you turn the rice into rice wine.' The best short films are pure rice wine – so concentrated and intoxicating that they take our breath away, while mediocre shorts that seem to go on forever, tediously belabouring their story, are like cooked rice. The great short films tell more in as little as four or seven minutes than many feature films. And the form is much freer, much less subject to formulaic storytelling patterns and conventions." (All killer no filler; An interview with Richard Raskin, Editor of Short Film Studies; http://www.intellectbooks.co.uk/MediaManager/File/filmcatalogue(web).pdf/ Accessed March 3, 2017. Reprinted by permission of Mr. Richard Raskin.)

Outcomes:

- A short live-action narrative film gives student-directors a capstone experience. Students' achievement, conventionally, has been assessed by examination, but for student-directors, the method of evaluation is the final project - a short live-action narrative film. It is a measure of the learning process.
- The creative and masterful interpretation, and transformation of the screenplay, demonstrating talent, artistic imagination, and technical skills in the storytelling area of the narrative film.
- A style-consistency film, which supports the unity of the film, and heightens the emotional impact on the audience.
- A unified and seamless film based on harmonizing all directorial components - directing actors, cinematography, shot design, and art direction.

Objectives:

- Practicing diverse specific directorial concepts and skills learned from this book, and from all hands-on exercises in one dramatic piece - in a short live-action narrative film.
- Testing the newly acquired theoretical and practical knowledge gained from all directing exercises and video assignments in a short live-action narrative film.

- Hands-on experience with working on a longer narrative piece from conception to completion. It will give student-directors hands-on experience as directors as they direct to finish a short live-action narrative film through pre-production, production, and post-production.
- Experiencing how own critical thinking, decision-making skills, new directorial skills, and proficiency with the equipment can shape own narrative product, and how that product (short live-action narrative film) can reflect own personality, talent, and imagination.
- To have one more piece to put into a portfolio, and perhaps some student-directors will produce a festival worthy film.

Goals:

- To creatively interpret a screenplay by applying many of the directorial concepts presented in the book.
- To develop the narrative filmmaking skills and visual storytelling abilities.
- To creatively master the relation of a shot to the emotional meaning of the situation.
- To translate scene components into a visual story, and present evolved the ability to tell a story visually, and visually express and communicate ideas, and meanings by filmmaking means.
- To translate inner feelings, motivations and insights of characters to the filmable situation.
- To skillfully use different visual strategies and methodologies in orienting and manipulating the audience's attention to the storyline and to all that is important for the story.
- To skillfully master different blocking, staging, and shooting methods, principles, styles, patterns, and strategies.

Description of a Short Live Action Narrative Film:

- **A: Auteur Film:**
  The student-director writes and directs the film. Interior and/or Exterior Dramatic Narrative Project, based upon an original screenplay written by the student himself/herself. The student-writer-director has an absolute degree of authorship over the entire film. The student-writer-director creates a film in accord with the "auteur theory", and he/she wants to stand out and be memorable in a good way.

How to set yourself apart from other directors? This section provides bulleted suggestions for you to grab and go:

- Find the story you love and tell it.
- Be curious, it will make you interesting.
- Apply your curiosity to things which may go unnoticed by others.
- Pay attention to notice things that usually go unnoticed.
- Question the status quo.
- Approach age-old problems with new solutions.
- Apply your own solution to an age-old ethical and philo-sophical problem.
- Be personal.
- Do it differently than others.
- Don't go with the flow.
- Separate yourself from the crowd.
- Stand out and take some chances.
- Apply your imagination.
- Separate yourself from others by style. Make sure that your style is different than anybody else's.
- Tell generic stories in a unique, unexpected way.
- Treat the story differently.
- Adopt rebelliousness.
- Challenge conventional wisdom.
- Adopt a radical form of self-presentation.
- Reject age-old schools of theoretical concepts.
- Ignore dogmas and scholasticism.
- Break free from an old world driven norms, paradigms and prejudice.
- See the beauty in patterns.
- Experiment.

This is what will get you on the radar! So, grab these suggestions and go with it. It's your time to shine. You cannot help but stand out and be memorable. Think also about the following in searching for the story you will be shooting as a Final Film:

- Unique theme or topic (something unique, never seen be-fore, or seen before but with a personal imprint imposed on it).
- New and unseen subjects.
- Turning generic themes into unique content.
- Meaningful, life-enriching story.

- Dealing with universal human subjects.
- Passing your sense of wonder and positivity onto others.
- Manifestations of humanity.
- Radical approaches.
- Something that reflects your identity, professionalism, artistry, and industry
- Innovations – the invention of a new language true to the nature of the film.
- Art-house approach.
- Art-cinema narration (breaking the conventional narration, chance events, fortuitous discoveries, subconscious, dreams, and emotions and not continuity and narrative logic as structuring devices).
- Crossover of genre visual style.
- Genre deviations.
- Stylistic replications.
- Rejections of standard conventions (a new system of conventions, a disorder as a rule).
- Breaking all the rules of conventional cinematographic practice set by traditional Hollywood filmmaking.
- Fully embracing new technologies.
- Artistic risks.
- A need to stand out from the crowd.
- A "wow" factor.

- **B: Original Screenplay:**

Interior and/or Exterior Dramatic Narrative Project, based upon an original screenplay written by somebody else, not by student-director.

- **C: Adaptation:**

Interior and/or Exterior Dramatic Narrative Project, based upon the pre-existing material of any kind, even a painting. A student-director can develop an idea from any existing screenplay, poem, short story, novel, Aesop's fable, myth, legend, fairy tale, radio drama, or even music or comics. (Make sure you have the legal right to use the pre-existing work of art. I encourage you to stay in compliance with the law. Even though you assume that the story, which was published a long time ago, may be now in the public domain that means no longer protected by copyright, it is safe to consult a copyright attorney, and make sure that story you are interested in is in public domain.)

- Pick a novel, or short story, or poem and adapt it to a screenplay, you will be shooting as a Final Film. You can strive to be "faithful" to the original written work, or your adaptation can be a "betrayal" of the original work. Your adaptation can be a straightforward adaptation, or distillation adaptation, or skeleton adaptation, or just freely reference to the source material. Do not fear to take an esteemed work of literature and make it your own.

- The point in working with story or script, written by somebody else is very simple:

  - to force yourself to find something, which will reflect your personal identity and can be recognized as something which belongs to you

  - to learn to find the core or meaning which is transferable from pre-existing work to the screen

  - to learn to work with somebody's else material

  - practice implementing your own vision, thoughts, and point of view into material that wasn't generated by you

  - practice imposing your own personal and professional imprint and mark on somebody's else material

- No doubts there are differences between designing a whole film and designing just one scene. If you plan to work only with one scene, or with a portion of a scene, pick a scene which will be convenient for the purposes of the Final Project:

  - a complete scene with a beginning, middle, and end (a portion of the scene must also satisfy this structure)

  - the scene must be based upon a screenplay or narrative text (fictional narrative story) or narrative art (narrative represented in painting or sculpture)

  - demand for the unity of space, time, and action doesn't have to be completely satisfied

  - demand for "traditional storytelling" must be satisfied, the continuity and narrative logic must be structuring devices – one event leads to the next event and so on, creating the chain of events linked or related to one another, a series of connected events leading to a conclusion

- no voice-over narration, no interior monolog

- abrupt discontinuity in the action, time and place must be adequately presented – no cinematic punctuation. But you can use fade-outs, fade-ins, dissolves, overlays, superimpositions, and jump cuts when you want to pace the action or externalize character's interiority.

- three characters at the same time - physically presented

- Any genre, any form, any poetic, and any style is acceptable.

- Style must not be presented as a substitute for a weak narration, style must not overwhelm the content.

- Fancy graphic design and attention-grabbing gimmicks with a tendency to mask narrative incapability and story-telling incompetence are forbidden.

- The cooperation with an actor is required.

- Cooperation with a DP is welcomed and recommended.

- The film must be edited by a student-director himself/herself or overseen by a student-director.

Technical requirements and key general duties:

- In case that you decide to go with the C: Adaptation, find a heavy dialogue-based scenes (scenes led by the dialogue, dialogue-driven scenes, scenes which look like everything is revealed through the dialogue), and unverbalize the scene.
- Originate artistic vision, and clearly articulating it to collaborators.
- Don't allow the content being carried only by dialogue. Emphasis is put on communicating meaning, even unspoken thoughts by visual means of film.
- Don't visually illustrate that characters are interacting.
- Create a believable illusion of the interaction, conversation.
- Utilize the editing technique, which helps to make a dialogue scene flow smoothly. Try to avoid "talking heads" and "ping-pong effect".
- Break an identical visual style of Cross-cutting dialogue situation.
- Break a visual limitation of dialogue scenes.

- Avoid having "too much on the nose."
- Make your film look unique.
- Find the way of communicating your messages with maximum effectiveness.
- Apply certain directorial concepts you have learned from the book and exercise your personal taste.
- Practice certain directorial methods and principles you have learned from this book.
- Carry out all director's duties and perform all the activities on a highest possible level, and accept all responsibilities.
- Guide, inspire and motivate the film crew members.
- Practice the decision-making, and exercise independent judgment.
- Be a strong and confident leader.
- Exercise competence.
- Exercise the powers for the reasons for which you are entitled to as a film director.
- Fulfill your vision.

Paramount Advice:

Try to create a richly textured film, do not rely only on the "power" of dialogue. Dialogue is just one of the film's expressive tools. Utilize a wide palette of narrative devices, which are at your disposal. Film communication is primarily a visual presentation, in spite of exploiting other differen*t* manners of presentation.

The Evils of dialogue:

- Dialogue is linear. Viewers comprehend the meaning of the dialogue, word by word, by the speed of how fast the dialogue is spoken. That means, very slowly.
- Dialogue kills a rhythm, tempo, and pacing. It definitely moves very slowly.
- Dialogue reveals a character rather than describing him/her.
- Dialogue reveals emotions, feelings, rather than dramatizing the situation.
- Dialogue overloads the intended meaning.
- Dialogue communicates the meaning instead of it being expressed.
- Dialogue shows conflict, instead of dramatizing it.
- Dialogue shows character, instead of portraying a real essence of a character.

- Dialogue suppresses subtext, instead of revealing it through gesture, intonation, and expression.
- Dialogue shows thoughts and attitudes, instead of them being physically or visually manifested.
- Dialogue externalizes feelings, instead of visualizing them.
- Dialogue verbally expresses internal, instead of reveling it externally.
- Dialogue shows inner motivation of a character, instead of rendering it through external events.

Some Thoughts of Accomplished Film Directors:

Dialogue should simply be a sound among sounds, just something that comes out of the mouths of people whose eyes tell the story in visual terms. – Alfred Hitchcock *(Psycho)*, English film director

I hate the idea of revealing the character's emotions through dialogue. I feel that expressing emotions through words rather than action is an easy option that cinema chooses more and more often. It's like a disease. - Emir Kusturica *(When Father Was Away on Business)* (Tirard, L. Moviemakers' Master Class: Private Lessons from the World's Foremost Directors, 1 edition; Farrar, Straus and Giroux; 2002, ISBN-10: 057121102X)

Too many films today strike me as being overly wordy ... I know what I am talking about since I'm aware of this destructive element in my own films. (...) In the first place, scenes in which there is a great deal of talk should be rendered as "dynamic" as possible via movement.
- Andrzej Wajda *(The Promised Land)*, (Wajda, A. (1992) Wajda on Film: A Master's Notes, 1 edition; Acrobat Books, 1992, ISBN 10: 0918226295)

Preliminary Work:

All preliminary work must be done in a timely manner. No one will get the permit to start shooting before all required work is turned in. When all preliminary work is turned, and all requirements related to the approval process are met, it automatically constitutes an official approval for the shoot, and no additional steps have to be taken.

- PHOTOSCRIPT
- VIDEO-STORYBOARD
- VIDEO STUDY OF CHARACTER
- VIDEO STUDY OF PLACE
- I, II, III, IV, V, VI, VII. STUDIO

Directing Crew:

You may direct alone or with the partner or in groups of three, maximum. If you are directing alone, all parts of the Final Film must be produced by you individually. If you are directing in a group, each group member will be responsible for contributing equally to the project, and only one Film Project is required for one group. I do not regard just editing, or producing as an equal contribution to the Final Film. Since you ran from the directing aspect as being "just" an editor or producer, you are losing a great benefit of a capstone experience by not participating in the directing aspect of the Final Film. In a group project, you have to direct a portion of that project. You, as a director, bear the full weight of responsibility for the ultimate success and failures of your film. Not just in this film, also in the real world.

What Students Said About a SHORT LIVE ACTION NARRATIVE FILM:

It was our thesis. The culmination of four years of education and experience, learning to form not just a perspective but a means of expressing it. Naturally, this film became something of the penultimate experience to graduation itself; something I looked forward to since I first realized that I wanted to study filmmaking. It would be the closest approximation yet of a real film. We were to be judged on its merits by collaborators, colleagues, professors, and most importantly ourselves; for in our education we naturally built up our facilities for self-critique, and this was essential in our journey of becoming better filmmakers, better artists, and better people. Reflecting on this process brings about the same feelings I had 12 years ago when I was knee deep in the middle of production: I am grateful to have had the guidance and tutelage of Professor Lubomir. He was the real deal, seamlessly merging aesthetic technique and lessons on theory with such passion and vitality, his students could only follow suit. In that, I found friends for life. As colleagues, we grew together, learned from one another and lifted each other up in the face of the many challenges that arose while making our films. Now, over a decade since graduation, many of these friends remain my closest collaborators, sharing a passion for the medium, instilled in us during our time with Lubomir. This class managed to be more than a foundation for me, and I look back to the wisdom gained from it with great reverence. It was there that I learned the vocabulary for not just making a film, but approaching the world as an artist. - Kevin Phillips *(Super Dark Times)*

My approach to storytelling has been and still is mostly non-traditional. 'Weird stuff' across many fields and platforms often alternating from a single screen to fully immersive interactive experiences. For me, my interest in moving and traditional arts started at a young age. I experimented with image, texture, sound, movement and space to elicit a feeling. It was odd, it was different, it was often terrible, but it was raw and how I liked to mix things together. This is where Directing the Narrative, and Prof. Lubomir Kocka played an important role in my development as an artist, not just as a filmmaker but across the other mediums I work in as well. I learned how to better translate ideas into the story by editing all of the same elements I had always worked with down to their raw purpose before designing what is actually needed and how to use it. Once planned, I am free to explore/play because the story is anchored. I learned how to manipulate and design using the tried and true techniques of visual narrative storytelling. It continues to elevate everything I do, both traditional and abstract. - Alexander Hammer - Artists he continually works with: Beyonce, Jay Z, Madonna, Katy Perry; Directors he continually works with: Jonas Akerlund, Dikayl Rimmasch.

When I arrived at SCAD, almost every film students were talking about Lubo's directing the narrative class. I can't stress enough how much this class impacted me as well. In fact, it was the best class I've ever had. The preliminary work, studio exercises and directing techniques were fundamental for me to become a director, and I'm still very proud of the final film I made in that class. Lubo gave us access to the world of cinema in a way that we felt like we were a part of it. We learned, we dreamed, worked hard, but it was always fun and exciting. I cherish the collaborations I got to be apart of with other students in that class. There was never a feeling of competition. We were a team. And we still are, as I very frequently work with my classmates to this day. Thank you so much, Lubo. Clemy Clarke - Writer director. Preparing two feature films. Past/current works include *Nudes (TV series to be released in 2019) After Anyuta (short film 2018) Hollywood (web/tv series 2016-2017) Dirty Sexy Children (short film 2013) Blue (short film 2013) My Only Cousin (short film 2011)*

After the first class of Directing the Narrative, I was completely traumatized. Students had a dense amount of information to absorb at an intense and fast pace. It was amazing! Young and careless, I created with just my intuition at hand. Whether I meant it or not, all my choices or my lack of choices were saying something. In this class, Lubo clearly labeled and categorized the different directorial concepts of filmmaking. We learned to control these with the purpose to achieve a goal. Identifying these notions gave me access to a bigger palette of choices. This allowed me precision and control. Making conscious choices forms a perspective; hence create a VISION. That's how I learned the most important aspect of directing. During the making of my final film for the class, I created a vision for the first time. You can only see what you can say. Thank you for making me see more. - Paloma López (Singer), *Sundance Ignite Fellow 2018*

Of all the classes and all the projects, I have had in my four years at SCAD the final project for my Directing the Narrative class was by far the project I have learned the most from. It was the first time we were given an assignment at the start of the quarter (more precisely a week prior to the start of the quarter) and were given the entire quarter to complete it. Not only that but for the first time, we were required to work with a separate DP and Editor. We had to take responsibility for ourselves and our project, do all of the preproduction and get everything together that we required to make the project possible on a larger scale. We were given the time to put all of the things we had learned from previous classes and throughout the quarter into practice and to really put a lot of thought and effort into this project. It was the first pitch I ever made, the first DP I ever worked with, the first time I did not write the script for my project and had to create a film based on someone else's work, and the first time I created video storyboards ahead of time preparing myself for issues and being able to compensate for them ahead of shooting, making the days of shooting more efficient. Most importantly, this project was unparalleled in preparing me for the work I would have to put into my Senior Film. Without this project, I would not have had the knowledge or experience to take a 25-person crew out to New Mexico in the dead of winter and come back with a festival worthy film that is truly a group collaboration, as any film should be. - Katherine Abshier Jones

I'm writing this in regards to the final project required for the Directing the Narrative class. I am in my senior year and must say that I have benefited greatly from this project. It was really the first time I had taken on a project of that size, and it helped me better understand the filmmaking process as a whole. It was also the first time I had a good-sized crew and a DP I had to collaborate with. This project provided an incredibly valuable experience that ushered me into the world of larger productions. Though I did not pursue the directing path, it helped me understand the directing process which in turn helped me better understand directors. This is invaluable to me now as a DP. Without this project, students would be missing a crucial step between the intro and mid-level courses and the advanced and senior courses. - Zak Ettlinger

SCAD remains a very special institution for studying film because it's one of the very few that allows each and every student the opportunity to control their own film, whether it be in the amateur stage during the intro to film/video or in directing the narrative. I recently completed my senior pro-

ject, and there is no doubt in my mind that 99% of its success rests on the skills and tools I learned from the experience of directing my own film. Without having the opportunity to be the sole creative mind behind my narrative film, my senior film would have failed. - Evan Watkins

I regard my Directing the Narrative Final as one the most important assignments I ever had. I always wanted to direct, but I never really knew if I could direct until I finished that project. The class gave me the tools and the techniques, but the project is where I learned how to apply those tools. While the project is demanding and requires a large amount of preparation, the end result is a learning experience that really shows you what you're made of. Sure, my project wasn't perfect, but I grew because of it. I learned from my mistakes, met actors and crew, and realized what was possible with next to no budget. All of which would prove vital to me for my Senior Film. Also, directors have very few chances to add to their reel, and this project is a great opportunity to enhance their portfolio. If it not been for my Directing Final, I would not have been properly prepared for the Senior Project Class, and my film would have suffered. - Daniel Etheridge

PART IV: STUDIO SCRIPTS

Compilation of six two and three-character scenes, which will be used by students-directors for shooting in-studio directing exercises. These scenes can be easily found and downloaded from the Internet.

- *Kramer vs. Kramer* - Screenplay by Robert Benton, based on the novel of the same name by Avery Corman.
  The breakup scene: Ted Kramer is a career man for whom his work comes before his family. His wife Joanna cannot take this anymore, so she decides to leave him. Ted has just landed a new account and the promise of a promotion. When he arrives home, he expects Joanna to share his elation, but that is instantly disrupted by Joanna's declaration that she's leaving him.

- *Sex, Lies, and Videotape* - Screenplay by Steven Soderbergh.
  A dinner scene: Ann and John are married. John is an attorney, and Ann is a housewife. Ann is in therapy, dealing with the stress. John is having an affair with Ann's sister, who works as a bartender, what Ann is unaware of. John reconnects with a close friend from college, Graham. They have not been in touch since Graham dropped out of college nine years ago. Graham has contacted John and asked to stay at his home. All three of them have a conversation at the dinner table. Reflexive comments on the specific events and incidents from the past, and indirect references to earlier events creates allusion. It is left to the audience to make the connections.

- *The Bridges of Madison County* - Screenplay by Richard LaGravenese, based on the novel of the same name by Robert James Waller.
  Scene: Friendly but awkward conversation between Robert, a traveling photographer and Francesca, a housewife. The early contours of the affair, of a loyal wife and a caring mother, taking place while her husband and children are at the state fair. This is the beginning of erotic fantasy, with little erotic touches that slowly escalate.

- *Closer* - Screenplay by Patrick Marber, based on his play of the same name.
  The breakup scene: Larry tells Anna about the prostitute he slept with only after he learns about her affair with Dan.

- *The Notebook* - Screenplay by Jan Sardi, based on the novel of the same name by Nicholas Sparks.

Two short scenes, EXT.HOUSE - DAY and EXT. HOUSE – NIGHT, back
to back: Martha goes over to Noah's house after he's reunited with Al-
lie, the love of his life, and asks to meet his "one." Martha is the
woman Noah has, but not the woman he wants, and she knows all
about it. After all, accepting that fact involves a process of grieving for
a lost self. The most difficult aspect of moving on is not the fact that
she is not the "one," and that Noah belongs to somebody else, but
how she will live now. Inexplicably, instead of being jealous, Martha
is inspired by the love she sees. Her parting words to Noah are: "For
the first time since I lost Richard, I feel like I've got something to look
forward to."

THE GOBLIN

Screenplay by Jana Kákošová

Directed by Lubomir Kocka

6 INT. SCHOOL OFFICE - DAY

6.1. MFS (50)

Peter standing by the door tediously watches as…

6.2.MCU (51)

…SECRETARY slowly types in his data to the computer.

                    SECRETARY
          Huska, Peter, seventh A … I will
          write out the cash account
          for lunch from today. Bring me
          the receipt tomorrow. Is that clear?

The Secretary squints at Peter off.

                    SECRETARY
          (obviously unhappy with something)
          Damn!

6.3.MFS-2MFS (52)

The door of the office opens and DANKO slips in.

6.4.CU (53)

SECRETARY

Stupid machine! Who has time to mess
with it?

6.5.M2S (54)

Danko moves toward Peter and whispers.

DANKO

286es were before the primates.

PETER

Seriously! … Old fashioned.

6.6.MS-M2S (55)

The Secretary stops paying attention to the computer.

SECRETARY

Don't be smart with me.

And what do you want Danko?

Danko walks into the shot and flashes a blue card.

DANKO

Cancel tomorrow's lunch for me.

The Secretary takes his card with annoyance and cop-
ies his number on a scrap of paper.

SECRETARY

I could do without these stupid

machine. Run, it's time for the bell.

The Secretary hands him the card.

6.7.MFS-2MFS (56)

Peter steps away from the door right when Danko passes him.

Peter takes a step toward the table as the Secretary writes his name on the yellow plastic card.

                          PETER
            What color is for middle school?

Without a word, the Secretary places the yellow card into a plastic cover and inserts it into the laminating machine.

                          PETER
                (Peter comments the color of the
                card.)
                That's like for toddlers.

6.8.ECU (57)

THE YELLOW CARD WITH THE NAME "PETER HUSKA' slides out of the machine.

6.9.M2S-MS (58)

Secretary, Peter.

                        SECRETARY
                Green is for teachers. If you
                don't like it, starve.

Peter pulls a sour face, takes the yellow card and walks out of the shot.

The Secretary looks in Peter's direction and turns back to the computer.

PART V: QUIZ, TESTS, CHARTS, TEMPLATES

The first section of this part contains a quiz. By taking this quiz, you will learn about your attitude toward the invisible film technique. The second section with multiple-choice questions contains six tests. The questions test your knowledge of material covered in this book. The point of taking these tests is to review the knowledge acquired from lectures, and from hands-on directed exercises linked to topics covered in particular chapters. How to do well on multiple-answer choice tests? If you apply the process of elimination in conjunction with guessing, it might lead you to gain points on tests. That will be most likely the strategy you will also employ in the real world when you are facing a few different approaches in making some important directorial choices, or in solving some creative dilemmas. You won't always know in advance, what is the best directorial choice. Well, probably not the best advice I can give you at this point, but give it a shot, and eliminate one or more answers and take your best guess, here in taking the test, and outside in making directorial choices. The third section of this part contains templates and charts for a shot list - chart, shot list - justification for crossing the line, verbal storyboard – chart, location survey checklist, genre breakdown – chart, conceptual map template for emotions – chart, harmonious portrait – chart, discordant portrait – chart, and proposal for the final project.

INVISIBLE TECHNIQUE
(Quiz)
**Take this quiz if you want to learn more about your attitude
toward the invisible film technique**

Every part of the statement must be True for the answer to be True. If any part of the statement is not true, then the answer is False. Choose true for statements with details and qualifiers like "often" and "usually." Choose false for statements that are shorter with absolutes like "always" and "never." When guessing, choose True because there are usually more True answers than False.

A. PART

1. I want to disguise how the film is created.
    T   F

2. I don't want to expose the mechanism of filmmaking and doing it divorced from the action.
    T   F

3. I want to emphasize the content, the development of the narrative.
   T   F

4. I would rather use the standard storytelling visual design/treatment as an uncomplicated that keeps faith with the expectations of most of its potential audience.
   T   F

5. I don't want to distract the audience by style, which would constantly remind them that they are watching a film.
   T   F

6. I don't want the audience to become aware of the methods of presentation, and suggests that the film is a piece of fiction, a fabrication of reality.
   T   F

7. I don't want to employ the style, which would continuously draw the audience's attention to the camerawork.
   T   F

A. PART Score: T:_____   F:_____

B. PART

8. I want to provoke the audience to wake up and examine what they are being told, how they are being told and why they are being told that particular story.
   T   F

9. I want to reject conventional visual and narrative codes and favor an indirect and oblique presentation.
   T   F

10. I don't want the audience to lose themselves in action.
    T   F

11. I want the audience to be constantly reminded that they are being told a story.
    T   F

B. PART Score: T:_____   F:_____

What's your score?

A. PART

- If you have 4 or more than 4 Ts answers in A. PART of the test:
  You are risk averse and rather worship for the invisible film technique. The III. STUDIO is exactly for you because it will teach you how to break the 180-degree Rule legally.

- If you have 4 or more than 4 Fs answers in A. PART of the test:
  You lean more toward the "aggressive" risk profile, definitely the III. STUDIO will help you because it challenges the 180-degree Rule.

B. PART

- If you have more than 2 Ts answers in B. PART of the test:
  You have enough courage to dare to take risks, and probably you are looking for ways to separate yourself from the crowd.

- If you have more than 2 Fs answers in B. PART of the test:
  You are inherently more conservative filmmaker.

A. PART + B. PART

- Now sum up Ts from A. PART and Fs from B. PART. If your number is 6 and higher, it looks like sticking to standard filmmaking approaches makes you feel safer and more secure and more powerful. Or you were born a scaredy-cat. To shine, you need to show that you have some original thoughts as well.

- Now sum up Fs from A. PART and Ts from B. PART. If your number is 6 and higher, it looks like a penchant for high risk makes you a fearless filmmaker, who is pushing the limits, and taking things too far. You understand that in order to be noticed, you need to stand out and take some chances. Or you were born a rebel. You are up for the challenge, a party animal, but people who don't know you may think that you are too pushy. First test the waters, before you jump in.

1ˢᵗ TEST – CAMERA

Circle the letter corresponding to the best or most nearly correct answer.

1. Aperture:
   a. Regulates the amount of light entering the camera.
   b. Regulates the length of time the light is allowed to enter the camera.
   c. All of the above.
   d. None of the above.

2. Shutter:
   a. Regulates the amount of light entering the camera.
   b. Regulates the length of time the light is allowed to enter the camera.
   c. All of the above.
   d. None of the above.

3. What is the relationship between aperture size, f-stop and depth of field?
   a. The smaller the aperture, the larger the f-stop, the greater the depth of field and vice versa.
   b. The smaller the aperture, the smaller the f-stop, the narrower the depth of field and vice versa.
   c. The smaller the aperture, the smaller the f-stop, the greater the depth of field and vice versa.

4. White balance controls:
   a. Shot exposure.
   b. Shot color.
   c. Shot focus.

5. By moving away from the subject matter and using a long focal length lens, the apparent speed of objects moving toward or away from the camera will appear:
   a. Reduced (slowed down).
   b. Sped up.
   c. Same.

6. Before setting up a shot.
   a. Zoom into the subject, focus the lens, then zoom out and compose the shot.
   b. Compose the shot and focus the lens.
   c. Focus the lens and then compose the shot.

7. Four factors affect the depth of field:
   a. Frame composition, Size of the shot, Vertical Camera Angle, Horizontal Camera Angle.
   b. Focal length of the lens, Distance from the camera to subject, The size of the aperture, Camera sensor size.
   c. Theme, Premise, Poetic, Style.
   d. Atmosphere, Mood, Tone, Feeling.

8. You must base your choice of using a "moving shot" or a "static shot" on:
   a. The type and needs of action, which is covering by a shot.
   b. The other types of shots used in the scene where this shot will be placed, and the rhythm of the action and the rhythm of the whole scene.
   c. All of the above.
   d. None of the above.

9. The wider the angle of the lens, the less annoying any camera jiggle will be in the image:
   a. True.
   b. False.

10. Shooting at long focal lengths requires that the camera must be:
   a. Handheld.
   b. Dolly-mounted.
   c. Very steady on a tripod.

2nd TEST - SHOT

Circle the letter corresponding to the best or most nearly correct answer.

1. **Shot from eye-level:**
   a. A shot taken from the eye-level of the camera operator.
   b. A shot taken from the eye-level of the actor or subject.
   c. A shot taken from beneath eye level with the camera looking up.

2. **Master shot is:**
   a. A shot, when the event is recorded in its entirety from a single camera position.
   b. A shot that shows the scene exactly the way a character sees it.
   c. A first shot in the scene, which establishes the scene's geographical and human context.

3. **POV shot is:**
   a. A shot, when the event is recorded in its entirety from a single camera position.
   b. A shot that shows the scene exactly the way a character sees it.
   c. A first shot in the scene, which establishes the scene's geographical and human context.

4. **Wide Angle Shot:**
   a. A shot made with a narrower field of action and depth of field.
   b. A shot that reproduces the perspective of the human eye.
   c. A shot made with a lens with greater depth of field and a wider field of action.

5. **Motivation of camera movement:**
   a. Story-teller's revelation.
   b. Character movement and eye line.
   c. All of the above.
   d. None of the above.

6. **Tracking back:**
   a. Draws viewer into a closer, more intensive relationship with the subject.
   b. Tends to create emotional distance and tends to divert attention to the edges of the screen.
   c. Draws attention to the camera itself.

7. Semi Profile:
   a. A side angle filmed directly from the side, creating a profile.
   b. A front angle.
   c. A forty-five-degree angle.

8. CLOSE UP is circumscribed by:
   a. Shoulder joint.
   b. Elbow joint, or hip joint.
   c. Knee joint, or ankle joint.

9. FULL SHOT is circumscribed by:
   a. Elbow joint, or hip joint.
   b. Knee joint, or ankle joint.
   c. Belongs to entire figure

10. Sequence
   a. A single run of the camera or the piece of the film resulting from such a run.
   b. A dramatic unit composed of a single or several shots.
   c. A dramatic unit composed of several scenes.

3rd TEST - COVERAGE

Circle the letter corresponding to the best or most nearly correct answer.

1. The purpose of the line of action:
   a. It creates a special directing style
   b. It organizes different camera angles to preserve consistent screen direction and space
   c. It makes the audience forget the sense of the direction in the last movement shown

2. The line of action is usually:
   a. The line between camera and subject in scene
   b. The line of sight between subjects featured in scene
   c. The line between two camera setups

3. Camera position within the established semicircle:
   a. Is permitted
   b. Is "over the line"

4. The *"triangle system"* is employed for:
   a. Dialog situation
   b. Action scenes
   c. All types of situations

5. Reverse shot:
   a. A shot taken from same camera position as the previous shot and with the exact angle
   b. A shot taken from same camera position as the previous shot with different angle and size of shot
   c. A shot with an angle of view directly opposite the previous angle of view and camera position

6. Open body position means that the actor:
   a. Faces the camera (audience)
   b. Has his back to the camera (audience)

7. The strongest camera position in "Triangle Principle" is:
   a. Camera set up on the apex of the triangle
   b. Position of the internal reverse angles (angular singles)
   c. Position of the external reverse angles (over the shoulder shots)

8. The way of covering the scene:
   a. A master shot registers the whole scene.
   b. A master shot is intercut with other master shot.

    c. A master shot is intercut with other shorter shots.

    d. All of the above.

    e. None of the above.

9. It is important for the Reverse shot to match:

    a. The camera position and the lens.

    b. The framing and the camera distance.

    c. The actor movement.

    d. All of the above.

    e. None of the above.

10. Subjective treatment

    a. The viewer is treated as an observer.

    b. The viewer is treated as a participant.

4th TEST - CONTINUITY

Circle the letter corresponding to the best or most nearly correct answer.

1. "Continuity" ensures that shots will:
   a. Provide coverage for the script.
   b. Play in a seamless, progressive and continuous manner when edited together.
   c. Be scheduled and shot in continual narrative order.

2. Rule of line:
   a. The rule, which only temporally overrides the rule of motion.
   b. The principal rule of composition, which takes you, where to place the horizon line.
   c. The most basic rule of camera placement. The camera must not cross the line if screen direction is to be maintained.

3. Which sentence best describes the *"Rule of Line"*?
   a. Screen direction of any shots obtained from one side of the line will be consistent with each other.
   b. Direction of movement should be the same in two consecutive shots.

4. Shots from opposite sides of the line (when two characters are looking at each other) will result to a reversal screen direction when cut together:
   a. True
   b. False

5. Techniques that can be used to cross the line:
   a. The camera visibly crosses the line.
   b. Crossing the line by sight of Player.
   c. Crossing the line by Neutral shot or Cut-away shot.
   d. Changing screen direction can be done if we see the change on screen.
   e. All of the above.
   f. None of the above.

6. Composition is stronger, if:
   a. The center of interest is somewhere along to horizontal lines.
   b. The center of interest is somewhere along to vertical lines.
   c. The center of interest falls near one of the four cross-points. (The rule of thirds.)

7. Proper *"Headroom"* is achieved when:
   a. Just a little space is left between subject's head and the top frame line.
   b. More space is left between subject's head and the top frame line.

8. Proper *"Leading space"* is achieved when:
   a. Just a little space is left in the frame in the direction that the subject travels.
   b. More space is left in the frame in the direction that the subject travels.

9. Matched cut:
   a. A cut joining two shots, whose compositional elements match, helping to establish strong continuity of action.
   b. A cut joining two shots, whose compositional elements match, helping to establish strong, realistic feeling.
   c. A cut joining two shots, whose compositional elements match, helping to confuse the viewers.

10. The ways how to establish a Match Cut:
   a. By Position.
   b. By Movement.
   c. By Look (dialog).
   d. All of the above.
   e. None of the above.

5th TEST – DEEP SPACE

Circle the letter corresponding to the best or most nearly correct answer.

1. **A shallow depth of field is often used as a technique to:**
   a. Provide coverage for the script.
   b. Focus audience's attention on the most significant aspect of a shot.
   c. Organize a film set.

2. **Central perspective:**
   a. Favors flat setups with the camera perpendicular to the background.
   b. Favors deep setups with the camera angular to the background.

3. **Benefits of deep staging:**
   a. It gives depth and a sense of dynamics.
   b. It establishes geography of a scene.
   c. It creates a special style.
   d. All of the above.
   e. None of the above.

4. **Strategy to create a deep space:**
   a. Stage on line.
   b. Move camera (parallel movement).
   c. Move camera (toward or away from actors; up or down).
   d. Move actors (Parallel movement of an actor to the picture plane).
   e. Do not overlap actors.

5. **By pulling the focus director can:**
   a. Shift the character perspective.
   b. Reveal new information related to the character.
   c. Externalize character's feeling, emotions, mental process, the inner state of mind.
   d. All of the above.
   e. None of the above.

6. **Pivotal Moment/Pivotal Beat in a scene can be visually rendered via:**
   a. Change in a visual pattern.
   b. Change in rhythm.
   c. All of the above.
   d. None of the above.

7. Change in a Visual Pattern is mostly a pattern change in shot design and it basically means:

    a. Instantaneous proximity to the characters (moving camera closer to the character or action).

    b. Shift from wider shots to tighter (using close-ups).

    c. Shift from regular/obvious camera angels to spectacular ones (using low angle, high angle, Dutch angle).

    d. Shift from Static Shots to Moving Shots.

    e. All of the above.

    f. None of the above.

6th TEST

CONCEPT OF CHARACTER PERSPECTIVE

Circle the letter corresponding to the best or most nearly correct answer.

1. Which model of character perspective is objective:
   a. Consistent Character Perspective.
   b. Neutral Stance.
   c. Fluid Character Perspective.

2. Consistent Character Perspective means:
   a. The events and emotions are rendered objectively.
   b. One character is favored in a scene.
   c. There is an alternation of Character Perspective within a scene.

3. Shift in a Character Perspective can be rendered via:
   a. Change in a visual pattern.
   b. Change in rhythm.
   c. All of the above.

4. Pseudo POV shot is:
   a. A shot, which shows, how the character seen in a shot, sees the situation.
   b. A shot, which shows how the character sees the situation.

5. The audience can align itself more with the character, who is in:
   a. Profile shot.
   b. OTS shot.
   c. Straight on Shot/Full Face Shot/Frontal View Shot.

6. A character in the center has:
   a. Less weight (visual) than one at the edge of the composition.
   b. More weight (visual) than one at the edge of the composition.

7. A character in the left of the frame:
   a. Has less compositional weight than a character positioned to the right of the frame.
   b. Has more compositional weight than a character positioned to the right of the frame.

8. Mood of the Scene means:
   a. The general feeling that a film scene creates within the viewer.
   b. Director's attitude/feel towards the subject and situation rendered in a film scene.

9. Atmosphere is:

a. Director's attitude/feel.

b. Audience's feeling.

c. The dominant tone or mood associated with a particular place.

10. Which statement is correct?

a. A particular environment/location creates the special mood, mood creates feeling, and feeling generates the atmosphere.

b. A particular environment/location creates the special atmosphere, atmosphere creates mood and mood generates a feeling.

c. A particular environment/location creates the special feeling, feeling creates atmosphere, and the atmosphere generates mood.

TEST ANSWERS - CORRECT ANSWERS

	1	2	3	4	5	6	7	8	9	10
1st TEST - CAMERA	1a	2b	3a	4b	5a	6a	7b	8b	9a	10c
2nd TEST - SHOT	1b	2a	3b	4c	5c	6b	7c	8a	9c	10c
3rd TEST – COVERAGE	1b	2b	3a	4c	5c	6a	7c	8d	9d	10b
4th TEST - CONTINUITY	1b	2c	3a	4a	5a	6c	7a	8b	9a	10d
5th TEST – DEEP SPACE	1b	2a	3d	4c	5d	6c	7e			
6th TEST CONCEPT OF CHARACTER PERSPECTIVE	1b	2b	3c	4a	5c	6a	7b	8a	9c	10b

SHOT LIST
(Chart)

TITLE:
Scene Number:
Director:

SHOT NUMBER	SIZE	ANGLE	TIME	MOVING/ STATIC	LENS	DOF	DESCRIPTION	STAGING AND BLOCKING

SHOT LIST
(JUSTIFICATION FOR CROSSING THE LINE)

Shot Number	Size of Shot	Description of the shot	Technique for Crossing the Line (Crossing the line by...)	Justification (motivation, desired effect) for crossing the line

VERBAL STORYBOARD

SCENE:
PRINCIPAL KEY:

DIRECTORIAL UNIT or SENTENCE or PHRASE or WORD or MEANING or EMOTION or ESSENCE or WHATEVER	INDICATED VISUAL IMAGE	VERBAL DESCRIPTION	ASSIGNED SHOT (use the chart for the SHOT LIST)

LOCATION SURVEY CHECKLIST

Scene(s)/Place:
Potential location of shooting:
Shooting Day/Time of Shooting:
Principal contact person:
Address:
Phone number:
E-mail address:

GENERAL:
How close does the location come to matching your vision?
Is the space big enough for camera movement and lighting set ups?
How much will it cost to dress the set?
Financial cost?
How far is it from your other locations?
How long can I use it?

CAMERA:
Where can the camera be placed?
What, if anything, is needed in the way of camera mounting devices or platforms?
What, if anything, is needed in the way of special lenses?
Will any objects interfere with the camera shots? If so, how can this situation be corrected?

LIGHTING:
What types of lights will be needed?
Where can the lights be placed?
What light stands or particular light holders will be needed?
What, if any, special lighting accessories will be needed?
How can any problems regarding mixing indoor and outdoor lighting be solved?
In what ways will the sun's position at different times of day affect the shooting?
What kinds of problems are shadows likely to cause?

POWER:
Is enough power available or will a generator be needed?
Where is the circuit breaker box?
Who can be contacted if a circuit blows?

Which circuits can be used and how many watts can be run on them?
How many, if any, extension cords will be needed?
What power outlets can be used?

SOUND:

Are there background noises that may interfere with audio? If so, how can
they be corrected?
Where can the microphones and cable be placed?
Are any particular microphone holders or stands needed?
What types of microphones should be used?
How much microphone cable will be needed?

MISCELLANEOUS:

Parking availability.
Weather conditions.

LOCATION - RISK ASSESSMENT:

The initial survey of possible filming locations should involve evaluating potential hazards to determine the need for special precautions or alternative
locations. Visibly mark in your screenplay all actions that may indicate an
unsafe or hazardous situation, or situations, which require a special treatment
like: guns, weapons of various characters (swords, knives, chains, bats and so
on); violent actions or action, which seems violent, or appears dangerous;
moving vehicles; minors; animals.

GENRE BREAKDOWN
(chart)

TITLE:
Scene:
DIRECTOR:

Genre:
Fundamental element of this genre: theme, dramatic components, narrative conventions, narrative style, dramatic action, dramatic structure, and tone of this genre.
Critical elements of this genre: conventional settings, conventional events, conventional roles, the qualities of the main character, the nature of the antagonist.
Some other main stylistic aspects or conventions of this genre (visual techniques, camera techniques, shot design):
Notable films:

CONCEPTUAL MAP TEMPLATE FOR EMOTIONS
(chart)

MOOD	EMOTIONS DESIGN (Physical and mental components of emotion; visual design; shot design)	ENHANCING EMOTIONS (Multiplying emotions)	EMOTION (Response or reaction triggered by stimulus)	ACCENTUATING/ INTENSIFYING STIMULUS (Engage as many of "senses" as you can)	STIMULUS (Emotional triggers)

HARMONIOUS PORTRAIT
(chart)

Virginia Woolf *(Mrs. Dalloway), English writer and one of the foremost modernists of the twentieth century,* once observed, *"Odd how the creative power brings the whole universe at once to order."*

HARMONIOUS PORTRAIT - all the elements that comprise the scene's mood and tone work together in unison, in order to intensify interest or emotion or drama.

Guidelines for creating a HARMONIOUS PORTRAIT of the scripted situation: Use all possible techniques and strategies to create a HARMONIOUS PORTRAIT of the scripted situation, and try to resolve any dissonance in the scene:

HARMONIOUS PORTRAIT	**PLACE** Choose the PLACE with the atmosphere, which will produce a pleasing mood, going hand in with the original mood; or distasteful mood, going hand in with the original mood. Create consonance, the harmony.
	VISUAL COMPONENTS Choose all the visual components (LINES and SHAPES, TONE, MOVEMENT and RHYTHM) and try to create affinity, which will go hand in with the original mood; or contrast, which will go hand in with the original mood. Create consonance, the harmony.
	COLORS Select the COLORS, which will produce a pleasing visual experience, highlighting the original mood; or distasteful visual experience, highlighting the original mood. Create consonance, the harmony.
	SOUND Select mood-setting SOUND, which will establish and maintain positive or negative attitude. Create consonance, the harmony.
	SHOT DESIGN Design each shot individually and organize all individual elements of the shot into a harmonious and unified whole.
	FINAL TOUCH Evaluate all employed elements and reexamine if all components are appropriately combined together and create a harmonious portrait of the scene.

DISCORDANT PORTRAIT
(chart)

DISCORDANT PORTRAIT - all the elements that comprise the scene's mood and tone contrast or work against each other in order to intensify interest or emotion or drama.

Guidelines for creating a DISCORDANT PORTRAIT of the scripted situation: Use all possible techniques and strategies to create a DISCORDANT PORTRAIT of the scripted situation, and try to heighten dissonance in the scene:

DISCORDANT PORTRAIT	**PLACE** Choose the PLACE with the atmosphere, which will produce an unpleasant-conflicting mood, contrasting the original mood; or pleasing-conflicting mood, contrasting the original mood. Create dissonance, the disharmony.
	VISUAL COMPONENTS Choose all the visual components (LINES and SHAPES, TONE, MOVE-MENT and RHYTHM) and try to create contrast, which will oppose the original mood; or affinity, which will oppose the original mood. Create dissonance, the disharmony.
	COLORS Use the COLORS in a discordant fashion, colors that clash with each other, contrasting the original mood; or use COLORS in a harmonious fashion, colors which work with each other, contrasting the original mood. Create dissonance, the disharmony.
	SOUND Select the SOUND, which will establish and maintain dissonance, disharmony.
	SHOT DESIGN Design each shot individually and organize all individual elements of the shot into a unified whole.
	FINAL TOUCH Evaluate all employed elements and reexamine if all components are appropriately combined together and create a discordant portrait of the scene.

PROPOSAL FOR THE FINAL PROJECT
SHORT LIVE ACTION NARRATIVE FILM

Student-Director:
Title:
Written by:
Date of submission:

A: Auteur Film:

B: Original Screenplay:
Screenwriter:
Writer permission to use the script:
The Collaboration Agreement:

C: Adaptation:
Pre-existing work:
Author of a pre-existing work:
Copyright Status: (Copyrighted Material; Public Domain; I don't know)
Original Genre:
Genre of Adaptation:

Synopsis: (A paragraph long summary of your project. Focus mostly on the story; describe the basic hero, situation(s), circumstance(s) and obstacle(s) he/she has to overcome in order to achieve or fail to reach the goal.)

Conflict: (Define where is the conflict and briefly describe the main source of dramatic tension in the story.)

The Story Outcome: (The plots of some stories start with a character's goal. A goal is something the character wants. The actions are what the character does to reach the goal. The outcome tells if the character reached the goal. Do your character's efforts to achieve the overall story goal result in Success or Failure?)

Character List with a Character Sketch:
- 1st Character:
- 2nd Character:
- 3rd Character:

Location(s):

Statement of Purpose/Statement of Intend:
- Briefly describe how the Final Film will fulfill the learning goals and further your education as a filmmaker:
- Briefly describe how the shooting of the Final Film supports your current strategic plan toward your future. (Identify the goals and strategies that the Final Film would support.):
- Film goals, fondest hopes and dreams:

EPILOGUE

I hope that I made it clear throughout this book that directing is a unique act of creation where talent, imagination, sensitivity, and workmanship play a vital role. At the same time, I said that directing is a painstaking process of translating your vision into film. It seems to me that I put sufficient emphasis on intuition, instinct, and improvisation as well.

You are already facing some creative dilemmas. You are in a constant dither, in pain and unbearable suffering over how to get the best out of your film. Suffer! That is part of creation. Eventually, when you find yourself stuck, let your instincts and intuition guide you. You'll be surprised how in the darkest situations, trusting your inner voice can lead you out into the light. Listen to your inner voice! Don't forget, directing is completely subjective. Your own temperament, emotionality, and mannerisms strongly affect the entire process of making a film, so be subjective and be emotional! Self-determination theory posits three universal psychological needs: autonomy, competence, and relatedness, and suggests that these must be satisfied for people to maintain optimal performance and well-being. According to this hypothesis, you will be more likely satisfied with your directing, if you feel in control of your directorial choices, good at what you do and closely connected to your viewers.

Mark Jonathan Harris, an Academy Award-winning documentary filmmaker, said:

> If you don't try to do new things, you don't grow as a filmmaker, as an artist. (...) When you make mistakes, I think that's the time you learn the most because when something you try doesn't work out, you are forced to examine "why".

You are going to shoot your film, your debut. You've prepared for this moment for a few months, if not years. Your experience, your knowledge, and your ability to hit the ground make you eminently qualified and capable. Your skilled artistry and high level of craftsmanship are unsurpassed for quality. But there is something else: Every film you will be directing is the chance to prove that you've got something to say. Before you get the specific language, think about what you want to say. Whether they love you or hate you, everyone wants to tune in to hear what you've gotten to say. So as you are looking for a theme for your film, consider this: you do not need to shock the audience. You need to surprise with sincerity. Tune in to the frequency of your heart and choose the theme close to your heart, something you are familiar with, something that is bothering you and you feel an unbearable need to shed light on it, tell everybody how you feel about old problems, ethical and philosophical problems; show them things no one else can see; discover things not seen, and show them to others; show them things they may go unnoticed by others without you; *make visible what, without you, might perhaps never have been seen.*

Remember what Fyodor Mikhailovich Dostoevsky *(The Idiot)*, the most important and influential writer who ever lived, said: "*Creativity isn't anything else but 2% of talent and 98% of sweat.*" Your talent, coupled with tenacity and the will to succeed, will bring the fruits. Your talent is your capital. The main question is how much capital you've got in the bank and how much time you have left to spend it. You have to cash it – I mean metaphorically (you might like to think also literally) – before the clock runs out. If you think that ample time has been granted to you, you are fatally mistaken. When you finish your studies, run out of the classroom and shoot your film. The main purpose of this book is to help you to reach your goal. And your goal is clear, am I right?

One of my director colleagues, back in Czechoslovakia, once responded to a harsh critic of his film: "*So what? A train also has a second railroad car.*" Wrong! Don't resign yourself to being a second railroad car! In all my years of directing and teaching, I have learned that it doesn't matter where you come from; all filmmakers share the same goal: to be good at what they do. Try to be the best at what you are doing, not just good. Keep in mind that the best films still remain unmade. Of course, they are waiting for you, and some of you will make them! Don't look around. I am talking to you. It might be YOU.

Sir Kenneth Robinson, an English author, speaker, and international advisor on education said, "*If you are not prepared to be wrong, you will never come up with anything original.*" You must believe in your quest, even if no one else does. Creative confidence is believing in in your own skills and that you can change the world around you. Napoléon Bonaparte, a French military leader and emperor who conquered much of Europe in the early 19th century said during his retreat from Russia, "*There is only one step from the sublime to the ridiculous.*" But from my perspective, "*It is better to fail in originality than succeed in imitation.*" as Herman Melville *(Moby-Dick)*, an American novelist, said.

Andrey Tarkovsky *(Stalker)*, one of Russia's most influential and renowned directors, left his artistic testament in his book *Sculpting in Time*. I am quoting this famous passage almost in full because it is often the subject of an incomplete or edited reference.

A director cannot be equally well understood by everyone, but is entitled to his own - more or less numerous – following among cinema-goers; this is the normal condition of existence for an individual artist, and of the evolution of cultural tradition in society. Of course, each of us wants to find the maximum number of kindred spirits, who will appreciate and need us; but we

*cannot calculate our own success, and we are powerless to select our work-
ing principles in such a way as to ensure it. As soon as one begins to cater
expressly for the auditorium, then we're talking of the entertainment industry, show business, the masses, or what have you, but certainly not of art
which necessarily obeys its own immanent laws of development whether we
like it or not. (...) Every artist performs his creative task in his own way;
whether he makes a secret of it or not, however, contact and mutual understanding with the audience is invariably the object of his hopes and dreams,
and all are equally downcast by failure. One remembers how Cezanne, recognized and acclaimed by his fellow-artists, was made deeply unhappy by
the fact that his neighbor didn't appreciate his paintings; not that he could
alter anything in his style. (...) A director is not entitled to try to please anyone. He hasn't the right to restrict himself in the process of his work for the
sake of success, and if he does he will inevitably pay the price: his plan and
purpose, and their realization will no longer have the same meaning for
him. It will be like a game of "give-away." Even if he knows before he starts
that his work is not going to have a wide appeal, he still has no right to
make changes in what he has been called to do.* (Excerpts from SCULPTING
IN TIME by Andrey Tarkovsky, translated by Kitty Hunter-Blair, translation
copyright © 1986, 1987 by Kitty Hunter-Blair. Used by permission of Alfred
A. Knopf, an imprint of the Knopf Doubleday Publishing Group, a division
of Penguin Random House LLC. All rights reserved.)

Polish film director Andrzej Wajda, whom I have quoted in this book a few
times, said in his book *Wajda on Film*:

*In my experience, most of misunderstanding that arise between the public
and the director derive precisely from filmmakers' tendency to mistake the
weaknesses in his film for originality. Any imprecision in the plot or action
relates to the "mystery" of his work. That is why I advise the young director
never resort to "That's just what I wanted" - for in the cinema the only judge
is the public. You'll realize the truth of that statement the first time you have
a successful picture and see long lines waiting to see it.*
(Wajda, A. *Wajda on Film: A Master's Notes*, 1st edition. Acrobat Books,
1992, ISBN 10: 0918226295)

Here is your chance to ask me anything you want, but if you could ask me just
one question, I think I know what it would be. *"Will I be a successful director if I
follow everything that you tried to teach us in this book?"* Let me answer your
question with the following story:

*A student asked his Zen master how long it would take to reach enlighten-
ment. "Ten years," the master said. But the student persisted, what if he*

studied very hard? "Then 20 years," the master responded. Surprised, the student asked how long it would take if he worked very, very hard and became the most dedicated student in the Ashram. "In that case, 30 years," the master replied. His explanation: "If you have one eye on how close you are to achieving your goal, that leaves only one eye for your task."

In order to answer your question in the most honest way, let me borrow gambling vocabulary for it. Why gambling? Because the film is as risky a business as gambling is. Regardless of the investment (bet), you don't know what to expect at the end. But you can't win unless you play! *"The biggest edge I live on is directing. That's the scariest, most dangerous thing you can do in your life,"* said the late American director Tony Scott *(Domino).* Will you win over your audience with your film? Let's presume that you have an amazing story and an amazing cast. Even though the finished film looks astonishing and the range of talent represented in your film is noteworthy, you can still fail. There are myriad reasons why you can fail – the current cultural atmosphere and political climate works against your film; you are ahead of your time with an unbiased and thought-provoking perspective, and the audience is not yet prepared to digest it; your film is too daring for its time; your film does not fit into the intellectual atmosphere of its time; your film is too harrowing for public consumption; you are simply on the wrong side of public opinion; or another film with the same theme was released one week before your film hit the movie theaters; you are a victim of bad timing. There are ample reasons out of your control that can negatively affect your film, or, better said, the audience's reaction to your film. In the arena of public opinion, you can lose for any reason or no reason at all. But it does not mean that your film is not good, even exemplary, or that you are not a good director. If your film is not well received by the audience, it does not mean that it is not excellent or exceptional. Know that the audience's attitude toward your film is in no way a reflection on the quality of your work or talent.

The graveyard of cinema is riddled with failed directors. And yet in Film Valley "failing fast" is heralded as a virtue and, sometimes, even failing slowly can have unforeseeable benefits. Cutting-edge films may die an embarrassing death, but they often also lay the groundwork for better, more well-timed ideas that flourish later on. There is a list of failures, yes, but failures that led to success or may yet still lead to something world-changing. That's why we are calling these films most successful failed films. Like an experiment gone awry, they can still teach us something.

I have borrowed this idea from *TIME* magazine's article *The 20 Most Successful Technology Failures of All Time,* from April 3, 2017. But do not forget the old saying when you seek credit for success: *"Success has many fathers, but failure is an orphan."*

In his book on winning roulette, M. Jensen says:

The probability of winning is equal to the number of ways to win, divided by the numbers of possible outcomes. (...) A gambler would say it is 1 chance out of 2. (Jensen, M. *Secret of Winning Roulette*, 2nd edition. Cardoza Publishing, 1992, ISBN-10: 1580420397)

I know that you don't like to see yourself as a gambler, but the sooner you adopt that idea, the better for you. Believe me, things will work out for you down the road; just follow your intuition and curiosity. Always remember that talent is not measured by success. Or maybe it's the other way around...

I used to conclude my film and television directing lectures in Europe with this statement: *"I don't think I've got anything else pretty cool to share with you today. Probably next time. Who knows? The class is over. See you tomorrow."*

Thank you for your attention and thank you for your hard work. I look forward to seeing you somewhere around – in the class, in the studio, in your film, in a movie theater watching your film, in a casino, or maybe in another world, illusion, or virtual reality. Acclaimed classical violin virtuoso Joshua Bell, in his 2013 interview for *TIME* magazine said, *"I'm addicted to the adrenaline of performing, and I think when you're used to having that high, you look for it in other things."* The rush you get from it is just so immense that you can't help but love it and want to do it again. You may not have the adrenaline junkie side, and may not want to make films for the rush, but for a living. But then you have to figure out how to balance what you really love and what the world pays you for.

I've learned that work is most fulfilling when it's a calling. And often, it's a calling because you find a deep sense of purpose and positive impact in your role. (Stevens, S. "The Difference Between a Job and a Calling." http://motto.time.com/4290610/find-a-sense-of-purpose/. Accessed March 16, 2017)

Enjoy and suffer. That's what film and television directing is all about. As Winston Churchill, former prime minister of the United Kingdom who led his country from the brink of defeat to victory in WWII, said, *"If you're going through hell, keep going."* Passion sparks interest and interest leads to success.

Enjoy this rare moment.

Lubomir Kocka

PHOTO ALBUM

1. Lubomir Kocka, Director

2. The 37th Student Academy Awards, 2010, Samuel Goldwyn Theater, Saturday, June 12, 2010. Narrative Bronze Medal, *The Lunch Box* by Lubomir Kocka, Jr.

3. Lubomir Kocka, Director with his parents and older brother

1.   **2.**   **3.**

On the set of TV Series *Mountain Rangers*, directed by Lubomir Kocka

On the set of TV miniseries *The Goblin*, directed by Lubomir Kocka

On the set of film *The Bridge*, directed by Lubomir Kocka

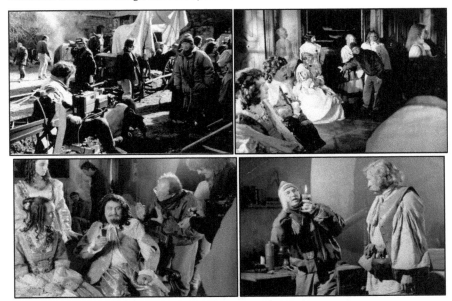

Aphrodite Film Posters

The Goblin Posters

The Bridge Film Poster

ABOUT THE AUTHOR

Lubomir Kocka (Slovak pronunciation: 'ʎubɔˌmiːr Kɔt͡ska), born in Žilina, Slovakia, is a Slovak-American director, screenwriter, professor, and producer. His films include: *Mountain Rangers* (Horská služba), *The Goblin* (Škriatok), *Aphrodite* (Afrodita), *The Bridge* (Most), *From Morning till Dawn* (Od rána do úsvitu), and *Fallacies of our Traditional Morale* (Omyly tradičnej morálky).

He graduated from the University of Muse and Dramatic Arts, Film and Television Department, Czechoslovakia, with a specialization in film and television directing. The school, along with the famous Film Academy FAMU in Prague, Czech Republic, educates highly professional filmmakers. He has a substantial career as a film and television director of produced fictional feature films – both inside the studio system and with independent films. He has directed nine feature films, 13 television dramas, and seven TV series and miniseries. His productions have been aired globally.

He has won numerous awards from international film and television festivals around the world: the Best Director Award for the film *How Julia Saved the Riddle Kingdom* and for *Aphrodite*, awarded by The Prize of Children Jury for the film. He was a director of many films chosen to be part of the official selections at international film and television festivals including Cannes, France; Monte Carlo, Monaco; Prix Italia, Italy; Reims, France; Golden Chest Plovdiv, Bulgaria; Varna, Bulgaria; Munich, Germany; Prix Danube Bratislava, Slovakia.

Aside from directing, he is also an author and co-author of several feature-length screenplays that went on to be produced. He produced Lubomir Kocka Jr.'s film entitled *The Lunch Box*, which was named a bronze medal winner in the narrative category for the Academy of Motion Picture Arts and Science's 37th Annual Student Academy Awards competition (2010).

In addition to his numerous directing credits, he is also an acclaimed film educator, with 17 years of teaching experience at the university level in Europe (Czechoslovakia and France) and 15 years in the USA at SCAD – altogether, 32 years of college teaching experience. Currently, he is based in Savannah, Georgia, USA, at the Savannah College of Art and Design (SCAD) as a Professor of Film and Television, where he has taught since 2002.

INDEX